4.20.77

A Hundred Years of Grand Opera
in New York
1825-1925

AMS PRESS

NEW YORK

A Hundred Years of Grand Opera in New York
1825-1925

A RECORD OF PERFORMANCES

By Julius Mattfeld
Music Division
The New York Public Library

New York
The New York Public Library
1927

Library of Congress Cataloging in Publication Data

Mattfeld, Julius, 1893-1968.
    A hundred years of grand opera in New York, 1825-
1925.

    Reprint of the 1927 ed. published by New York Public
Library, New York.
    Bibliography: p.
    Includes index.
    1. Opera—New York (City) —History and criticism.
I. Title.
ML1711.8.N3M25   1976   782.1'09747'1   74-24146
ISBN 0-404-13038-0

Reprinted from an original copy in the collections
of the Boston Public Library

From the edition of 1927, New York
First AMS edition published in 1976
Manufactured in the United States of America

AMS PRESS, INC.
NEW YORK, N.Y.

1955226

TABLE OF CONTENTS

ERRATA AND ADDENDA

p. 23, *for* Pearmann *read* Pearman.

p. 32, Luigi Ravaglio:
> This singer's name is also spelt Ravaglia in contemporary newspapers.

p. 35, Mlle. Calvé:
> This singer also appeared in French opera in Philadelphia in 1843 and 1845. Armstrong (A Record of the Opera in Philadelphia, p. 44) says of her: "Mlle. Calvé was equally charming as a vocalist and actress. She was a graceful and light soprano, and was a great favorite."

p. 48 and 69, *for* Le Pardon de Poërmel *read* Le Pardon de Ploërmel.

p. 56, *for* Griselides *read* Grisélidis.

p. 61, Lucia di Lammermoor:
> This opera was broadcast by radio in its entirety, in Italian, by the Civic Opera League, on Aug. 21, 1925, through station WMCA, New York.

p. 61, Ma tante Aurore:
> An earlier performance of this opera was given at the Park Theatre, New York, July 18, 1827. It was preceded by a comedy, "Beneficiare," and followed by a French vaudeville, "Theolon." The initial productions of the French opera company which played at the Park Theatre during July, 1827 (see p. 24–25) received at first scant notice by the contemporary English newspapers of the city, but soon attracted the attention of the latter, because of the merit of its performances.

p. 66, *for* La Niege *read* La Neige.

p. 74, *insert after* Il Segreto di Susanna:
> **Semiramide:**
> Italian opera in 2 acts, libretto by Gaetano Rossi, founded on Voltaire's play, "Semiramis;" music by G. Rossini. (Venice, Teatro La Fenice, Feb. 2, 1823.) Palmo's Opera House, Jan. 3, 1845, in Italian.
>> Performed in New Orleans, May 1, 1837.
>> Various selections from this opera were sung by Clementina Fanti, Julia Wheatley, Ravaglio, Porto and Ferrero, at Fanti's benefit on April 29, 1835, at the Italian Opera House, New York.
>> A duet from this opera was sung on Jan. 9, 1834, at a concert by the Italian Opera company at the Euterpean Hall, 410 Broadway, New York.
>> This opera has been confused by many writers with Manual Garcia's opera, "La Figlia dell' aria," performed at the Park Theatre, New York, April 25, 1826, of which Semiramide is also the heroine Rossini's opera was never produced in the United States by Garcia's company.

p. 80, *for* Die Wiederspentigen Zaehmung *read* Die Wiederspenstigen Zaehmung.

A HUNDRED YEARS OF GRAND OPERA IN NEW YORK
1825–1925
A Record of Performances

By Julius Mattfeld
Music Division

INTRODUCTION

THE subject of opera has always been a fascinating one. Ever since the little group of sixteenth century enthusiasts met in the salon of Count Bardi's legatine palace in Florence, men and women of all ranks and station and types have found in it an attraction and sought to draw from it artistic and personal benefits. The story is still untold in its entirety, so varied has been the career of opera and so extended its ramifications. It is a story full of glamor, aspirations, individual triumphs — and failures, managerial achievements and debacles, machinations and saddening episodes — a story for a writer alive with human sympathies and equipped with the knowledge of a musical scholar.

To-day opera is an integral part of the musical life of nearly every civilized country. It has attained to great heights; and it has fallen to exceedingly low depths, lapsing lamentably from the high conceptions which actuated its first successful founders. Yet the Greek ideals of this group which brought it into being under the patronage of a secular-minded churchman of the Italian Renaissance are, perhaps, being slowly realized in our day, in a different connotation than they conceived it, in the open-air productions of opera and its Icarian flight through the air on the wings of the radio. In the former aspect, it is finding a place in the life of the community; in the latter, it is becoming a companion of the home. Either aspect, it is not too rash to speculate, may develop a newer type of entertainment and source of edification. Whereas the early innovators of opera transferred the Greek method of production in the open air of an amphitheatre to the enclosed space of the indoor theatre, the modern attempts at open-air performances are, in a measure, a return to the classic precedent. The motion picture, also, may not be without effect on future operatic production.

The following compilation was prepared in commemoration of the one hundredth anniversary of the introduction of Italian opera in the United States. Four other coincident events of the year are notable in this connection. The first in point of time is the death of Gustave Garcia, the grandson of New York's first opera impresario; the second, the decision to raze the Academy of Music, the former seat of grand opera in New York and the predecessor of the Metropolitan Opera House. The third is the disposal of the plot at 17–21 John Street, the site of New York's first theatre, from 1767 to 1798, known as the John Street Theatre, which Washington is said to have visited while President and a resident of New York. In this theatre was acted on April 16, 1787, Royall Tyler's comedy, "The Contrast," the first play by a native playwright to be produced in America. A house of two floors occupies the plot at present. A seventeen-story skyscraper is to be erected in its place — strangely realizing the title of Tyler's piece! — to be called the Tyler Building in honor of the dramatist. The fourth is the demolition of the one-time fashionable concert room, Steinway Hall, on Fourteenth Street. Here Dickens gave a series of readings from his novels, Mark Twain delivered his first New York lecture, General William T. Sherman thrilled his audience with a recital of his famous March to the Sea, Henry M. Stanley told of "The Horrors of the Slave Trade in Central Africa," and Adelaide Ristori, the renowned Italian tragedienne, made her first bow to the American public. Here Christine Nilsson made her first American appearance on Sept. 23, 1870, the composer-pianist, Anton Rubinstein, drew his first American admirers in 1872, and the boy Fritz Kreisler, a virtuoso of thirteen years, first ravished the ears of New York's music lovers. Many another concert, vocal and instrumental, by Theodore Thomas, Anton Seidl and others, filled the capacity of the auditorium.

This compilation is an alphabetical and chronological record of one hundred years of operatic production in New York. Lack of space forced the list to be confined to grand opera. Light opera is excluded, however important in its own sphere. In adhering to this plan, the compiler was compelled to omit the comic operas of such composers as Offenbach, Johann Strauss, Sir Arthur Sullivan, Reginald DeKoven, Victor Herbert, and others, as well as the myriad tuneful musical comedies of lesser men, despite the fact that many operas herein listed are of less significance historically and as works of the operatic stage.

Sundry exceptions to the above have been made, particularly in regard to the operas produced at the Opéra Comique of Paris and the compositions in dramatic form by Beethoven, Weber, Mendelssohn, Schumann and other outstanding figures in the history of music, such as "Egmont," "Midsummer Night's Dream" and "Manfred," and operas performed in New York in concert form, as Berlioz's "Les Troyens à Carthage," and Rubinstein's "Der Thurm zu Babel."

The compiler has also attempted to add three features of interest to musicians and writers on music. The first includes notices of certain musical dramatic works, never performed in New York, of which either the overture or vocal or instrumental selections were rendered in concerts during the first years of opera production in New York. The second is a mention of the open-air productions of opera in New York and the third, references to the operas broadcast by radio stations in New York.

The material offered here, then, may seem at first glance a duplication of the writings of Frederic Louis Ritter, Henry Edward Krehbiel, Esther Singleton, Henry C. Lahee, and others. A comparison of the present compilation with the labors of these authors will disclose, however, not only a difference in plan and execution, but a wealth of material insufficiently, even inadequately, treated by them. This compilation, in its restricted form, endeavors to supply for a period of one hundred years, from 1825 to 1925, a list of references to operatic performances which will supplement the work so thoroughly inaugurated by O. G. Sonneck's "Early Opera in America." The operatic doings of the first quarter of the nineteenth century are not touched upon in the present compilation, as outside of its scope, and find only an occasional note.

In the preparation of this work, the compiler has consulted the following two classes of material. The first embraces the books and magazine articles dealing with the subject, listed in the selected bibliography appended to this introduction. To these should be added, among others too numerous to mention, F. Clément and P. Larousse, "Dictionnaire des Opéras" (edited by A. Pougin); H. Riemann, "Opern-Handbuch"; G. Albinati, "Piccolo Dizionario di Opere Teatrali"; the compilations by W. G. Armstrong and G. H. Wilson; George P. Upton, "Musical Memories," and various magazine articles, dealing with musical life and conditions in New Orleans and San Francisco. The second class includes the newspapers and periodicals of the period covered by this compilation, namely, "The Euterpeiad," "The New York Musical Review and Gazette," "The American Art Journal," "Freund's Musical Weekly," "Freund's Music and Drama," "Musical America," "Musical Courier," "Musikalisches Wochenblatt," "Signale für die musikalische Welt," "Anglo-American," "The Albion," "The New York Spy," "The New York Mirror," "Morning Courier and Enquirer," "The New York Dramatic Mirror," "The Evening Post," "The New York Herald," "The New York Times," "The New York Tribune," "The Commercial Advertiser" and "New Yorker Staats Zeitung." The chief source of the compiler's information is the second group.

Among the works consulted by the present compiler, J. N. Ireland's "Records of the New York Stage, from 1750 to 1860," and T. A. Brown's "A History of the New York Stage from its First Performance in 1732 to 1901," have been of inestimable value. Bristling with facts and data, they aggregate 1,403 and 1,846 pages respectively. Unfortunately, these writers, though giving attention to operatic performances, are not always dependable or specific in their reports. They pass over many details of interest and importance and in some instances omit the dates of American premieres of well-known European operas. Not infrequently, too, they err in the date of a premiere by basing their record on the advertisement of a production which they failed to verify with a review or notice of the actual performance itself, in some cases occurring several days later on account of a postponement.

Typographical errors, partly occasioned, perhaps, by a misreading of their notes or due to an oversight in proofreading, are to be found. Strange to say, in common with later writers, they have ignored the bulk of early French operas performed in New York by the company from New Orleans. Nevertheless, despite these discrepancies, their compilations cannot be too highly recommended.

In 1882, the "Century Magazine" published in four installments a story of "Opera in New York," by Richard Grant White. The account is weak in dates of first performances, but informative and illustrated. As an early essay to tell the incidents of New York's operatic beginnings, the article was an aid to later writers. Its value has now been lessened by the subsequent results to which it contributed, often without an acknowledgement of indebtedness on the part of the borrowers.

Ritter's "Music in America" deals with operatic history in New York from the middle of the eighteenth century to the spring of 1889. In his treatment, he gives an extended account which is fairly trustworthy on the whole, but not always reliable in details. The author was seriously handicapped by the material at hand. He admittedly made use of the Drexel music collection, then in Philadelphia and at present incorporated in the Music Division of The New York Public Library. Unfortunately, Drexel's collection was not extensive in American sources. "Dwight's Journal of Music," "The Euterpeiad," and the "New York Musical Review and Gazette" were the only larger periodicals of the time in the collection which could furnish Ritter with reports of contemporary musical events in the United States. As a result, Ritter's account of opera in New York is general rather than specific.

In December, 1898, Miss Esther Singleton wrote in the "Musical Courier" (New York) a long magazine article under the title, "History of the Opera in New York from 1750 to 1898." The story covers fifteen large folio pages, two columns to a page, with illustrations. In its allotted space it is by far one of the best and most useful accounts yet written, covering the subject period by period, but necessarily restricted in details. As a pilot to H. E. Krehbiel's leviathan "Chapters of Opera" and its continuation, "More Chapters of Opera," Miss Singleton's article should not be overlooked, supplementing the work of the eminent critic in many departments and supplying a vast amount of information and data of which he took no cognizance.

The late Henry Edward Krehbiel was New York's chronicler of opera par excellence. His "Chapters of Opera" and "More Chapters of Opera" narrate the tale of operatic production in New York with all its glamor and shortcomings, managerial rivalries and enormous expenditure of money. The story in the first volume is, generally, more entertaining than historical; in the second, it is more critical of the operas performed at the Metropolitan and Manhattan opera houses. The first volume begins with the performances at the Park Theatre in 1825, taking up in turn the events at the Richmond Hill Theatre, Palmo's Opera House, the life of Lorenzo da Ponte (Mozart's librettist and the first professor of Italian at Columbia University) in New York, the Astor Place Opera House and the Academy of Music (soon to be razed), as a prelude to the operatic history of the Metropolitan Opera House. The performances in the smaller houses on the Bowery and along Broadway, like the New York Stadt Theatre, the German Opera House (the old Wallack's Theatre), Haverly's Fifth Avenue Theatre and the Théâtre Français, do not come in for consideration. Like Ireland, Brown, Ritter, White, and Miss Singleton, Krehbiel omits mention of the early French productions of 1827, 1833 and later. He makes use of Ritter's "Music in America" and follows a straight line to 1918. In his account of productions prior to the opening of the Metropolitan Opera House, he gives little attention to the dates of first performances or to the productions in other languages of the same operas. In the second volume, "More Chapters of Opera," the story is more fully told. No one who has in any way entered this field will underestimate the value of Krehbiel's work or can be without a sense of gratitude to him for it.

This compilation does not presume to take the place of the preceding publications. Its purpose is wholly dissimilar. In this compilation, the writer has sought to present briefly in a systematic form for quick reference:

1. A list of the operas and other musical dramatic works performed in New York, their number of acts, librettists and composers, and, in parentheses, the place and date of first performance.
2. The place and date of the first performance in New York, and a record of the language in which it was sung in New York.
3. The earliest dates of subsequent performances in New York in other languages.
4. The dates of open-air performances in New York.
5. The dates of broadcastings by radio stations in New York.
6. The dates of performances in other cities in America.
7. A review of the principal writings on the subject of opera in New York.
8. A selected bibliography of works dealing with the operatic life of New York.
9. A brief historical survey of the establishment of grand opera in New York.
10. A chronology of the grand operas performed in New York from 1825 to 1925.

The dates offered in this compilation have been for the most part verified in the newspapers and the musical journals. The dates which have been accepted by other writers and are either incorrect or have been differently fixed by the present compiler are quoted in parentheses. The asterisk (*) before a New York date indicates the first performance in the United States, which in most cases is the first in the western hemisphere. The date of the first performance in this part of the globe when definitely known, is specified in the notes. The dates of the first performances in New York are reasonably positive. On the other hand, absolute accuracy cannot always be attached to the secondary dates (those of performances of operas in other languages), as being the first performance in a given language. That some may be earlier is not unlikely; but the compiler vouches for a certainty that a performance in that language on the date noted actually did take place.

The compiler desires to thank Dr. Otto Kinkeldey, head of the music department at Cornell University, for his interest and helpful suggestions, Mr. Waldemar Rieck, of "Musical America," for exchange of courtesies, and Mr. Daniel C. Haskell for his assistance in the preparation of the writer's manuscript. Finally, the compiler wishes to express his indebtedness to all writers, mentioned or unnamed, whose labors have aided in the collection of the matter offered here.

A SELECTED BIBLIOGRAPHY OF WRITINGS DEALING
WITH GRAND OPERA IN NEW YORK

Arditi, Luigi. My reminiscences. Edited and comp. with introduction and notes by the Baroness von Zedlitz. New York: Dodd, Mead and Co., 1896. xxii, 314 p. illus. 8°.   * MEC

The **Art** of music: volume 4. Music in America. Department editors: Arthur Farwell and W. Dermont Darby. Introduction by Arthur Farwell. New York: The National Society of Music [cop. 1915]. xxix p., 1 l., 478 p. 8°.   * MF

Boyd, Charles Newell. *See* **Pratt,** Waldo Selden, and C. N. BOYD.

Brown, Thomas Allston. A history of the New York stage from its first performance in 1732 to 1901. New York: Dodd, Mead & Co., 1903. 3 v. 8°.   * R – NBL

Champlin, John Denison. Nearly two centuries of music. illus. (In: J. G. Wilson. The memorial history of the city of New York, from its first settlement to the year 1892. [New York:] New-York History Co., 1893. v. 4, p. 165–187.)   * R – Room 328

D., H. N. Theatres in 1825 and 1826. (In: Old New York, a journal relating to the history and antiquities of New York City. New York, 1889. 4°. v. 1, p. 116–126.)   IRGC
Reprinted from "The New York Mirror," Jan. 26, 1856.

Elson, Louis Charles. The history of American music. New York: The Macmillan Co., 1904. xiii, 380 p. illus. 8°.
"Opera in America," p. 95–122.   * MF

—— —— New York: The Macmillan Co., 1925. xiii, 423 p. new ed. illus. 8°.   * MF

Farrar, Geraldine. Geraldine Farrar; the story of an American singer. Boston: Houghton Mifflin Co., 1916. ix(i) p., 1 l., 114 p., 1 l. illus. 8°.   * MEC (Farrar)

Francis, John Wakefield. Old New York; or, Reminiscences of the past sixty years. Being an enlarged and revised edition of the anniversary discourse delivered before the New York Historical Society (November 17, 1857). New York: C. Roe, 1858. 384 p. 12°.   IRGC

—— Old New York: or, Reminiscences of the past sixty years. With a memoir of the author. New York: W. J. Widdleton, 1865. cxxxvi, 400 p. 4°.   IRGC

Griggs, John Cornelius. Studien über die Musik in Amerika. Leipzig: Breitkopf & Härtel, 1894. iv, 91(1) p. 8°.   * MF
"Konzerte und Opern," p. 71–81.

Hess, C. D. Early opera in America. illus. (Cosmopolitan. New York, 1901–02. 8°. v. 32, p. 139–152.)   * DA
The author was an impresario, head of the opera troupe, C. D. Hess & Co., and one of the directors of "The Parepa-Rosa Grand English Opera Company" in America.

Hoexter, Hermann H. English grand opera in America. A condensed history. (Century opera magazine. New York, 1914. Season 1914–15. Sept. 14, 1914, p. 9, 11, 19; Sept. 21, 1914, p. 9, 11, 19; Sept. 29, 1914, p. 9, 11, 19, 30, 32.)   * MBD

Howard, Kathleen. Confessions of an opera singer. New York: A. A. Knopf, 1918. 5 p.l., 13–273 p. illus. 8°. * MEC

Ireland, Joseph Norton. Records of the New York stage, from 1750 to 1860. New York: T. H. Morrell, 1866. 2 v. 8°.
                                        * R – NBL

Kahn, Otto H. An interview with Otto H. Kahn on operatic and dramatic art in America, and other art topics. [New York:] Publishers Press, 1911. 20 p. 8°.
                                 * MFC p.v.2, no.9
Reprinted from "The New York Times."

—— The Metropolitan Opera. A statement. [New York: The Metropolitan Opera Co., 1925.] 24 p. 8°.   * MFC p.v.6, no.1.

Selected Bibliography of Writings Dealing with Grand Opera in New York, continued.

Key, Pierre Van Rensselaer, and BRUNO ZIRATO. Enrico Caruso; a biography. Boston: Little, Brown and Co., 1922. xv, 455 p. illus. 8°.   *** MEC (Caruso)**

Klein, Hermann. Unmusical New York: a brief criticism of triumphs, failures and abuses. London: J. Lane, 1910. xi, 144 p., 1 port. 12°.   *** MG**

Kobbé, Gustav. Putting on grand opera. illus. (Cosmopolitan. New York, 1901–02. 8°. v. 32, p. 247–256.)   *** DA**

—— Signora. New York: T. Y. Crowell and Co. ₁cop. 1907.₁ 2 p.l., 205 p. illus. 8°.   **NBO**
A musical novel, written around the Metropolitan Opera House. Published in 1902 under the title, "Signora, a child of the opera house" (New York: R. H. Russell).

Krehbiel, Henry Edward. Chapters of opera; being historical and critical observations and records concerning the lyric drama in New York, from its earliest days, down to the present time. New York: H. Holt and Co., 1909. xvii, 435 p. illus. 8°.   *** MFC**

—— —— New York: H. Holt and Co., 1909. xvii, 435 p. 2. ed. illus. 8°.   *** MFC**

—— More chapters of opera; being historical and critical observations and records concerning the lyric drama in New York from 1908 to 1918. New York: H. Holt and Co., 1919. 3 p.l., ix–xvi, 474 p. illus. 8°.   *** MFC**

—— Opera in the United States. (In: Grove's Dictionary of music and musicians, edited by J. A. Fuller Maitland. New York: The Macmillan Co., 1907. 8°. v. 3, p. 466–.472.)   *** MD**
A continuation of this article will be found in "Grove's Dictionary of music and musicians," American supplement, v. 6, p. 292–296.

—— Review of the New York musical season 1885–1886 ₁to 1889–1890₁. Containing programmes of noteworthy occurrences, with numerous criticisms. New York: Novello, Ewer & Co., 1886–90. 5 v. 8°.   *** MGD**

Lahee, Henry Charles. Annals of music in America; a chronological record of significant musical events, from 1640 to the present day, with comments on the various periods into which the work is divided. Boston: Marshall Jones Co., 1922. vii p., 1 l., 298 p. 8°.   *** MF**

—— Grand opera in America. Boston: L. C. Page & Co., 1902. vi, 7–348 p. illus. 12°. (Music lovers' series.)   *** MFC**

—— The grand opera singers of to-day; an account of the leading operatic stars who have sung during recent years, together with a sketch of the chief operatic enterprises.

Boston: The Page Co., 1922. x p., 1 l., 543 p. illus. new rev. ed. 8°.   *** ME**
"The Metropolitan Opera House," p. 1–120, 260–356, 455–497.
"The Manhattan Opera House," p. 121–259.

Lilienthal, A. W. Led Philharmonic when overture to "Tannhäuser" was called "impossible." An appreciation and reminiscences of Carl Bergmann...port. (Musical America. New York, 1916–17. f°. v. 25, no. 2, p. 13–14.)   *** MA**

Mackinlay, Malcolm Sterling. Garcia, the centenarian and his times; being a memoir of Manuel Garcia's life and labours for the advancement of music and science. Edinburgh: W. Blackwood and Sons, 1908. xii p., 3 l., (1) 4–335 p. illus. 8°.   *** MEC (Garcia)**

Mapleson, James Henry. The Mapleson memoirs, 1848–1888. London: Remington & Co., 1888. 2 v. 2. ed. 8°.   *** MFC**

Maretzek, Max. Crotchets and quavers; or, Revelations of an opera manager in America. New York: S. French, 1855. 346 p. 12°.   *** MFC**

—— Max's memories. The veteran Maretzek talks of old-time opera. (American art journal. New York, 1892. f°. v. 59, p. 93–94.)   *** MA**

—— "Sharps and flats;" a sequel to "Crotchets and quavers." v. 1. New York: American Musician Publishing Co., 1890. 1 p.l., 87 p. illus. 8°.   *** MFC**
No more published.

—— *See also* **Rieck,** Waldemar.

Marzo, Eduardo. A golden winter 39 years ago. illus. (Musical America. New York, 1918. f°. v. 28, no. 11, p. 11.) *** MA**

—— Touring the states with Strakosch's stars in '73. illus. (Musical America. New York, 1918. f°. v. 27, no. 14, p. 8, 11.)   *** MA**

—— When Campanini and Maurel stirred New York; "touring the provinces" with a noted troupe. illus. (Musical America. New York, 1918. f°. v. 27, no. 19, p. 11.)   *** MA**

—— When New York repudiated Offenbach as a conductor. illus. (Musical America. New York, 1918. f°. v. 27, no. 24, p. 9, 11.)   *** MA**

The **Metropolitan** Opera House fire. Whether it will be rebuilt in doubt — its history. (American art journal. New York, 1892. f°. v. 59, no. 21, p. 485–488.)   *** MA**

Morris, William H. Memories of the old Park Theatre. illus. (American art journal. New York, 1892. f°. v. 59, p. 14–16.)   *** MA**

New York Academy of Music. (New York musical review and choral advocate. New York, 1854. 4°. v. 5, p. 353–354.)   **Drexel 417**

Selected Bibliography of Writings Dealing with Grand Opera in New York, continued.

New York's first 'Lohengrin.' Mr. Habelmann tells of an event of 37 years ago. [New York, 1908.] 2 l. 4°.
* MFC p.v.2, no.10.
Clipping from The Sun, New York, July 5, 1908.

Pratt, Waldo Selden, and C. N. BOYD. Grove's dictionary of music and musicians. American supplement, being the sixth volume of the complete work. New York: The Macmillan Co., 1920. vii, 412 p. illus. 8°.
* MD (Grove)
Contains much information about American opera companies.
"The Metropolitan Opera House in New York," p. 292–296, is a continuation of H. E. Krehbiel's "Opera in the United States" in "Grove's Dictionary of music and musicians," v. 3, p. 466–472.

Richard Wagner's erste Apostel in New York. [New York, 1908.] 3 l. 4°.
* MFC p.v.2, no.11.
Clipping from the New Yorker Revue, July 19, 1908.

Rieck, Waldemar. Max Maretzek — impresario, conductor and composer. illus. (Musical courier. New York, 1922. f°. v. 84, no. 25, p. 6–7, 47.)   *** MA**

—— When Bristow's "Rip" was sung at Niblo's Garden. illus. (Musical America. New York, 1925. f°. v. 43, no. 7, p. 3, 19.)
* MA

—— When Italian opera came to New York a century ago. illus. (Musical America. New York, 1925. f°. v. 42, no. 26, p. 3, 14.)   *** MA**

Ritter, Frédéric Louis. Music in America. New York: C. Scribner's Sons, 1883. xiv, 423 p. 8°.   **Drexel 1907**

—— —— New edition, with additions. New York: C. Scribner's Sons, 1890. xiv, 521 p. 8°.   *** MF**

—— —— New York: C. Scribner's Sons, 1900. xiv, 521 p. 8°.   *** MF**

Rogers, Francis. America's first grand opera season. (Musical quarterly. New York, 1915. 8°. v. 1, p. 93–101.)   *** MA**

Saerchinger, César. Musical landmarks in New York. illus. (Musical quarterly. New York, 1920. 8°. v. 6, p. 69–90.) *** MA**

Serruys, Margaret. Italian opera introduced to New York 100 years ago. [New York, 1925.] 2 l. 4°.   *** MF p.v.6**
Clipping from The New York Times, July 19, 1925.

Singleton, Esther. The Garcia centenary. illus. (Musical courier. New York, 1925. f°. v. 91, no. 23, p. 7, 41.)   *** MA**

—— History of the opera in New York from 1750 to 1898. (Musical courier. New York, 1898. v. 37, no. 23. [15 p.])   *** MA**

Sohn, J. Music: lessons of the operatic season. Opera in New York. (The Forum. New York, 1903. 8°. v. 34, p. 561–575.)
*DA

—— —— Extract.   *** MFC p.v.1, no.16.**

Somigli, Carlo. L'attuale situazione e la nuova produzione operatoria teatrale negli Stati Uniti dell' America del Nord. (Rivista musicale italiana. Torino, 1912–16. 8°. anno 19, p. 898–915; anno 20, p. 354–376; anno 21, p. 513–569; anno 22, p. 651–689.)
* MA

Sonneck, Oscar George Theodore. Early American operas. (Internationale Musik-Gesellschaft. Sammelbände. Leipzig, 1904–05. Jahrg. 6, p. 428–495.)   *** MA**
With musical examples.
Reprinted in his "Miscellaneous studies in the history of music," New York: The Macmillan Co., 1921, p. 16–92, *MGA.

—— Early opera in America. New York: G. Schirmer [1915]. viii, 230 p. illus. 8°.
* MFC
The first part of this work appeared in the "New music review," New York, June – Aug., 1907.

—— Pre-Revolutionary opera in America. (New music review. New York, 1907. v. 6, p. 438–444, 500–506, 562–569.)   *** MA**
These studies were incorporated in his "Early opera in America" (above).

Sotheran, Charles. The theatres of New York. illus. (In: J. G. Wilson. The memorial history of the city of New York, from its first settlement to the year 1892. [New York:] New York History Co., 1893. v. 4, p. 456–497.)   *** R – Room 328**

Stuerenburg, E. New Yorker Opernpioniere. Aus Geschichte und persönlichen Erinnerungen. New York, 1908. 2 p. illus. f°.   *** MFC**
Extract from the "Sonntagsblatt der New Yorker Staats-Zeitung," Nov. 1, 1908.

Wemyss, Francis Courtney. Twenty-six years of the life of an actor and manager. Interspersed with sketches, anecdotes and opinions of the professional merits of the most celebrated actors and actresses of our day. New York: Burgess, Stringer and Co., 1847. 2 v. in 1. 12°.   **AN**
Although chiefly an account of theatrical life in Philadelphia, this book contains information about singers who appeared in English opera in New York.

White, Richard Grant. Opera in New York. (Century. New York, 1882. 8°. v. 23 [new series, v. 1], p. 686–703, 865–882; v. 24 [new series, v. 2], p. 31–43, 193–210.)
*DA

Young, James C. Academy of Music bows to a new era. Its old walls, soon to be torn down, hold wealth of stage history. [New York, 1925.] 3 l. 4°.   *** MF p.v.6.**
Clipping from The New York Times magazine, Aug. 30, 1925.

Zirato, Bruno. *See* **Key,** Pierre Van Rensselaer, and BRUNO ZIRATO.

THE ESTABLISHMENT OF GRAND OPERA
A Brief Historical Survey

O N Tuesday, Nov. 29, 1825, at 8 o'clock in the evening, Mr. Nathaniel De Luce rapped for the attention of the twenty-five musicians who constituted the orchestra of the Park Theatre in New York. They responded with the two incisive chords that introduced the orchestral prélude of the evening's theatrical entertainment. From the orchestra pit ascended the strains of the overture of Rossini's unsuccessful opera, "Elisabetta, Regina d'Inghilterra," which he transferred bodily to his operatic masterpiece, "Il Barbiere di Siviglia." A few moments later, the curtain rose, revealing a scene in a Spanish courtyard before the house where the Count Almaviva had gathered a group of guitarists to serenade, in Italian, his beloved Rosina. Soon the village barber, Figaro, happens along and with the help of the gay and boisterous factotum, the amorous Count and his fiancée, after sundry adventures and escapades, are united to the gradual satisfaction of her guardian — to the evident delight of the spectators and Mr. Price, the manager of the theatre.

The performance was a memorable one for New York. The fashionables of the city had come to what was then the finest place of theatrical presentation in the metropolis (there were only two) to hear the florid vocalization of Rosina, the rattling recitatives of Figaro, the sonorous pomposities of Dom Bartolo and Basilio, and the adroit combination of all their parts in effective ensembles. A gala event, assuredly! "An assemblage of ladies," reported the "New-York Evening Post" the next day, "so fashionable, so numerous, & so elegantly dressed, was probably never witnessed in our theatre." The audience was "surprised, delighted, enchanted." "The repeated plaudits with which the theatre rung were unequivocal unaffected bursts of rapture."

Not only had these well-dressed ladies and their handsome male escorts witnessed the first performance in America of Rossini's ever-popular opera, "Il Barbiere di Siviglia," in Italian, but they had also applauded the efforts of the first real grand opera troupe in New York. The event was significant, historically, socially, and artistically. Among the spectators, says General James Grant Wilson ("The Life and Letters of Fitz-Greene Halleck," New York, 1869, p. 282), was no less a personage than Joseph Bonaparte, the ex-King of Spain; and the American poet, Fitz-Greene Halleck, and his friend, the novelist Fenimore Cooper, "who sat side by side," were "delighted listeners to the magnificent singing of the celebrated Signorina

Garcia." This brilliant gathering not only witnessed and applauded a new phenomenon in the musical life of the city, but became on that night, perhaps unaware of the fact, the first of New York's countless opera-going audiences.

The opera on this historic occasion was cast as follows:

Almaviva - - - - - - - -	Manuel Garcia, sr.
Rosina - - - - - - - -	Maria Garcia
Figaro - - - - - - - -	Manuel Garcia, jr.
Bertha - - - - - - - -	Mme. Garcia
Bartolo - - - - - - - -	Signor Rosich
Basilio - - - - - - - -	Signor Angrisani
Fiorello - - - - - - - -	Signor Crivelli, jr.

Although a contralto, Signorina Garcia sang soprano roles, like that of Rosina above, which were within the compass of her voice.

The performance was enthusiastically received by the audience and the press. The "New-York Review and Atheneum Magazine" (Dec., 1825) realized the historic importance of the event:

The twenty-ninth of November, 1825, will constitute a very interesting era in the history of Music... We do not say, that Europe cannot furnish a more finished Soprano voice than Signorina Garcia's, or a more astonishing Tenore than her father's, or a more extraordinary bass than Signor Angrisani's; but we do say, and that without fear of contradiction, that if their superiors can any where be found, they must be sought singly and separately at such places as the perpetual struggle of European competition may have made it their interest to visit.

The "New York Evening Post" on Nov. 30, 1825, wrote:

In what language shall we speak of an entertainment so novel in this country, but which has so long ranked as the most elegant and refined among the amusements of the higher classes of the old world? All have obtained a general idea of the opera from report. But report can give but a faint idea of it. Until it is seen, it will never be believed that a play can be conducted in recitative or singing and yet appear nearly as natural as the ordinary drama... There were no less than six [singers] whom we would esteem in the ordinary comedy, performers of the first order, considered merely as actors and independently of their vocal powers. Their style or manner of acting differs widely from any to which we have been accustomed. In the male performers you are struck with the variety, novelty and passion of their expressive, characteristic and unceasing gesticulation. The female performers, on the contrary, appeared to us to have less action, though quite as much expression as any we had ever before seen. There is indeed in their style of acting a most remarkable chasteness and propriety; never violating good taste nor exceeding the strictest bounds of female decorum...

The "New York Mirror and Ladies' Literary Gazette," on Dec. 3, 1825, reported to its readers:

The impression made upon the audience was novel and decidedly favourable. We were at a loss which to admire most, the powerful vocal talents of the operatic corps, or the galaxy of fashion and beauty that listened with admiration and applause.

The "New-York Literary Gazette and Phi Beta Kappa Repository" of Dec. 17, 1825, dissented from the general point of view:

The Italian opera has lately been introduced into this country: from what we had previously read of it, we always esteemed it a forced and unnatural bantling; seeing it, has not changed our opinion. It has grieved us to go to that house, where Shakespeare, Massinger, Lee, Sheridan, Cumberland, and a host of others have so long shone in the splendour of genius, and see anything unnatural presented. We have always looked on farce, melo-drama, and opera, with dissatisfaction — nothing but the old English tragedy and comedy ever afford us amusement ... Let us turn to the good old time when Shakespeare played...

The genuine drama is a natural-born subject — it represents the actions and passions of men as we see them in the world at large, and whatever is natural will delight. Is the false Italian school of opera natural? What man ever sung out his fit of passion? Who in jealousy, ambition, or revenge, ever vented his feelings in song? ...

The style of singing now introduced is, in a measure, new to this country, and the science they display, wonderful. For ourselves (ignoramuses that we are!) we do not relish the music, because we do not understand the Italian. There are those, no doubt, who can, or pretend, to follow the composer through all his passages, even without a syllable of language: we have not so much skill, and never delight in vocal music without the words. There are some sweet English, Scotch, and Irish melodies which touch us deeply, and make us feel the poetic influence of music, and long after the strain has ceased, reverberate on the heart ...

Signorina Garcia, however, had gratified the musical predilections of the former writer at the performance of "Il Barbiere di Siviglia" on Dec. 10, 1825, by interpolating in the lesson scene in the second act two songs which radiated "the poetic influence of music," to which he reacted:

On Saturday evening last...she sang a favourite Scotch song with great feeling and effect; and such was the stillness and attention of the audience, that the gentlest sigh would have been heard. When she finished, she rose from the piano amid the plaudits of all; and "encore" was sounded from every part of the house: cheerfully and gracefully she seated herself again, and sung "Home, sweet home," with more science and effect than we ever heard it before. These two songs made us deeply lament that the other parts of her performance were both in song and language so unintelligible to us.

Dr. John Wakefield Francis, an eminent New York physician, who ministered to the Garcia family among other notables, recalling the first opera performance in New York in a lecture before the New York Historical Society in 1857, declared in contrast to the above quotation:

From the moment that first night's entertainment closed, I looked upon the songs of Phillips (which made Coleman, the editor, music-mad), the melodies of Moore, and even the ballads of Scotland, as shorn of their popularity, and even now I think myself not much in error in holding to the same opinion. The Italian opera is an elaboration of many thoughts, of intelligence extensive and various; while it assimilates itself by its harmonious construction and entirety, it becomes effective by external impression and rational combination. It blends instruction with delight; if it does not make heroes, it at least leads captive the noblest attributes of humanity.

The singers were equally lauded. Dr. Francis held them all in high opinion:

The indomitable energy of Garcia, aided by his melodious strains and his exhaustless powers, the bewitching talents of his daughter, the Signorina Garcia, with her artistic faculties as an actress, and her flights of inspirations, the novelty of her conception, and her captivating person, proved that a galaxy of genius in a novel vocation unknown to the New World, demanded now its patronage. To these primary personages, as making up the roll, were added Angrisani, whose bass seemed as the peal of the noted organ at Haerlem; Rosich, a buffo of great resources; Crevelli, a promising *debutante;* the younger Garcia, with Signora Garcia, and Madame Barbiere with her capacious tenor [sic!], constituting a musical phalanx which neither London nor Paris could surpass, nay, at that time could equal.

By a strange coincidence, "The Harmonicon" of Nov., 1825 (p. 200–201) published a "catalogue of the stops in the great Organ at Haarlem."

What circumstances operated in bringing to our shores a European opera troupe singing in a language foreign to the majority of the resident population, is a point upon which, in the absence of positive information, one can now only speculate. Dr. Francis, recalling the event some thirty-two years later, declared that "we were indebted to the taste and refinement of Dominick Lynch, the liberality of the manager of the Park Theatre, Stephen Price, and the distinguished reputation of the Venetian, Lorenzo Da Ponte." Ritter summarily points out that the latter seems not to have been directly involved in the negotiations which brought Garcia's troupe to America. That he was, however, a factor in encouraging the scheme is not to be denied. Indeed, to establish Italian opera in New York was, as he himself phrased it in his "Memorie" (v. 3, p. 42), "il desideratum del mio sommo zelo"—the object of all his aspirations. As a poet of the Viennese court, the librettist of Mozart's operas, "Don Giovanni" and "Così fan tutte," and finally the compiler of a pasticcio which had been performed in the Kaiser-Stadt, he had reason to move with pardonable pride in the social circles of the day, especially in a city where the art of music was still in the crude stages of development. For such an one, the local theatres had little to offer. The contemporary musical productions, for the most part, were meagre and mediocre in comparison with the repertoire of Vienna. They consisted of English ballad operas, truncated versions of continental operas and plays with incidental songs, called melo-dramas. Each evening's principal entertainment was invariably preceded by a farcical curtain-raiser or followed by a silly after-piece, all delivered in a language strange to his ears. What more laudable or justifiable desire, then, could he entertain than to see the works in which he collaborated and the gorgeous operas by his countrymen performed in the city which he had chosen for his home. He must have known Price, a man of the theatre, and met his friend, Lynch, with both of whom he certainly would have discussed a project which engrossed his mind.

Dominick Lynch, the first member of the group mentioned by Dr. Francis, was a wealthy New York wine dealer. He seems to have been inordinately fond of music, particularly in its operatic form, for we find him connected with a subsequent and larger venture along the same lines. According to Dr. Francis, he "was the acknowledged head of the fashionable and festive board, a gentleman of the *ton,* and a melodist of great powers and of exquisite taste;

he had long striven to enhance the character of our music; he was the master of English song, but he felt, from his close cultivation of music and his knowledge of the genius of his countrymen, that much was wanting, and that more could be accomplished. . . " Not unlikely, through his interest and possibly with his funds, he was instrumental in winning Price to look with favor on Da Ponte's "desideratum." At all events, he went for Price to London, where the manager of the New York Park Theatre was well remembered, to engage singers for such an enterprise. He was undoubtedly the "agent of Mr. Price," of whom "The Harmonicon" (London, October, 1825, p. 194) speaks.

The company which Dominick Lynch recruited in the British capital consisted of eight members: two sopranos, one alto, two tenors, and three basses. It consisted of the Garcia family: Manuel, sr., aged 50, tenor; his wife, Joaquina Sitchès Garcia, soprano; their 20-year-old son, Manuel, jr., bass; their 17-year-old daughter, Maria (Marietta) Felicità, alto; Mme. Barbieri, soprano; Giovanni Crivelli, tenor; Felix Angrisani and Paolo Rosich, basses. "The Harmonicon," cited above, expressed surprise that so small a troupe should set out to produce opera. It adds, ungracefully: "But our trans-atlantic brethren have no experience in this kind of musical representation, and, therefore, will not perhaps be very nice."

Of the Garcia family, we need not speak in detail here. Suffice it to say, the elder Manuel had already enjoyed a wide career as a singer and a composer. He was a Spaniard who had identified himself with Italian opera. His wife had appeared in minor roles in Paris and "made an unsuccessful attempt in the same," according to "The Harmonicon," "in London." Their daughter, Maria, had been on the stage from her fifth year. She had made her debut in London at Her Majesty's Theatre on June 7, 1825, which year also witnessed her advent across the Atlantic. She was then on the threshold of a marvelous career, which was prematurely to be cut short by death eleven years later. Their son, Manuel, jr., was still a novice. He was to make his first appearance on the stage on the opening night of his father's first season in America. The younger Crivelli (the "New-York Evening Post" gives his first name as Giovanni) had sung previously to his New York engagement in secondary parts at the King's Theatre in London. Paolo Rosich had an occasional appearance in London in 1824, and, though re-engaged for the next season in 1825, at a salary of £50, did not return to the boards. Angrisani was an experienced singer, of whom "The Harmonicon" made no disparaging comment. He had been a leading bass in the Italian opera at the King's Theatre, in London, from 1817 to 1821, and, perhaps, later.

Garcia, sr., also, had sung at the King's Theatre in London and was heard in Rossini's "Il Barbiere di Siviglia." "The Harmonicon" (1830, p. 248) said of him:

He was half worn out; if he had ever possessed the power of sustaining a note, it is now entirely gone and he endeavoured to conceal the defect by the utmost profusion of florid ornament. It must be acknowledged, however, that, in the novelty, variety, and taste of his divisions, he has been excelled by no tenor of our time; and if the power of multiplying beautiful roulades were sufficient of itself to constitute a great singer, he had every title to the distinction.

Dominick Lynch seems to have justified the trust vested in him by Price in his efforts to get together an adequate company, as it proved, for New York's first season of grand opera. Among the renowned singers he is said to have endeavored to engage were Mme. Pasta, Mme. Caradori-Allen, the young Signora Marinoni, and others. Mme. Caradori (afterwards Caradori-Allen) had made her operatic debut in the Italian opera at the King's Theatre in 1822, singing with Angrisani. She came to America in 1837. Returning to England, she sang in the first production of Mendelssohn's oratorio, "Elijah," at Birmingham, on Aug. 26, 1846, under the composer's direction. Sufficient evidences, indeed, of Lynch's "taste and refinement," as Dr. Francis characterized his qualities.

Whatever may have been the merits of the individual members of the troupe they started for America, setting a precedent which has never been eradicated. "The sums said to be secured to these persons," commented the same "Harmonicon," "are past belief, all circumstances considered. We have hitherto been the laughing-stocks of Europe, for the preposterous manner in which we pay foreign singers, but the ridicule will now be transferred to the Western continent, if the statements put forth — which we cannot credit — should actually prove true." The fortune of Dominick Lynch and the liberality of Stephen Price are reflected in these words.

Accompanied by Lynch, the company embarked on the packet ship, "New York," on or about Oct. 1, 1825, from Liverpool. On Oct. 28, the "New-York Evening Post" communicated the fact that berths had been erected, fore and aft, on the packet, for the accommodation of her passengers. The boat with its galaxy of singers, passengers and merchandise reached New York on Sunday evening, Nov. 6. As members of the Garcia-Lynch-Price opera troupe were also listed Señor and Señora Ferri, Don Fabian, Giuseppe Pasta, Giovanni Cardini and Cristofaro Constantino "of the Italian Opera." These names are not to be found in the casts of the operas performed by Garcia's company during its first and only season in New York.

On Nov. 17, the first announcement of the plans of the "Italian *troupe* (among whom are some of the first artists of Europe)" was published in the "Evening Post." On the editorial page of the same issue appeared a letter reprinted from the "New York American." It explained the different types of arias in Italian operas and retold the circumstances surrounding the production of Europe's first opera, "Eurydice," by Ottavio Rinuccini [sic]. The communication was signed "Musœus." Query: was the letter inspired by Garcia and written by Price (or one of his assistants)?

Da Ponte was not slow in making the acquaintance of Garcia. He introduced himself as "the author of the libretto of Don Giovanni, and the friend of Mozart." Garcia is said to have embraced him, singing the beginning of the "champagne" aria, "Finch'han dal vino." No doubt, Garcia outlined his repertoire and the poet must have felt gratified in at least one of his secret ambitions to learn that "Don Giovanni" was a forthcoming production.

The season began at the Park Theatre on Nov. 29, 1825, with the first performance in America of Rossini's opera, "Il Barbiere di Siviglia," in Italian, as described above. The doors of the theatre opened at 7.30 p. m. The performance commenced at 8 o'clock and ended about half an hour before midnight. The opera itself was not entirely new to the theatre populace. It had been heard on the same stage six years earlier, on May 17, 1819, in an abridged English adaptation.

The orchestra at the Park Theatre for these opera performances was no "scratch" band, even though it was lacking in some of the instruments required by the operas rendered by the singers, and needed a piano to strengthen and unite its elements. The leader, who was also the principal violinist, was Nathaniel De Luce. His orchestra consisted of the following musicians: violins, Dumahault, Hill, Hollaway, jr., Milon, Moriere, W. Taylor; violas, Hollaway, sr., Nicolai; violoncello, Bocock, [Peter F.] Gentil, [P. K.] Moran; double bass, Davis, Greer; flute, [Francis] Blondeau, P. Taylor; clarinet, Beck, Mertine; bassoon, [John] Hornung; horn, Eberle, sr., Eberle, jr.; trumpet, [Raymond] Metz, Peterson; kettledrum, [John S.] Carroll; piano, [D. G.] Etienne. The first names or initials in brackets are supplied from the city directories of the time and may not be correct in all cases. Oboes, rare instruments in the New York orchestras of those days, were noticeably absent. One wonders, too, how De Luce, whose orchestra likewise lacked trombones, managed the supposedly horrific and fateful blasts on these instruments at the entrance of the ghost in "Don Giovanni!"

The personnel of the Garcia-De Luce orchestra was fairly international. De Luce was the regular leader of the Park Theatre orchestra. His wife appeared here in the English adaptation of Weber's opera, "Der Freischütz," in 1825, creating the role of Aennchen, called Linda in the version. Among the musicians, W. Taylor was undoubtedly the William Taylor who had conducted concerts in New York and played the overture of Beethoven's "Prometheus" for the first time in New York, according to the announcement on the programme, on March 20, 1823. Etienne was another active musician who appeared in the capacity of an orchestral leader and participated on many programmes. During the 40's, he figured both as a soloist and conductor of The Philharmonic Society of New York. As a composer he published a number of piano pieces. Gentil was probably the same who gave concerts and appeared as a conductor. P. Taylor was very likely the P. H. Taylor, a noted flute soloist during the first quarter of the century. Hornung, the bassoon player, according to the city directory, was also a grocer. Who the Eberles were is doubtful; a Jacob Eberle, musician, appears in the directories for 1825, a Frederick in 1826.

From the start, Garcia showed himself an enterprising impresario. Said the "New-York Review and Atheneum Magazine" (Dec., 1825):

Signor Garcia has shewn great judgment in the selection of the first opera. The music of "Il Barbiere di Siviglia" has always been extremely popular... The music...is of the sort which is almost immediately appreciated by the most unpractised ear (provided it be naturally a good one), and fixes itself firmly in the least retentive memory.

The choice of "Il Barbiere di Siviglia" was the more appropriate when we recall that Garcia himself created the role of the Count Almaviva at the original production of the opera at the Teatro Argentina in Rome on Feb. 5, 1816.

For his repertoire, Garcia had chosen only such operas which, with exception of two, had proven unmistakable successes in Europe. In course of his season he brought out no less than seven standard Italian operas and two of his own composition. Rossini was then the foremost operatic composer in Europe, and Garcia, besides playing his "Il Barbiere di Siviglia," put on his "Tancredi," "Il Turco in Italia" and "La Cenerentola" which in numerous English adaptations was one of the most popular operatic productions in New York for nearly half a century. He mounted also Zingarelli's "Romeo e Julietta" and Mozart's "Don Giovanni."

After playing Rossini's "Il Barbiere di Siviglia" five times, Garcia essayed what in modern journalese phraseology is designated a world premiere. It was an Italian opera in two acts, "L'Amante Astuto," the music of which was written by Garcia himself to a libretto by his basso buffo, Paolo Rosich. On April 25, 1826, Garcia brought forward another world premiere, his own "La Figlia dell' Aria," for which Paolo Rosich had again provided the libretto. This opera, founded on the story of Semiramis, has been consistently confused by all writers on the subject, including Krehbiel, with Rossini's "Semiramide" and ascribed to the swan of Pesaro. Garcia never played Rossini's opera. It was first introduced in New York at Palmo's Opera House on Jan. 3, 1845.

Although the season began auspiciously, local interest in the novelty of opera gradually waned. The company, generally, played on Tuesdays and Saturdays, alternating with English drama and comedy on the other nights. The performances usually began at 7.30 o'clock. The prices of admission were: boxes, $2; pit (orchestra) $1; gallery, 25 cents. An increase in prices, however, was found necessary and a new scale was arranged accordingly, 1st and 2nd tier boxes, $2; 3rd and 4th tier, $1; pit $1; gallery, 25 cents. The practice of selling opera librettos of a performance began on the first night: "Books of the opera can be procured at the theatre — price 37¾ cents," read the advertisement in the newspapers. The season came to a close on Sept 30, 1826, with a performance of the season's initial production, "Il Barbiere di Siviglia." The total receipts for the ten months were $56,685. The largest attendance after the opening night, paid $1,962; the smallest, $250. The opening night netted $2,980.

Nine operas were performed. "Il Barbiere di Siviglia" was the company's best asset. It was played twenty-three times. According to most writers 79 performances were given; according to Miss Singleton, 76. The present compiler tabulates 80 complete performances and one split bill, including two benefits. The record for the season is as follows:

1825 — Nov. 29; Dec. 3, 6, 10, 13, "Il Barbiere di Siviglia"; Dec. 17, 20, "L'Amante Astuto"; Dec. 24, 27, "Il Barbiere di Siviglia"; Dec. 31, "Tancredi."

1826 — Jan. 3, 10, 17, "Tancredi"; Jan. 21, "Il Barbiere di Siviglia"; Jan. 24, Feb. 4, "Tancredi"; Feb. 7, 11, 14, 18, "Otello"; Feb. 25, "Il Barbiere di Siviglia"; Feb. 28, "Tancredi"; March 2, "Otello"; March 4, one act of "Il Barbiere di Siviglia" and "Otello"; March 7, "Otello"; March 11, "Tancredi"; March 14, "Il Turco in Italia"; March 18, "Tancredi"; March 21, 28, "Il Turco in Italia"; April 1, "Il Barbiere di Siviglia"; April 4, "Tancredi"; April 8, "Otello"; April 10, "Il Turco in Italia"; April 15, "Il Barbiere di Siviglia"; April 22, "Tancredi"; April 25, 29, May 2, "La Figlia dell' Aria"; May 6, "Il Barbiere di Siviglia"; May 9, "La Figlia dell' Aria"; May 13, "Otello"; May 16, "Il Barbiere di Siviglia"; May 23, 27, 30, "Don Giovanni"; June 3, "Il Barbiere di Siviglia"; June 6, "Otello"; June 10, "Don Giovanni"; June 17, "Il Barbiere di Siviglia"; June 20, "Don Giovanni"; June 24, "Tancredi"; June 27, "La Cenerentola"; July 1, "Tancredi"; July 3, "Il Barbiere di Siviglia"; July 10, "La Figlia dell' Aria"; July 12, 14, "La Cenerentola"; July 17, "Otello"; July 19, "Il Barbiere di Siviglia"; July 21, "Don Giovanni"; July 24, "La Cenerentola"; July 26, "Romeo e Giulietta"; July 28, "Don Giovanni"; July 31, "Romeo e Giulietta"; Aug. 2, "Tancredi"; Aug. 3, 4, "Il Barbiere di Siviglia"; Aug. 7, "La Cenerentola"; Aug. 9, "Don Giovanni"; Aug. 11, "Il Barbiere di Siviglia"; Aug. 12–28, theatre closed; Aug. 29, "La Figlia dell' Aria"; Sept. 2, "La Cenerentola"; Sept. 5, "Don Giovanni"; Sept. 9, "Otello"; Sept. 12, "Il Barbiere di Siviglia"; Sept. 16 (benefit of Manuel Garcia, jr.), "Il Barbiere di Siviglia"; Sept. 19 (benefit of Mme. Garcia), "Il Barbiere di Siviglia"; Sept. 26, "Romeo e Giulietta"; Sept. 30, "Il Barbiere di Siviglia."

No performances took place on Jan. 7, 1826; Jan. 14, 28 and 31; April 18, and May 20, on account of the indisposition of Manuel Garcia, sr. He announced a benefit for himself on Sept. 23, with "Tancredi," but cancelled the performance, because of illness. On June 13, 1826, and July 8, Signorina Garcia was indisposed and no performances were given. Dr. Francis, who attended the Garcia family, asserted that its members "possessed good constitutions and took little physic."

When Garcia's season ended on the night of Sept. 30, 1826, the redoubtable impresario decided to try his fortunes in Mexico. He departed with his company to Mexico City, where he played with his troupe until 1828. He left his daughter, Maria, behind. Of his singers, Angrisani and Rosich only seem to have returned to the scene of their first American triumphs, for both reappeared with Mme. Feron at the Bowery Theatre two years later, in 1828.

Maria Garcia remained in New York because she had been married before the French consul on March 23, 1826, to a French merchant, named Eugene Malibran, by which name she subsequently became best known. (J. G. Prod'-homme gives M. Malibran's Christian name as Louis.) Maria was eighteen years of age at the time of her marriage. Her husband was several decades her senior. His affairs were in a bad state and the marriage proved to be an unhappy one for the girl, whom the "New-York Evening Post" described as a "cunning pattern of excelling nature." She acquired a knowledge of English and appeared in the English ballad operas, "The Devil's Bridge" and "Love in a Village," at the Bowery Theatre. She was paid $500 for each performance, approximately the same sum she received at the height of her career in Paris and Naples. She — the great contralto! — also sang on Sundays with the choir of Grace Church in New York.

Toward the end of the year, Maria Garcia, now Mme. Malibran, decided to return to Europe — to quit the American continent and her superannuated spouse. Her farewell performance took place at the Bowery Theatre, not, as usually stated, on Sept. 28, 1827, but on Oct. 29, 1827, a month and a day later. On Sept. 28, the twelfth performance of an Asiatic ballet with the same title as Boieldieu's opera, "The Caliph of Bagdad," and with music by Rossini (!), was danced. On the occasion of her farewell appearance Mme. Malibran sang in the first performance in America in English of Boieldieu's two-act opera, "Jean de Paris," which had been just introduced in New York in the original French version at the Park Theatre on Aug. 6 of that year. A miscellaneous programme of vocal compositions in Italian, Spanish and German rounded out the evening's bill. Worthy of note is the fact that she sang in German the aria, "Und ob die Wolke sich verhülle," from the third act of Weber's opera, "Der Freischütz."

Mme. Malibran arrived in Paris sometime toward the end of November. She soon made the acquaintance of Charles de Beriot, a clever young violinist, aged twenty-five. A mutual attachment sprang up between them. Fortunately for Maria, rumors and news travelled slowly across the Atlantic. At any rate, they were very late in reaching Malibran, who, obligingly, as it were, had remained behind at 86 Liberty Street, New York — unless, indeed, Maria Felicita ran away. When, at length, his sentiments were sufficiently roused, he went in pursuit of his prima donna wife. He set out for Paris in December, 1830. Thereupon Mme. Malibran began to institute proceedings for divorce. To aid her cause, she sought the legal advice of Lafayette, the dignified soldier and statesman of seventy-odd years, whose knowledge of American law would prove an asset to the prosecution. J. G. Prod'homme published in "The Chesterian" (London, Sept., 1919) a resumé of the affair based upon certain unpublished letters. Eleven letters of the correspondence which passed between Mme. Malibran and Lafayette are now in the Library of Congress, Washington, D. C. They were made public in "The Chesterian" (nos. 44–45) in 1925, by Mr. Carl Engel, head of the Music Division of the Library of Congress.

The success of Italian opera in New York did not deter the managers of the English opera companies. On the contrary, they were bold enough to vie with it in the presentation of at least three of its best examples in English versions. "Il Barbiere di Siviglia" was revived, and "Don Giovanni," in Sir Henry Rowley Bishop's vile adaptation, followed at the Chatham Theatre on May 29, 1826. Mozart's "Le Nozze di Figaro," though not in Garcia's repertoire, was a representative Italian opera which was resuscitated in English in New York and elsewhere. A host of excellent singers, among them Mrs. Hackett, Mrs. Austin, Mrs. Knight, Mrs. Sharpe, Miss Kelly, and Messrs. Pearmann, Philipps, Incledon and Charles Edward Horn in turn invaded the local theatres to the delight of all who subscribed to the opinion of the writer in the "New-York Literary Gazette and Phi Beta Kappa Repository." They succeeded, at any rate, in delaying the recurrence of organized Italian opera in New York for nearly six years.

Weber's opera, "Der Freischütz," was performed in English on March 2, 1825, at the Park Theatre, in advance of Garcia's arrival. Weber's "Abou Hassan" (invariably misspelt "Abon Hassen") came on Nov. 5, 1827. Other operas performed between Garcia's period and the advent of the next season of Italian opera in New York were: "The Castle of Andalusia," "No Song, No Supper," "Fontainebleau," "Alfred the Great," "Artaxerxes" and "Dido." The revival of Cherubini's "Lodoiska" introduced an astonishing proceeding. The overture of the opera was wedged into the opera itself, and to its fine strains, two of the principal male characters fought a much advertised broadsword combat!

Although grand opera was an innovation for New York's theatre-going public, it was no new form of entertainment in the United States. As far back as 1791, a company of French actors and singers produced drama, opera and ballet at the Théâtre St. Pierre in New Orleans. A more pretentious structure, called the Théâtre St. Philippe, after the name of the street on which it stood, and owned by a Frenchman, named Croquet, was erected in 1808. Three years later, in 1811, one John Davis, from San Domingo, came to New Orleans and built of brick the Théâtre d'Orléans, which was opened in 1813. Within four years, it was destroyed by fire. The undaunted John Davis at once conceived a new project, and reared at the cost of $180,000 a more substantial structure on the spot of the old theatre, retaining its name. The people of New Orleans heard, among others, such operas as Paisiello's setting of "The Barber of Seville," Zingarelli's "Romeo and Juliet," first introduced in New York in Italian by Garcia, and Cherubini's "Les Deux Journées." In New York, a so-called American opera, "The Archers of Switzerland," composed by Benjamin Carr, to a libretto by William Dunlap, had been performed on April 18, 1796. In the same year, on Dec. 19, another American opera, by Pellisier, was tried out. These operas, however, were not of the type with which Garcia made America acquainted. The list can be lengthened by several other interesting American specimens. They are described in O. G. Sonneck's "Early American Operas." (Consult the bibliography included in the present work.)

In the New York theatres, the operatic pieces by Samuel Arnold, Stephen Storace, Sir Henry Rowley Bishop, William Shield, Michael Kelly, Joseph Mazzinghi, and others had repeatedly delighted the populace. Even an English version of Rousseau's "Pygmalion" had gone over the boards. Mozart's "Le Nozze di Figaro," in Bishop's perversion, gave New York an idea of the composer whose sacred music had figured on many a local concert. But none of these productions, least of all Mozart's opera, were attempts at grand opera in Garcia's manner, but makeshifts adapted, pruned and spliced to fit the exigencies of the companies performing them. They were, in form, little better than modern musical comedies, abounding in spoken dialogue and other stage business. Arias which taxed the powers of the singers were omitted and popular airs of the day inserted to replace them. The performances usually began at 7.30 o'clock and the evening's entertainment was rounded out with either a curtain-raiser or an after-piece. Sometimes both figured on a bill. This procedure explains how an opera like Mozart's "Le Nozze di Figaro," which in a regular European opera house filled the entire evening, was billed in America with fore and after comedies and farces. Most writers on this subject have ignored this phase of theatrical production and created an erroneous impression when noting the first performance of a grand opera during the early years of opera in America.

French opera next claimed the attention of New York. It followed closely upon the departing shadow of Italian opera. On July 13, 1827, a French company from New Orleans opened at the Park Theatre with Nicolo's opera, "Cendrillon," introducing a new foreign element in the operatic life of the city. There was a patronage for French opera in New York at the time, not extensive, perhaps, but sufficient to warrant the risk of bringing a company from the West. French musicians had played in Garcia's orchestra. Two of its members, Messrs. Etienne and Gentil, were both active independently of each other and had arranged concerts for the local French Benevolent Society and for other purposes. Other French names are to be met on the roster of the next larger Italian venture.

All writers on opera in New York have either ignored this first season of French opera or glossed over it with a mere mention. The company was composed of Mesdames Millon, Paradole and Chollet and MM. Alexandre, Blonze, Gontier, Notaire, and Richard, among others. Their repertoire included, besides French dramas, farces and vaudevilles which figured on every bill, the operas, "Cendrillon," "Les Deux Journées," "Joconde," "Ma Tante Aurore," "La Dame Blanche," "Le Caliph de Bagdad," "Le Maçon,"

"Le Petit Chaperon Rouge," "Aline, Reine de Golconde," and others. (For a partial list, consult the chronology, appended to this work.)

In the fall of the year, Mme. Malibran made her farewell appearance in America and departed for France. She was rejoined in Paris by her parents late in the autumn of 1828. Her divorce from Malibran was finally granted by the French courts on March 26, 1836. Three days later she married De Beriot. But fate laid a heavy hand on her. On Sept. 23 that year, she died in Manchester, England, from the effects of a fall from a horse.

To return to opera in New York in 1827 — on Dec. 24, Paer's opera, "Il Fuorusciti di Firenze," was performed at the Bowery Theatre, in English, under the title, "The Freebooters."

In 1829, Italian opera was announced by Mme. Feron, Mme. Brichta, Charles Edward Horn, Rosich, and Angrisani at the Bowery Theatre "for 5 nights only, previous to their departure for Europe." The singers had been living in New York, singing at concerts and appearing on programmes of sacred music, called "oratorios." The days of performance were to be Monday, Thursday, and Saturday. The opening night was April 20, 1829. An operatic piece, "Il Trionfo de la Musica" (also known as "Il Fanatico per la Musica"), was given for the first time in America. William Taylor, who had been a violinist in Garcia's orchestra, conducted. The newspapers reported favorably on the performance. Rosich, in particular, was singled out for especial laudation. The "Morning Courier and New-York Enquirer" said of him the next day:

And who had forgotten Rosich? jovial, facetious Rosich — the Bartolo of the Garcia *troupe.* He is a host of himself, and one glance at his jolly face, and one of his buffo songs, are werth [sic] a ticket of themselves.

The same paper on the 20th declared, " . . . we are well satisfied that the house on Thursday will present as great a display . . . " But was there a performance on Thursday, the 23rd? An examination of the contemporary papers discloses no record of one. A performance was announced for Saturday, the 25th. The same problem confronts the investigator. On Monday night, the 27th, Mme. Feron's benefit took place. A one-act operetta, "The Quartette," in English, by C. E. Horn, received its initial rendition, and "Il Trionfo de la Musica" was repeated. On the ensuing Wednesday, the 29th, Horn's benefit took place with "an Italian opera" and the English adaptation of "The Marriage of Figaro." The advertisements did not reveal the name of the Italian opera; probably, "Il Trionfo de la Musica" was again sung. Thus ended the *stagione.*

Da Ponte meanwhile was not to be satisfied with but one season's fulfilment of his "desideratum." He now brought his niece, Giulia Da Ponte, from Italy. She was a soprano, a pupil of Bagioli, and Da Ponte determined on launching her on an operatic career in America. She made her first appearance in a concert of instrumental and vocal selections at the Bowery Theatre in New York on March 31, 1830, assisted by Rosich and Angrisani, who apparently had not departed for Europe, a Mr. Hagenmacher, a Mr. Metz (the same who played in Garcia's orchestra?), and others. The Frenchman, Etienne, who was ubiquitous in all the city's musical affairs, was at the piano. A lecture on "Shakespeare's Early Days" introduced the evening's programme. A farce, "Wm. Thompson," closed the entertainment.

The "New-York Evening Post" the following day reported:

> The gifted debutante fully realized the expectations of her friends, and judging from the impression it made upon her audience . . . it must be pronounced complete.

With the help of his niece, Da Ponte ventured to put on an Italian opera. For the signorina's second appearance, he revived his pasticcio, "L'Ape Musicale," which had been· performed in Vienna forty-one years earlier, in 1789. The performance took place at the Park Theatre on April 20, 1830, "after being delayed from night to night," as the "Morning Courier and New-York Enquirer" (April 20, 1830) informed its readers, "in consequence of the Opera being in a fit state for representation." Nevertheless, the young singer "drew a full and fashionable house." The "New-York Evening Post" reported:

> She was welcomed with deafening applauses, and her performance increased the favorable impression already made.

But a note of concealed diffidence marked the criticism of her performance. The "Morning Courier and New-York Enquirer" (April 22, 1830) said:

> The second effort of the Signorina Da Ponte was altogether happier and more successful than her first.

The programme which her uncle devised for the occasion was ill-assorted. The "Morning Courier and New-York Enquirer" severely denounced its heterogeneous array of selections. Among other pieces, she sang an aria from Rossini's "Semiramide."

On her third appearance, Giulia took a benefit. A concert was arranged on April 29, 1830, at the Park Theatre. She sang arias from "L'Inganno Felice" and "Francesco da Rimini" and repeated the excerpt from "Semiramide." A comedy, "Popping the Question," opened the programme; a farce, "My Master's Rival," closed it. A "strong and effective" chorus took part and Rosich assisted.

She again appeared in public on May 10, 1830, at the Park Theatre, at Rosich's benefit. She was featured with Mrs. Austin and sang a duet with Angrisani. The programme was the usual miscellaneous musical hotchpotch. The next night saw Giulia singing at the annual spring concert of the New-York Musical Fund Society at the City Hotel. The artistic fraternity surrounding her included Mrs. Knight, Rosich, Angrisani, and a pianist, Miss Sterling, among others.

Elson ("The History of American Music," p. 102) calls the Signorina Giulia Da Ponte a good soprano; on what authority he fails to indicate. She seems not to have sustained herself before the public. As Ireland says ("Records of the New York Stage," p. 627), she "gracefully retired into the more congenial shades of private life." So, her uncle's second dream of Italian opera in New York passed like a mirage.

New York at this time was no longer a city of average size. It had reached a plane from which a prophetic vision of its present greatness was no idle dream. It had become the commercial and trading centre of the East and was already looked upon as a rival of the principal cities of Europe. In 1820, New York state became the largest in population in the union. The census figures were set down as 1,372,111. In 1800, New York had been third, Virginia being first and Pennsylvania second. Ten years later, it was second, with a population of 959,049, being exceeded by Virginia's 974,600. In 1830, the census reached the then staggering count of 1,918,608. In the decade between 1820 and 1830, the population of New York city almost doubled. The limit of its fashionable residential section was Warren Street, and the Broadway stage coaches did such a thriving business that a regular line of stages was established between Bowling Green and Bleecker Street in 1830.

In 1825, the year of the introduction of grand opera in New York, John Quincy Adams, of Massachusetts, son of the second president, was inaugurated as the sixth President of the United States, with John C. Calhoun as vice-president and Henry Clay, of Kentucky, as the secretary of state. On Oct. 6, five days after Garcia sailed from Liverpool, the Erie Canal in New York was completed. De Witt Clinton was the governor of the state. The year saw the opening of the Sante Fé trail, as a result of the strenuous efforts of Senator Benton of Missouri, while Great Britain hailed the operation of Robert Stephenson's first steam locomotive over the Stockton and Darlington Railway in the north of England.

In 1830, the "Euterpeiad" (New York, p. 86) said:

There has been no Opera at [the Park Theatre] since the opening of the present season; and nothing, therefore, would appear to require a passing notice from us at this time...

Opera we shall have, undoubtedly, during the present autumn and coming winter. For it is not the character of the managers of this house to suffer the public taste to remain ungratified in any respect...

A footnote (on p. 148) definitely declared:

Opera in New York is now under a cloud; perhaps all the patronage is reserved for Cinderella.

This was Rophino Lacy's English adaptation of Rossini's "La Cenerentola." Lacy's version proved an unprecedented success and was performed at the Park Theatre as late as 1845. It was one of the main pieces in the repertoire of the English opera companies which played uninterruptedly during the trials and vicissitudes of Italian opera.

Da Ponte was, however, not disheartened by his recent ill-luck:

> Two distinguished performers, one tenor, the other bass, have been engaged at Venice, through the exertions of professor Da Ponte. . .

said the "Euterpeiad" on June 1, 1830 (p. 27). His restless disposition is even reflected in his moving about the city from house to house. During the preceding six years he changed his place of residence no fewer than five times. He had been an unsuccessful merchant in Elizabethtown, N. J., in 1805 and the cities beyond the Hudson were no mere names to him. He now turned his eyes to Philadelphia.

An Italian drama which his son, Lorenzo L. Da Ponte, had written for his cousin, Giulia, seems to have been considered for production in the Quaker City. For this drama, the elder Da Ponte arranged an interpolation, "something similar to the one in Shakespeare's Hamlet," with music selected by him from Rossini, Vaccai, Generali, Mercadante and Mozart. Was the piece his "L'Ape Musicale" again? Whether or not the younger Da Ponte's drama was performed in Philadelphia, the present writer has not been able to learn. The younger Da Ponte was also a professor of Italian in New York, teaching in the University of the City of New York for a number of years prior to his death in 1840.

English opera now emerged triumphant. The Italian Opera House became the National Theatre. Many eminent singers arrived from Europe and new musical dramatic pieces were tried out. Barnet's opera, "The Mountain Sylph" was mounted at the Park Theatre on May 11, 1835. Bellini's "La Sonnambula" was heard there in English on Nov. 13, 1835. Auber's "Le Dieu et la Bayadere," under the title, "The maid of Cashmere," was interpreted at the National Theatre, late Italian Opera House, on Oct. 3, 1836. Among the singers who were newly welcomed was Mme. Caradori-Allen, whom Dominick Lynch endeavored to secure for Garcia. In 1838 came Richings and later his daughter, Caroline, who gave readings of Longfellow's "Hiawatha." Then the Seguins with Miss Jane Shireff and Mr. Wilson drew full houses at the National Theatre. In 1839, New York became acquainted with an arrangement of Beethoven's only opera, "Fidelio," which enjoyed a run of fourteen consecutive nights. Braham, the once popular English singer and composer of operettas, also appeared in America at this time, singing in concerts at Niblo's Garden before approving audiences.

The setback which Italian opera had just experienced in New York was only temporary — like the lull which precedes a coming storm. Phoenix-like and irrepressible, it showed its countenance in 1832 and spread its wings over the Richmond Hill Theatre. Da Ponte was its oracle; one Giovanni Battista (?) Montressor, a tenor (was he the tenor to whom the "Euterpeiad" referred?), its prophet.

The company opened at the Richmond Hill Theatre on Oct. 6, 1832, with Rossini's "La Cenerentola." It was a regularly equipped opera organization, the second of its kind in New York. The roster of singers included, among others, Adelaide Pedrotti, Albina Stella, Mme. Brichta (she, too, apparently, had remained in America), Lorenza Marozzi, Enchritta Salvioni, Teresa Verducci, Signora Saccomani, Montressor himself, Signor Fornasari, Giuseppe Corsetti, Francesco Sapignoli, and Signor Orlandani.

The orchestra was under the able direction of Bagioli and the leader was the violinist, M. Rapetti, afterwards conductor of the orchestra at the Astor Place Opera House, New York, and a soloist of the Philharmonic Society of New York. There were twenty players, among them the trombonist Cioffi, whose performances of solos afterwards became notable in New York. The orchestra also boasted of two oboes, the first to be heard in the city. An anonymous but ostensibly well-informed writer in the "New-York Mirror" (Jan. 3, 1834, p. 211) wrote:

. . . we have had a specimen of what a band ought to be, in that led by Rappetti, at the Richmond-hill theatre, the best, we do not hesitate to say, that ever played dramatic music in America.

The Richmond Hill Theatre gloriously changed its name to the Italian Opera House. On April 10, 1833, the company transferred its activities to the American or Bowery Theatre. On Dec. 14, 1832, Signor Rapetti took a benefit with the sixth performance of Bellini's "Il Pirata." The season ended, according to the announcement, on Dec. 21, 1832. The next day the company performed Rossini's "Mosè in Egitto," in concert form as an oratorio, at the Masonic Hall, New York. The opera-oratorio was repeated by them on Jan. 5, 1833, in the Assembly Room of the City Hotel, New York. On Jan. 2, 1833, the soprano, Adelaide Pedrotti, took a benefit with Mercadante's "Elisa e Claudio." On the 10th, Montressor followed with a manager's benefit at the Bowery Theatre with "Il Pirata:" On the 12th, the company sang its farewell in "Elisa e Claudio" and departed to Philadelphia to inaugurate there at the "Italian Opera-House, late Chestnut Street Theatre" on Jan. 23, 1833, with "Elisa e Claudio" the first season of Italian opera in the city founded by William Penn (W. G. Armstrong, "A Record of the Opera in Philadelphia," p. 21).

The company returned to the American or Bowery Theatre on April 10, 1833, and played until May 11, 1833, closing with the first performance in America of Rossini's "L'Inganno Felice" and the second act of "Il Barbiere di Siviglia." On May 9, 1833, Montressor took a second benefit. "Il Barbiere di Siviglia" was performed and the first music from Meyerbeer's pen was, according to the bill, heard in America. The overture of his "Il Crociato in Egitto" was played by the orchestra. Montressor reimbursed himself with the proceeds of a third benefit on May 16, 1833. Rapetti was last in line with a benefit concert on the 27th at the Masonic Hall, New York.

Philip Hone, one-time mayor of New York and afterwards a box-holder at Montressor's Italian Opera House, was not impressed with the company's leading prima donna. He was severe in his strictures to the point of ungallantry. It seems he had been invited to a reception in Park Place, and there met, as he underscored her in his diary (Nov. 13, 1832), "*The Pedrotti*, the *prima donna* of the Italian opera." Apparently, she had declined an invitation to sing for the guests, whereupon our diarist found her to be "wretchedly out of place, with her immense vulgar figure, staring eyes, and tawdry dress, amongst the lovely, modest, and graceful women with whom she was associated. And she refused to sing, too, after Mrs. Parish and Helen McEvers had kindly set her the example. If she did not sing, why was she there? And then the elegant amateurs of Italian music pretend to compare this woman to Fanny Kemble; nay, pretend to say that, independently of her singing, she plays better and has more grace! She is no more comparable to her than I to the Apollo Belvidere, a sunflower to a violet, a cart-horse to the Bussorah Arabian, an ale-house sign to a landscape of Claude, or Jane, our chambermaid, to Mrs. Gardiner Howland."

Montressor's company gave about fifty performances, not including benefits and concerts. He introduced in America for the first time four operas, Rossini's "L'Italiana in Algeria" and "L'Inganno Felice," Mercadante's "Elisa e Claudio," and Bellini's "Il Pirata." They represented the company's chief productions. The other operas in its repertoire were "La Cenerentola" and "Il Barbiere di Siviglia." After the collapse of the enterprise, not a few of its singers and instrumentalists settled in New York.

As in 1827, French opera again trailed the Italian season. A strong company from New Orleans engaged the Park Theatre in August, 1833. They gave New York its second glimpse of the French form of opera. As before, writers on local operatic matters have ignored their productions. They gave the first performance in New York of "Le Philtre" and "La Fiancée," both by Auber, Hérold's "Zampa," Rossini's French opera, "Le Comte Ory," and Castil-Blaze's pasticcio, "Les Folies Amoureuses." New York also heard from them "Fra Diavolo" and "La Dame Blanche" in their original French versions. The company played in Philadelphia in September.

The Italian and French opera performances were not without a beneficial effect on local musical dramatic productions in English. The merits of the foreign renditions created an artistic standard by which the English performances were measured — and the latter were found wanting in method and in presentation. The "American Monthly Magazine" (New York, 1833, p. 191) observed this condition. It said, in this serpentine manner:

We had begun to congratulate ourselves and the public that a taste for the science of music had sprung up among us, and that the light and frivolous tinkling which had so long pervaded our drawing rooms, would soon give place to a better state of things; — that mere melody however excellent in itself, as far as it goes, would now be conjoined with harmony, delighting the imagination as well as the ear, and that the *remembrance* of our musical entertainments would remain with us, on which to employ the scrutiny of criticism, thus giving a mental treat as well as a mere gratification of the senses, instead of a repetition of those evanescent pleasures which are forgotten with the sounds that gave them birth, leaving not an impression behind, which could convey the idea of an artist's hand, or of a composer's skill. We hailed with the most sincere pleasure the prospect of the efforts of those children of harmony, the Italians, in our city, and every day added to the satisfaction of our minds on finding that their first performances were attended with crowded houses in the certain expectation that our taste for that most social of all accomplishments would now rise in dignity, and change from rude noises to refined and bewitching sounds.

A desire for more genuine operatic works, in contrast to the current mutilated versions and dramatic pieces interspersed with songs and choruses, was beginning to make itself felt. Weber's "Der Freischütz" was put on with great scenic display. The incantation episode, in particular, afforded an opportunity for stage management and caused a sensation. Meyerbeer's "Robert le Diable," in an English adaptation by Rophino Lacy, was another work of this type. Auber's "Fra Diavolo" and his "Masaniello" next intrigued the managers. Boieldieu's "La Dame Blanche" also held the boards effectively, under the title, "The White Lady or The Spirit of Avenal," in an English translation by John Howard Payne, the author of the words of "Home, Sweet Home." Even Mozart's opera, "Die Zauberflöte," in an arrangement by the indefatigable Charles Edward Horn, was not too much to attempt. Other instances might be enumerated. "Nothing," as Arthur Elson said ("The History of American Music," p. 102), "was too high game for the 'adaptors' to fly at." Such was the state of operatic affairs in New York when the next season of Italian opera followed closely upon the financial failure of Montressor's enterprise.

The year 1833 was not to close ignominiously with Montressor's fiasco. Before the lapse of many months, New York was to behold a building devoted exclusively to the production of grand opera, i. e., Italian opera. Da Ponte was once more the leading spirit of the movement. He, now a bookseller at 336 Broadway, had succeeded in interesting several wealthy New Yorkers to support a theatre of this kind. Not to repeat the catastrophe which befell the former undertaking with Montressor, he persuaded them, in the bargain, to finance this latest venture. Among the "backers," as they would nowadays be called, were Philip Hone, once a mayor of New York, and Da Ponte's old stand-by and friend, Dominick Lynch.

The new opera house was a handsome structure, erected at the corner of Church and Leonard streets. The name adopted by the Richmond Hill Theatre was transferred with justification to this edifice. It was known as the Italian Opera House.

On Sept. 15, 1833, the drawing for the stalls at the above house occurred. Philip Hone describes the event in his diary:

September 15, 1833. — The drawing for boxes at the Italian Opera House took place this morning. My associates, Mr. Schermerhorn and General Jones, are out of town, and I attended and drew No. 8, with which I am well satisfied. The other boxes will be occupied by the following gentlemen: Gerard H. Coster, G. C. Howland, Rufus Prime, Mr. Panon,

Robert Ray, J. F. Moulton, James J. Jones, D. Linch, E. Townsend, John C. Cruger, O. Mauran, Charles Hall, J. G. Pierson and S. B. Ruggles.

They constituted, under the circumstances, New York's first horseshoe circle. The house opened on Nov. 18, 1833. Ritter gives a careful description of the interior ("Music in America," p. 208):

The auditorium was different in arrangement than any hitherto seen in America. The second tier was composed entirely of private boxes, hung with curtains of crimson silk; and the first tier communicated with the balcony and pit, thus making the first advance toward the long-desired privilege of the ladies occupying that portion of the house. The whole interior was pronounced magnificent, and the scenery and curtains were beautiful beyond all precedent. The ground of the front-boxes was white, with emblematical medallions and octagonal panels of crimson, blue, and gold. The dome was painted with representations of the Muses. The sofas and pit-seats were covered with damask, and the floors were all carpeted.

The opera of the gala opening was Rossini's "La Gazza Ladra," performed for the first time in America. "Il Barbiere di Siviglia" was revived on the 25th. Another novelty arrived on Dec. 16, 1833, Rossini's "La Donna del Lago," founded on Sir Walter Scott's poem, "The Lady of the Lake." Cimarosa's "Il Matrimonio Segreto" followed on Jan. 4, 1834. Pacini's "Gli Arabi nelle Gallie" came on the 20th. On Feb. 10, the fifth novelty, Rossini's "Matilde di Shabran," with a miscellaneous musical programme, was forthcoming. In April, the company went to Philadelphia and played at the Chestnut Street Theatre, returning to New York on May 24. The months of June and July were almost entirely devoted to benefits. On July 22, Clementina Fanti, the prima donna of the troupe, sang in concert at Niblo's Garden, New York. Her colleagues followed her example and during the temporary cessation of the performances at the Italian Opera House, eked out their earnings by singing selections from Italian operas at this Germanic rendezvous.

On Aug. 4, a concert was arranged for the benefit of Alberto Bazzini, the costumer of the troupe. Bellini's "La Straniera" was put on for its first American production on Nov. 10th, and on the 25th, Rossini's "Eduardo e Cristina" was first heard. The season terminated with a benefit for the manager on Dec. 23, with a double bill consisting of the last named opera and "L'Inganno Felice."

The company was under the management of Rivafinoli and Da Ponte. Rivafinoli was probably the same with whom Da Ponte had dealings regarding Italian books ("Memorie," v. 3, p. 25). The principal singers were Clementina Fanti, soprano; Rosina Fanti, second soprano; Luigia Bordogni, mezzo soprano; Mme. Schneider-Maroncelli, contralto; Luigi Ravaglio and G. B. Fabi, tenors; and De Rosa and A. Porto, basses. The musical director was Carlo Salvioni, who took a benefit on March 22, 1834, when his opera, "La Casa da Vendere," followed by a miscellaneous musical programme, received its world premiere. On Feb. 1, 1834, he produced his Italian scene, "Coriolanus before Rome; or, Filial Love," for tenor solo sung by Luigi

Ravaglio and chorus "in full costume," between the acts of Pacini's "Gli Arabi nelle Gallie." The scene was repeated at the City Hotel on Feb. 15, 1834, at a concert for the benefit of Eugene Guillaud, who had been a clarinetist in Rapetti's orchestra at the Richmond Hill Theatre.

The season under Rivafinoli and Da Ponte lasted six months, ending on April 4. The management was re-organized and passed into the control of Porto, the bass of the company, and its treasurer, Sacchi. They re-opened on May 24, with several additions among the singers, the new members being Miss Julia Wheatly, an American and the daughter of the manager of the Park Theatre, and Signori L. Monterasi and S. Ferrero. The re-organized troupe played until Dec. 23, 1834, as noted above. The company put on Rossini's "L'Assedio di Corinto" on Feb. 6, 1835, and journeyed to Albany in April ("The American Musical Journal," New York, 1835, p. 144).

The orchestra consisted of twenty-five musicians: seven violins, two violas, two violoncellos, two double basses, two flutes, a third flute to replace oboe parts, two clarinets, one bassoon, two horns, two trumpets, three trombones, kettledrum and harp. Oboes were again absent. Boucher, the principal violoncellist, was the leader. He was afterwards one of the conductors of The Philharmonic Society of New York and occasionally appeared as a chamber music soloist on its programmes.

The new opera house incurred the displeasure of its subscribers. Ritter ("Music in America," p. 210) quotes a notice to this effect, which appeared in one of the periodicals of the time:

> An opinion prevails pretty generally among opera-goers that the proprietors of this house are retarding the very object for which they built it by their injudicious retaining the whole second row of boxes. It is said that this arrangement operates injuriously in several ways, and that it would be much more advantageous to the managers to pay a rent fully equal to the interest of the capital invested on the building.

Ritter informs us (p. 212):

> The manager paid no rent in cash for the house: but the proprietors reserved to themselves the exclusive use of twenty boxes in the second tier, with the privilege of a hundred and sixteen free tickets for each night, all transferable; which tickets, calculated at the same rate as the sofa-seats were the previous season, make sixty-eight representations, a sum equal to $15,776.

A most preposterous deal! In it can again be seen Da Ponte's impractical business methods. Under such circumstances, financial prosperity could only have been the last thought.

Rivafinoli, as if in self-defense for the collapse of his management, published in the New York newspapers a table of the receipts and expenditures of his enterprise — a highly illuminating document. Too long to be re-printed here, it can be consulted in Ritter's "Music in America," p. 211–212. The total expenses for eight months amounted to $81,054.98. Of this sum, $9,476.54 was still due by the manager to different singers, chorus-singers, orchestra and other persons. The receipts aggregated $51,780.89, which included the income derived from thirteen benefits, twelve concerts, one

oratorio performance and one rendition of a mass. Rivafinoli's deficit was
$29,275.09.

The whole undertaking seems to have disgruntled Hone. Having been a
box-holder, one can suspect the source of his grievances. The picture which
he gives of the time, in his diary (Nov. 11, 1835), and the attitude of the
patrons of opera, as well as his criticism of the management of the opera
company, is instructive:

> . . . The avidity with which people crowd to hear these oratorios [as the concerts of sacred
> music were called, — not to be confused with its formal meaning], and the immense houses
> which Mr. and Mrs. Wood bring nightly to the Park, prove that the New Yorkers are not
> devoid of musical taste, notwithstanding that the Italian opera does not succeed, and the pro-
> prietors are about selling their opera-house (the neatest and most beautiful theatre in the
> United States, and unsurpassed in Europe); but there are two reasons for this, both of which
> savour much of the John Bullism which we have inherited from our forefathers. The first
> is, that we want to understand the language; we cannot endure to sit by and see the performers
> splitting their sides with laughter, and we not take the joke; dissolved in "briny tears," and
> we not permitted to sympathize with them; or running each other through the body, and we
> devoid of the means of condemning or justifying the act. The other is the private boxes, so
> elegantly fitted up, which occupy the whole of the second tier. They cost six thousand dollars
> each, to be sure, and the use of them is all that the proprietors get for their money; but it forms
> a sort of aristocratical distinction. Many people do not choose to occupy seats (more pleasant
> and commodious than they can find in any other theatre) while others recline upon satin
> cushions, and rest their elbows upon arm-chairs, albeit they are bought with their own money.
> These causes have prevented the success of the Italian opera, and I do not wonder at it. I like
> this spirit of independence which refuses its countenance to anything exclusive. "Let the pro-
> prietors," say the sovereigns, "have their private boxes and satin cushions; they have paid well
> for them and are entitled to enjoy them. We will not furnish the means of supporting the
> establishment, but go to the Park Theatre, where it is 'first come, first served'; where our dol-
> lar will furnish us with 'the best the House affords,' and where the Woods will provide us with
> that dollar's worth of something we can understand without the aid of a bungling translation."

Italian opera in New York went down completely. It lost its champion,
too. Da Ponte died on Aug. 17, 1838, at the age of eighty-one, in the city
for whose musical entertainment he had labored so assiduously during his
last years. His theatre, the elegant Italian Opera House (renamed the National Theatre) likewise disappeared in ashes. On Sept. 23, 1839, at 5 o'clock
in the evening, it burned to the ground, setting fire to the African Methodist
Church on the opposite side of Leonard Street, the French church, Du Saint
Esprit, on the corner of Franklin Street, and the incomplete Dutch church
on the same street, as well as a large number of dwellings. On Jan. 20, 1840,
Stephen Price passed away.

The English productions of the next years differed in no wise from those
already recounted. Operas by Balfe, Rooke, Benedict and others followed
each other in rapid succession. Horn continued to be prolific as an operatic
arranger and a composer of operas of his own, the most pretentious being
"Ahmed al Kamel" (1840) and "The Maid of Saxony" (1842). Two other
productions of this period need only detain us here. Rophino Lacy, whose
version of Rossini's "La Cenerentola" as "Cinderella" haunted the wings of

almost every local theatre like a hybrid afrit and dogged Italian opera whenever it threatened to take root, conceived for the Seguin troupe, in English, "a sacred music drama." The term suggests at once that which Wagner was later slowly to evolve by devious processes of philosophizing — and he was at this time preoccupied in writing operas on Italian and French models to test their effectiveness as vehicles for a music drama. Lacy's "sacred music drama," however, was a conglomerate pot-boiler. It was put on with scenery at the Park Theatre on Oct. 31, 1842, and proved a box-office attraction for many nights. The chorus which participated in the production numbered fifty-five and the orchestra, thirty-five musicians. The music was selected by Lacy from Handel and Rossini. What a team for the chariot of a muse! On Nov. 21, Handel's "Acis and Galatea" was performed at the Park Theatre.

French opera returned from New Orleans in 1843. The chief singer of the company was an inimitable Mlle. Calve, who captured New York as did her greater namesake in present-day memory. The company played from May to October, with interruptions, at Niblo's Garden and introduced in French the first performances of the Italian operas, "Lucia di Lammermoor," "Gemma di Vergy" and "Anna Boleyn," besides the French operas, "La Fille du Régiment," "Le Domino Noir," "L'Éclair," "Le Pré aux Clercs," "Le Châlet," "Les Diamants de la Couronne," "L'Ambassadrice" and lesser works.

The vacillating interest in Italian opera in New York once more gathered momentum — this time as a consequence of the success of French opera. It was sponsored over the white table cloths of an Italian eating-house on Broadway near Duane Street, emblazoned with the dazzling French appellation, Café des Mille Colonnes. The guiding spirit was the proprietor of the establishment himself: short of stature, high in ideals and more than amply supplied with funds provided by hungry patrons. A new headquarters for Italian opera went up on Chambers Street, a little further north than the former Italian playhouse. Palmo's Opera House, he called it, and near enough to his Duane Street café for his musically sated opera guests to retire after the performance to satiate their material appetites and to aid unwittingly the box office of the opera house. The shrewd little restaurateur avoided the box system which caused such dissatisfaction at Da Ponte's Italian Opera House, and enhanced the interior with only two private boxes. The price of the seats was uniform throughout the house.

Palmo's season was inaugurated with eclat on Feb. 3 (not 2 or 5), 1844, with the first American production of Bellini's "I Puritani." All of the now traditional difficulties and problems of Italian opera in New York beset Palmo's efforts. Four years after its opening Palmo's Opera House was abandoned to be reopened under the name of Burton's Theatre. On Feb. 3, 1854, Shakespeare's "Midsummer Night's Dream," with Mendelssohn's incidental music, sold the house out for a prosperous run.

The operas which Palmo introduced in New York for the first time, besides "I Puritani," were "Beatrice di Tenda," "Belisario," "Lucrezia Borgia," "I Lombardi," "Nina Pazza per Amore," "Linda di Chamounix" and "Chiara di Rosemburgh."

While Palmo was seeking to delay the inevitable end, English opera in New York became more firmly intrenched with the American production of Balfe's still delightful English opera, "The Bohemian Girl," at the Park Theatre on Nov. 25, 1844, by the Seguin company. It was one of its principal successes until 1846 when it popularized Donizetti's Italian opera, "Don Pasquale," in English. The Seguin troupe toured the United States extensively and was a prototype of many subsequent travelling companies, such as the Emma Abbott Opera Co., Clara Louise Kellogg Opera Co., Parepa-Rosa Opera Co., Emma Juch English Opera Co., American Opera Co., National Opera Co., Castle Square Opera Co., the Italian San Carlo Opera Co. to-day, and others, bringing to countless cities and towns the operas which the larger centres are privileged to enjoy. These companies, for the most part, sang in English.

German opera was late in making its appearance in New York. It made up for this tardiness during the Damrosch regime at the Metropolitan Opera House. It made its entry in New York at Palmo's Opera House for a number of nights late in Dec., 1845, and early in Jan., 1846. All writers have overlooked this season. Weber's opera, "Der Freischütz," once so popular in English, was sung for the first time, as far as the present writer has been able to trace, in its original tongue on Dec. 8, 1845. Weigl's "Die Schweizer Familie," was an offering on Dec. 17th. For lack of patronage the season was short-lived.

Another German season was inaugurated in 1855 at Niblo's Garden. Flotow's "Martha," which initiated at that theatre the transcontinental career of the English singer, Anna Bishop, in 1852, under Bochsa with whom she eloped, was performed in German on March 13, 1855. Adam's French opera, "Le Brasseur de Preston," was also in the repertoire in German.

A third attempt followed late in 1856 at the old Broadway Theatre. "Fidelio," the company's initial production, was then performed for the first time in New York, in German, on Dec. 29th. Lortzing's "Czar und Zimmermann" was tried out for its American premiere on Jan. 9, 1857. The same composer's "Alessandro Stradella" and "Undine" were put on in German on Sept. 20th and Oct. 9th, respectively, at Niblo's Garden.

A more ambitious season of German opera sought to establish itself in 1862 at 485 Broadway, Wallack's old theatre, renamed the German Opera House. Mozart's opera, "Die Entführung aus dem Serail," was the first novelty on Oct. 10th. Mehul's French "Joseph" was sold to his brethren in German on Feb. 16, 1863.

Wagner came to New York in an operatic guise in 1859 at the New York Stadt Theatre in "Tannhäuser." Carl Bergmann conducted and the local Arion singing society supplied the choruses. It was the first of Wagner's operas to be heard in America. His "Lohengrin" arrived on our shores at the same theatre on March 12, 1871. Six years later, on Jan. 26, 1877, "Der Fliegende Holländer" sailed into port on the stage of the Academy of Music. On April 2, "Die Walküre" sent their cries over the same footlights to the wand of Adolph Neuendorff — an inadequate performance. There, too, "Rienzi" fought his political opponents on March 4, 1878. The story of the introduction of subsequent Wagner operas belongs to a later era.

Russian opera feebly sought recognition on Dec. 15, 1869. Verestowsky's "Askoldowa Magila" (Ascold's tomb) was staged at the Théâtre Français, on Fourteenth Street, by the Slaviansky Russian Opera Co. The libretto in an English translation by Mme. Olga Agreneff was published in New York for the occasion (a copy is in the Music Division of The New York Public Library). The attempt proved abortive.

During the years briefly outlined in the preceding paragraphs, grand opera in foreign languages became firmly rooted in New York. Palmo's efforts showed the way. While he was seeking to hold his audiences downtown at Chambers Street, the northward expansion of the city indicated the advisability of following its trend. A move sponsored by one hundred and fifty men of wealth resulted in the erection of a new opera house in Astor Place. The seating capacity was nearly fifteen hundred and prices ranged from one dollar to two dollars. The house was built by Messrs. Foster, Morgan and Colles and opened on Nov. 22, 1847, with Verdi's "Ernani." Rapetti, of Montressor's Richmond Hill venture, was the leader of the orchestra. The opening night presaged a successful future. The company was strong in all its departments and included the Barilis and Pattis. But again the same old story! Palmo's years were four and those of the Astor Place Opera House numbered five. In 1852, the place was forsaken. It was metamorphosed into the Clinton Library.

While Italian opera was being performed regularly at the Astor Place Opera House, other Italian opera troupes visited New York from time to time, playing wherever a theatre could be found. The management of the Astor Place Opera House, experiencing this rivalry, was constrained to compel public attention. It resorted to a questionable method, unquestioned in Europe at the time, and obtaining to this day, to insure success for its singers, a device which misled not a few of the unsophisticated contemporary music critics. The presence of professional applauders, known as the *claque*, became as active a factor in American operatic productions during the next decades as in European houses. The "New York Herald," of Feb. 2, 1848, summarized the situation clearly:

> By the by, the musical criticisms of some of the journals are quite amusing, more especially those of the *Courrier des Etats Unis*. In some of the articles that appear in that delectable paper concerning the opera, there is such good nature, and amiable combinations of sense and silliness, of absurdity and critical acumen, of learning and lumbering, that they seem to be

more a sort of half-formed literary articles, than real musical *critiques*. One very sensible remark made in these *critiques*, must strike every person as rather correct, viz.: that the refined audience of the Astor Place Opera applaud seldom when applause is deserved, and fail to condemn when condemnation is merited. In fact, the critic thinks the audiences there would relish much better, and be better judges, of a mere English ballad, than they would be of the finished musical compositions called Italian operas. There is more truth than poetry in this remark; and the following advertisement is proper: —

> WANTED IMMEDIATELY. — A few young gentlemen, with real moustaches, and also some old boys, with deep dyed moustaches, who can officiate as *claquers* at the Italian Opera. They must furnish their own gloves. Apply at the office of the managers.

The lares of the Astor Place Opera House were not long to be without shelter. They found a new, finer, more commodious abode in Fourteenth Street near Third Avenue. An application for an Act of incorporation was made to the legislature and the charter was granted on April 10, 1852. The building operations commenced in May, 1853, and the Academy of Music was completed, at a cost of $335,000, in 1854. The grand inauguration was set for Oct. 2, 1854, and Grisi and Mario, two of the greatest singers of the age, sang grand opera into permanence in New York. The house has enjoyed a glorious history. It was afterwards superseded as an operatic centre by its rival, the Metropolitan Opera House, built about a mile and a half to the north, and opened on Oct. 22, 1883, at a total cost of $1,732,978.71. Like other vestiges of by-gone days, the Academy of Music is shortly to be razed.

The story of opera at the Academy of Music is that of history subsequent to the establishment of grand opera in New York. The events at the Astor Place Opera House, Academy of Music, Metropolitan Opera House, the incursion of the Manhattan Opera House and the seasons of light opera at the Century Opera House, under the auspices of grand opera management, are too numerous, diversified and extensive to permit of a cursory treatment. The subject can be pursued in Henry Edward Krehbiel's "Chapters of Opera" and "More Chapters of Opera" and other writings, listed in the bibliography included in the present work.

GRAND OPERA IN NEW YORK

1825-1925

A basso porto (At the lower harbor).

Italian opera in 3 acts, libretto by Eugenio Checchi, founded on the play by Goffredo Cognetti; music by N. Spinelli. (Cologne, Stadttheater, April 18, 1894, in German; Rome, Teatro Costanzi, March 11, 1895, in Italian.) American Theatre, Jan. 22, 1900, in English, preceded by Jacques Offenbach's one-act operetta, "Le chanson de Fortunio," in English, as "The magic melody," in two acts.

First performed in America: St. Louis, Exposition Music Hall, Jan. 8, 1900, in English for the first time on any stage.

Abou Hassan.

German opera in 1 act, libretto by Franz Carl Hiemer; music by C. M. von Weber. (Munich, June 4, 1811.) *Park Theatre, Nov. 5, 1827, in English, preceded by John O'Keefe's English operatic piece, "Fontainebleau."

Performed in Philadelphia, Nov. 21, 1827.

Acis and Galatea.

English pastoral serenata in 2 acts, libretto by John Gay, with additions by Alexander Pope; music by G. F. Handel. (Sung in concert form at the Duke of Chandos's palace, 1720-21; acted at the Haymarket Theatre, London, May 17, 1732.) *Park Theatre, Nov. 21 (not 22), 1842, in English, followed by a farce, "Meet me by moonlight."

The operatic version of this serenata bore at its first production in America the sub-title, "The fiend of Mount Etna."

This serenata was performed in concert form on Feb. 14, 1839, Charles Edward Horn conducting, as the first part of a concert, at the Lyceum Building, New York.

Adel (Adele) di Lusignano.

Italian opera in 2 acts, music by Ramon Carnicer. (Barcelona, Casa Teatro, May 15, 1819.)

Never performed in New York.

A duet for tenor and bass from this opera was sung "by particular request" on Dec. 19, 1833, by Signor G. B. Fabj and Signor A. Porto at Euterpean Hall, New York, in a concert by the Italian Opera Co.

Adina. *See* L'Elisir d'amore.

Adolphe et Clara; ou, Les deux prisonniers.

French opera in 1 act, libretto by Benoit Joseph Marsollier des Vivetières; music by N. Dalayrac. (Paris, Opéra Comique, Feb. 10, 1799.) Park Theatre, Aug. 23, 1827, in French, preceded by Molière's comedy, "Tartufe."

Adriana Lecouvreur.

Italian opera in 4 acts, libretto by Arturo Colautti, founded on the play by Augustin Eugène Scribe and Ernest Legouvé; music by F. Cilea. (Milan, Teatro Lirico Internazionale, Nov. 6, 1902.) Metropolitan Opera House, Nov. 18, 1907, in Italian.

First performed in America: New Orleans, French Opera House, Jan. 5, 1907.

L'Africaine (L'Africana; Die Afrikanerin).

French opera in 5 acts, libretto by Augustin Eugène Scribe; music by G. Meyerbeer. (Paris, Opéra, April 28, 1865.) *Academy of Music, Dec. 1, 1865, in Italian; New York Stadt Theatre, May 2, 1871, in German.

Performed in Philadelphia, Academy of Music, Jan. 2, 1866; Chicago, Crosby's Opera House, June 17, 1866; New Orleans, French Opera House, Dec. 18, 1869.

Ahmed al Kamel; or, The pilgrim of love.

American opera, libretto by Henry J. Finn, founded on Washington Irving's "Tales of the Alhambra;" music by C. E. Horn. First performed: New National Opera House, Oct. 12 (not 20), 1840, in English, preceded by a comedy, "Perfection."

Aïda.

Italian opera in 4 acts, libretto translated from the French of Camille Du Locle by Antonio Ghislanzoni; music by G. Verdi. (Cairo, Egypt, Dec. 24, 1871, at the inauguration of the new opera house.) *Academy of Music, Nov. 26, 1873, in Italian; Haverly's Fifth Avenue Theatre, March 9, 1881, in English; Academy of Music, April 29, 1881, in French; Metropolitan Opera House, Nov. 12, 1886, in German.

An open air performance of this opera was given on Aug. 16, 1919, in Italian, at Sheepshead Bay Speedway, and on June 20, 1923, in Italian, at the Polo Grounds, New York. Another open air performance of this opera was given on Aug. 1, 1925, in Italian, at Ebbets Field, Brooklyn.

This opera was broadcast by radio on May 26, 1925, in Italian, through station WGBS, New York. This opera was again broadcast by radio on June 30, 1925, in Italian, in tabloid form, with reduced orchestra, through station WEAF, New York. The open air performance in Italian at Ebbets Field, Brooklyn, was broadcast by radio through station WNYC, New York. The indoor performance of this opera on Sept. 7, 1925, in Italian, by the Boston Civic Grand Opera Co., at the Manhattan Opera House, New York, was broadcast by radio, in its entirety, through station WJZ, New York.

A curious performance of this opera was given in concert form, in English, on May 15 and 16, 1925, at the Boston Opera House, Boston. The triumphal scene in the second act of the opera was presented with appropriate settings and costumes, and a ballet. During the other scenes of the opera, the chorus and soloists, dressed to represent Egyptians, were arranged as during the performance of an oratorio.

Grand Opera in New York, 1825–1925, cont'd.

The soloists sat in a row of chairs at the front of the stage, rising to sing their parts; the chorus, which was recruited from various local singing societies, was grouped behind them.

Performed in Philadelphia, Academy of Music, Dec. 12, 1873; Chicago, 1874; New Orleans, French Opera House, Dec. 6, 1878; Boston, Globe Theatre, Nov. 8, 1880, in English.

Verdi's opera was performed in New York before it was produced either in Paris or London.

L'Ajo nell' imbarazzo.

Italian opera in 2 acts, libretto by Jacopo Ferretti; music by G. Donizetti. (Rome, Teatro Valle, Feb. 4, 1824.)

Never performed in New York.

The overture of this opera was played on May 27, 1833, at the Masonic Hall, New York, at the benefit of Signor M. Rapetti, leader and violinist of the Italian Opera House, corner Church and Leonard streets.

Alessandro Stradella.

German opera in 3 acts, libretto by W. Friedrich; music by F. von Flotow. (Paris, Palais Royal Théâtre, Feb., 1837; Hamburg, Dec. 30, 1844, in expanded form.) *Niblo's Garden, April 12, 1855, in German; Winter Garden, April 20, 1860, in Italian.

Performed in Philadelphia, Academy of Music, Jan. 28, 1863.

Aline, reine de Golconde.

French opera. Park Theatre, Aug. 29, 1827, in French, followed by a play, "Werter; ou, Les égaremens d'un coeur sensible."

Query: By whom?

There are three French operas of the same title, all in 3 acts: (1) libretto by Michel Jean Sedaine, music by P. A. Monsigny; performed in Paris at the Opéra, April 15, 1766; (2) libretto by Vial and Edmé Guillaume François de Favières, music by H. M. Berton; performed in Paris at the Théâtre Feydeau, Sept. 2, 1803; (3) same libretto as preceding, music by A. Boieldieu, performed in St. Petersburg, March 5, 1804.

According to Noel Straus (New York *Times,* Dec. 6, 1925; section 8, p. 10), Berton's opera was performed in the Spring of 1825 at the Théâtre d'Orléans, New Orleans, during Lafayette's visit to the city. A French company from New Orleans played during the Summer of 1827 at the Park Theatre, New York. Not unlikely the opera noted above was Berton's work.

L'Amante astuto.

Italian opera in 2 acts, libretto by Paolo Rosich; music by M. Garcia. First performed: Park Theatre, Dec. 17, 1825, in Italian.

L'Ambassadrice (The Ambassadress).

French opera in 3 acts, libretto by Augustin Eugène Scribe and Jules Henri Vernoy de Saint Georges; music by D. Auber. (Paris, Opéra Comique, Dec. 21, 1836.) Niblo's Theatre (not Garden), May 26 (not 25), 1843, in French; Brougham's Lyceum Theatre, Jan. 27, 1851, in an English version by George Loder.

Performed in Philadelphia, Chestnut Street Theatre, Sept. 14, 1843.

L'Amico Fritz.

Italian opera in 3 acts, libretto by P. Suardon; music by P. Mascagni. (Rome, Teatro Costanzi, Oct. 31, 1891.) Carnegie Music Hall, Jan. 31, 1893, in Italian, for the benefit of the Young Men's Hebrew Association and the Hebrew Institute.

First performed in America: Philadelphia, Grand Opera House, June 8, 1892.

Amilie; or, The love test.

English opera in 3 acts, libretto by John Thomas Haines; music by W. M. Rooke. (London, Covent Garden, Dec. 2, 1837.) *National Theatre, Oct. 15 (not 13), 1838, in English.

Performed in Philadelphia: Walnut Street Theatre, Nov. 19, 1838.

L'Amore medico.

Italian comic opera in 2 acts, founded on Molière's play, "L'amour médecin," libretto by Enrico Golisciani; music by E. Wolf-Ferrari. (Dresden, Hofoper, Dec. 4, 1913, in German translation by Richard Batka, as "Der Liebhaber als Arzt.") *Metropolitan Opera House, March 25, 1914, in Italian.

L'Amore dei tre re.

Italian opera in 3 acts, libretto by Sem Benelli; music by I. Montemezzi. (Milan, Teatro alla Scala, April 11, 1913.) *Metropolitan Opera House, Jan. 2 (not 14), 1914, in Italian.

Performed in Boston, Boston Opera House, Feb. 9, 1914.

L'Amour des trois oranges.

Russian opera in a prologue and 4 acts, founded on Carlo Gozzi's "Fiaba dell' amore delle tre melarancie;" libretto and music by S. Prokofieff. (Chicago, Auditorium, Dec. 30, 1921, in the French translation by Véra Janacopulos and the composer.) Manhattan Opera House, Feb. 14, 1922, in French.

The Andalusian; or, The young guard.

English opera, libretto by George Loder; music by Edward Loder. Brougham's Lyceum Theatre, Jan. 15, 1851, in English, preceded by a play, "David Copperfield."

Andrea Chenier.

Italian opera in 4 acts, libretto by Luigi Illica; music by U. Giordano. (Milan, Teatro alla Scala, March 28, 1896.) *Academy of Music, Nov. 13, 1896, in Italian.

Anima allegra (The joyous soul).

Italian opera in 5 acts, libretto by Giuseppe Adami, founded on a story by the brothers Quintero; music by F. Vittadini. (Rome, Teatro Costanzi, April 15, 1921.) *Metropolitan Opera House, Feb. 14, 1923, in Italian.

Performed in San Francisco, Civic Auditorium, Sept. 26, 1925.

Grand Opera in New York, 1825–1925, cont'd.

Anna Bolena (Anna Boleyn).

Italian opera in 2 acts, libretto by Felice Romani; music by G. Donizetti. (Milan, Teatro Carcano, Dec. 26, 1830.) Niblo's Garden, Aug. 2, 1843, in French, followed by a miscellaneous musical program; Park Theatre, May 6, 1844, in English, followed by an English farce, "The young scamp;" Astor Place Opera House, Jan. 7, 1850, in Italian.

The overture of this opera was played "for the first time in this country," according to the announcement, on May 27, 1833, at the Masonic Hall, New York, at the benefit of Signor M. Rapetti, leader and violinist of the Italian Opera House, corner Church and Leonard streets. At the same concert, Signor G. B. Montresor sang a tenor aria, "Vivi tu te ne scongiuro," from the second act of this opera.

Performed in Philadelphia, Chestnut Street Theatre, April 12, 1844, in an English translation by Joseph Reese Fry.

Antigone.

Greek tragedy by Sophocles, adapted to the English stage by William Bartholomew; incidental music by F. Mendelssohn. (Potsdam, Neue Palais, Oct. 28, 1841; Berlin, Royal Opera, Nov. 6, 1841.) *Palmo's Opera House, April 7, 1845, in English.

L'Ape musicale.

Italian musical "revue" by Lorenzo Da Ponte, introducing popular selections from contemporary Italian operas, principally by G. Rossini, performed in Vienna. (Vienna, during the Lenten season, 1789.) *Park Theatre, April 20, 1830, in Italian.

Aphrodite.

Spectacular French play in 3 acts and 7 scenes, book by Pierre Frondaie, founded on the novel by Pierre Louÿs; music by H. Février; American version by George C. Hazelton, with additional music by Anselm Goetzl. (Paris, Théâtre de la Renaissance, March, 1914.) Century Theatre, Dec. 1, 1919, in English.

Aphrodite.

French opera in 4 acts and 5 scenes, libretto by Louis de Gramont, founded on the novel by Pierre Louÿs; music by C. Erlanger. (Paris, Opéra Comique, March 27, 1906.) *Lexington Theatre, Feb. 27, 1920, in French.

Gli Arabi nelli Gallie; ossia, Il trionfo della fede.

Italian opera in 4 acts, founded on d'Arlincourt's novel, "Le renégat;" music by G. Pacini. (Milan, Teatro alla Scala, March 8, 1827.) *Italian Opera House, Jan. 20, 1834, in Italian.

Performed in Philadelphia, Chestnut Street Theatre, April 23, 1834.

Ariane et Barbe Bleue.

French opera in 3 acts, libretto by Maurice Maeterlinck; music by P. Dukas.

(Paris, Opéra Comique, May 10, 1907.) *Metropolitan Opera House, March 29 (not Feb. 3), 1911, in French.

Armida.

Italian opera in 3 acts, libretto by Schmidt; music by G. Rossini. (Naples, Teatro San Carlo, Nov. 9, 1817.)

Never performed in New York.

A duet for soprano and tenor from this opera was sung on Dec. 19, 1833, by Signorina Clementina Fanti and Signor Luigi Ravaglia at Euterpean Hall, New York, at a concert by the Italian Opera Co. The number was repeated at Euterpean Hall on Jan. 9, 1834.

The duet was again sung on Dec. 7, 1842 by Mme. Otto and Charles Edward Horn at the Apollo Rooms, New York, at the first concert of the Philharmonic Society of New York.

Armide.

French opera in 5 acts, libretto by Philippe Quinault; music by C. W. Gluck. (Paris, Académie royale de musique, Sept. 23, 1777.) *Metropolitan Opera House, Nov. 14, 1910, in French.

Aroldo.

Italian opera in 4 acts, libretto by Francesco Maria Piave; music by G. Verdi. (Rimini, Teatro Nuovo. Aug. 16, 1857, at the inauguration of the theatre.) *Academy of Music, May 4 (not April 15), 1863, in Italian.

Artaxerxes.

English opera in 3 acts, founded on Metastasio's Italian libretto, "Artaserse," libretto and music by T. Arne. (London, Covent Garden, Feb. 2, 1762.) Park Theatre, Jan. 31, 1828, in English, with Charles Edward Horn's orchestration, preceded by an English piece, "The blue devils," and Stephen Storace's two-act ballad opera, "No song, no supper."

Ascold's tomb (Askoldowa magila).

Russian opera in 3 acts and 4 scenes (or 4 acts), libretto by Zagoskin; music by A. M. Verstovsky. (Moscow, Sept. 15, 1835.) Théâtre Français, Dec. 15, 1869, in Russian.

Asrael.

Italian opera in 4 acts, libretto by Ferdinando Fontana; music by A. Franchetti. (Reggio Emilia, Teatro Municipale, Feb. 11, 1888.) *Metropolitan Opera House, Nov. 26, 1890, in Italian.

L'Assedio di Corinto; ossia, Maometto II (Le siège de Corinthe).

French opera in 3 acts, libretto by Alexandre Soumet and Giuseppe Luigi Balochi, translated into Italian by Calisto Bassi; music by G. Rossini. (Paris, Opéra, Oct. 9, 1826.) *Italian Opera House, Feb. 6, 1835, in Italian.

This opera was an adaptation by Rossini of an earlier dramatic work, "Maometto Secondo," performed in Naples, Teatro San Carlo, Dec. 3, 1820.

Performed in Albany for the first time by the New York company, April 6, 1835.

Grand Opera in New York, 1825–1925, cont'd.

At the lower harbor. *See* **A basso porto.**

L'Attaque du moulin.

French opera in 4 acts, libretto by Louis Gallet, founded on the story in Émile Zola's "Soirées de Meudon"; music by Alfred Bruneau. (Paris, Opéra Comique, Nov. 23, 1893.) *New Theatre, Feb. 8, 1910, in French.

Performed in New Orleans, French Opera House, Jan. 19, 1911.

Attila.

Italian opera in a prologue and 3 acts, libretto by Temistocle Solera; music by G. Verdi. (Venice, Teatro La Fenice, March 17, 1846.) *Niblo's Garden, April 15, 1850, in Italian.

The date of the first performance of this opera in America has been incorrectly reported as March 15, 1850 and April 16, 1850.

Azael, the prodigal. *See* **L'Enfant prodigue.**

Azora.

American opera in 3 acts, libretto by David Stevens; music by H. K. Hadley. (Chicago, Auditorium, Jan. 7, 1918.) Lexington Theatre, Jan. 26 (not 28), 1918, in English.

Der Bajazzo. *See* **Pagliacci.**

Un Ballo in maschera (The masked ball; Der Maskenball).

Italian opera in 3 acts, libretto by Antonio Somma; music by G. Verdi. (Rome, Teatro Apollo, Feb. 17, 1859.) *Academy of Music, Feb. 11, 1861, in Italian; Academy of Music, Feb. 5, 1871, in English; Metropolitan Opera House, Dec. 11, 1889, in German.

Performed in Philadelphia, Academy of Music, April 18, 1861; New Orleans, French Opera House, Feb. 1, 1867.

I Banditi.

Italian opera in 2 acts, music by M. Garcia.

According to Clément and Larousse's "Dictionnaire des opéras" and Hugo Riemann's "Opern-Handbuch," this opera was performed in New York in 1827. The date cannot be substantiated by a search in the New York newspapers and periodicals of the time. Garcia's first and only opera season in New York closed on Sept. 30, 1826. As far as records go, this opera was never performed in New York.

The Barber of Seville. *See* **Il Barbiere di Siviglia.**

Der Barbier von Bagdad.

German opera in 2 acts, libretto and music by P. Cornelius. (Weimar, Hoftheater, Dec. 15, 1858.) *Metropolitan Opera House, Jan. 3, 1890, in German.

Performed in Chicago, Auditorium, May 5, 1890.

Il Barbiere di Siviglia (The barber of Seville).

Italian opera in 2 acts, libretto by Pietro Sterbini, founded on Pierre Beaumarchais's

play, "Le barbier de Séville;" music by G. Rossini. (Rome, Teatro Argentina, Feb. 5, 1816.) *Park Theatre, May 17, 1819, in English; Park Theatre, Nov. 29, 1825, in Italian; Academy of Music, Dec. 4, 1863, in German.

A cavatina from this opera was "sung by a young lady," in Italian, at Mr. Huerta's concert in the Concert Room, corner Reed street and Broadway, opposite Washington Hall, New York, on Oct. 12, 1825.

This opera was broadcast by radio on June 2, 1925, in Italian, in tabloid form, with reduced orchestra, through station WEAF, New York.

Il Barbiere di Siviglia. *See also* **The Two Figaros.**

Il Barone di Dolsheim.

Italian opera, music by G. Pacini. (Milan, Teatro alla Scala, Sept. 23, 1818.)

Never performed in New York.

A duet for mezzo-soprano and bass from this opera was sung on Dec. 19, 1833, by Signorina Rosina Fanti and Signor DeRosa at Euterpean Hall, New York, at a concert by the Italian Opera Co.

The Bartered Bride. *See* **Die Verkaufte Braut.**

The Basket maker's wife.

English opera, libretto by Alfred Bunn; music by W. M. Balfe. (London, Surrey Theatre, 1847.) Niblo's Garden, Dec. 17, 1852, in English.

This little opera, or rather, operetta, is better known by the title, "The Devil's in it," or "The Devil to pay."

"The subject, originally Spanish, was translated into French, and then rendered into English by Charles Coffey in the early part of the 18th century, under the title of 'The Devil to pay.' Scribe translated this farce, and Auber set it to music as 'La Part du Diable.' Balfe altered the title afterwards to 'Letty the basket maker.'" — *W. A. Barrett, Balfe; his life and work* (London: Remington and Co., 1882), p. 192.

Bastien und Bastienne.

German opera in 1 act, libretto by Andreas Schachtner, founded on Weiskern's German translation of a French parody, by Mme. Favart, of Jean Jacques Rousseau's "Le devin du village;" music by W. A. Mozart. (Vienna, in a garden house on Landstrasse, 1768.) Empire Theatre, Oct. 26, 1916, in an English translation by Alice Mattulath, followed by Mozart's one-act operetta, "The impresario," in Louis Schneider's adaptation.

La Bayadere. *See* **Le Dieu et la Bayadere.**

Beatrice di Tenda.

Italian opera in 3 acts, libretto by Felice Romani; music by V. Bellini. (Venice, Teatro La Fenice, March 16, 1833.) Palmo's Opera House, March 18, 1844, in Italian.

First performed in America: New Orleans, Théâtre d'Orléans, March 21, 1842.

The Beautiful Galatea. *See* **Galatée.**

Belisario.

Italian opera in 3 acts, libretto by Salvatore Cammarano; music by G. Donizetti.

Grand Opera in New York, 1825-1925, cont'd.

(Venice, Teatro La Fenice, Feb. 4, 1836.) *Palmo's Opera House, Feb. 14, 1844, in Italian.

This opera was announced in rehearsal in German at the New York Stadt Theatre early in 1871, but not performed.

Performed in New Orleans, March 10, 1845, in Italian; April 7, 1853, in French.

Belmonte and Constanze. *See* Die Entfuehrung aus dem Serail.

Betly.

Italian opera in 2 acts, founded on A. Adam's opera, "Le châlet;" libretto and music by G. Donizetti. (Naples, Teatro Nuovo, Aug. 24, 1836.) Academy of Music, Oct. 28, 1861, in Italian, preceded by Massé's one-act opera, "Les noces de Jeannette."

Performed in Philadelphia, Academy of Music, Oct. 25, 1861.

Bianca.

American opera in 1 act, libretto by Grant Stewart, founded on Carlo Goldoni's play, "La locandiera" ("The mistress of the inn"); music by H. K. Hadley. First performed: Park Theatre, Oct. 18, 1918, in English.

Bianca e Faliero; ossia, Il Consiglio dei tre.

Italian opera in 2 acts, libretto by Felice Romani; music by G. Rossini. (Milan, Teatro alla Scala, Dec. 26, 1819.)

Never performed in New York.

A quartet from this opera was sung on Jan. 9, 1834, in Italian, by Signora Clementina Fanti, Signora Luigia Bordogni, Signor G. B. Fabj and Signor A. Porto, at the Euterpean Hall, New York, in a concert by the Italian Opera Co. The quartet was repeated "by particular desire" on Jan. 25, 1834, by the same singers, at the postponed concert of the Musical Fund Society at the City Hotel, New York.

Boabdil, der letzte Maurenkönig.

German opera in 3 acts, libretto by Carl Wittkowsky; music by M. Moszkowski, op. 49. (Berlin, Königliches Opernhaus, April 21, 1892.) *Manhattan Opera House, Jan. 24, 1893, in English.

La Bohème.

Italian opera in 4 acts, libretto by Giuseppe Giacosa and Luigi Illica, founded on Henri Murger's novel, "La Vie de Bohème;" music by G. Puccini. (Turin, Teatro Regio, Feb. 1, 1896.) Wallack's Theatre, May 16, 1898, in Italian; American Theatre, Nov. 28, 1898, in English.

This opera was broadcast by radio on Oct. 30, 1925, in Italian, in tabloid form, through station WRNY, New York.

First performed in America: Buenos Aires, June 16, 1896.

First performed in the United States: Los Angeles, Los Angeles Theatre, Oct. 14, 1897, in Italian.

Performed in San Francisco, California Theatre, Nov. 6, 1897; Boston, Boston Theatre, Jan. 25, 1899, in English; New Orleans, Jan. 31, 1901.

This opera was performed in Mexico before it was produced in the United States.

The Bohemian girl (La zingara).

English opera in 3 acts, libretto by Alfred Bunn; music by W. M. Balfe. (London, Drury Lane Theatre, Nov. 27, 1843.) *Park Theatre, Nov. 25, 1844, in English; Academy of Music, Jan. 10, 1859, in Italian.

A burlesque of Balfe's opera, in 3 acts, was performed in English at the Buckley's Serenaders' New Hall, New York, Nov. 24, 1856.

This opera was broadcast by radio on July 7, 1925, in English, in tabloid form, with reduced orchestra, through station WEAF, New York.

Performed in Philadelphia, Chestnut Street Theatre, Dec. 30, 1844.

Boris Godounoff.

Russian opera in 3 (4) acts, founded on the play by Alexander Pushkin; libretto and music by M. Moussorgsky. (St. Petersburg, Imperial Opera House, Jan. 24, 1874, first time in its entirety.) *Metropolitan Opera House, March 19, 1913, in Italian; New Amsterdam Theatre, May 11, 1922, in Russian.

At the Russian production of the opera at the New Amsterdam Theatre, seven scenes from the opera were performed.

Performed in Philadelphia, Metropolitan Opera House, March 10, 1914.

Le Bouffe et le tailleur.

French opera in 1 act, libretto by Gouffe and Villiers; music by P. Gaveaux. (Montasier, June 21, 1804.) Park Theatre, Aug. 20, 1827, in French, preceded by a play, "Maria Stuart."

Le Brasseur de Preston (The brewer of Preston; Der Brauer von Preston).

French opera in 3 acts, libretto by Adolphe de Leuven and Brunswick [pseud. of Léon Lévy, called Lhérie]; music by A. Adam. (Paris, Opéra Comique, Oct. 31, 1838.) Park Theatre, March 23, 1846, in English; Niblo's Garden, March 20, 1855, in German.

Performed in Philadelphia, Chestnut Street Theatre, May 6, 1846.

Briséïs.

French opera in 3 acts, libretto by Ephraïm Mikhaël and Catulle Mendès; music by E. Chabrier. (Incomplete; performed at the Concerts Lamoureux, Paris, Jan. 31, 1897.) Performed in concert form by the Schola Cantorum at Carnegie Hall, March 3, 1911, in French.

The Bronze horse. *See* Le Cheval de bronze.

La Buona famiglia.

Italian opera in 1 act, music by M. Garcia.

According to Clément and Larousse's "Dictionnaire des opéras" and Hugo Riemann's "Opern-Handbuch," this opera was performed in New York in 1827. The date cannot be substantiated by a search in the New York newspapers and periodicals of the time. Garcia's first and only opera season in New York closed on Sept. 30, 1826. As far as records go, this opera was never performed in New York.

Grand Opera in New York, 1825-1925, cont'd.

Buy it dear, 'Tis made of Cashmere. *See* Le Dieu et la Bayadere.

Le Caïd.

French opera in 2 acts, libretto by Thomas Marie François Sauvage; music by A. Thomas. (Paris, Opéra Comique, Jan. 3, 1849.) Niblo's Garden, June 28 (not 30), 1852, in French, preceded by a farce, "Naval engagements."

Le Calife de Bagdad (The caliph of Bagdad).

French opera in 1 act, libretto by Claude Godard d'Aucour de Saint-Just; music by A. Boieldieu. (Paris, Opéra Comique, Sept. 16, 1800.) Park Theatre, Aug. 27, 1827, in French, preceded by a vaudeville, "L'homme gris;" Park Theatre, Oct. 14, 1829, in an English version by Thomas John Dibdin.

Camille; ou, Le souterrain.

French opera in 3 acts, libretto by Benoît Joseph Marsollier des Vivetières, founded on Mme. de Genlis's novel, "Adèle et Théodore;" music by N. Dalayrac. (Paris, Théâtre Italien, March 19, 1791.) Park Theatre, Sept. 8, 1827, in French, followed by vaudeville, "Je fais mes farces."

Il Campanello di notte (The night bell).

Italian opera in 1 act, founded on a French vaudeville, "La sonnette de nuit;" libretto and music by G. Donizetti. (Naples, Teatro Nuovo, June 1, 1836.) Empire Theatre, May 7. 1917, in English, preceded by Pergolesi's two-act opera, "La serva padrona."

The Canterbury pilgrims.

American opera in 4 acts, libretto by Percy Mackaye; music by R. DeKoven. First performed: Metropolitan Opera House, March 8, 1917, in English.

Performed in Philadelphia, Metropolitan Opera House, March 20, 1917.

Les Caprices d'Oxane. *See* Cherevicky.

I Capuletti e Montecchi (Romeo und Julie).

Italian opera in 2 acts, libretto by Felice Romani, founded on the play by Shakespeare; music by V. Bellini. (Venice, Teatro La Fenice, March 11, 1830.) Astor Place Opera House, Jan. 28 (not Feb. 1), 1848, in Italian; Niblo's Garden, April 10, 1855, in German.

The German performance of this opera was announced for April 3, 1855, but postponed because of Holy Week.

The cavatina, "L'amo, l'amo e m'è più cara," for tenor, from the first act of this opera was sung, in Italian, on May 27, 1833, by Signor G. B. Montresor at the Masonic Hall, New York, at the benefit of Signor M. Rapetti, leader and violinist of the Italian Opera House, corner Church and Leonard streets.

Performed in Philadelphia, Walnut Street Theatre, Aug. 6, 1847.

Il "Carillon" magico.

Mimetic symphonic comedy in a preamble and 1 act by R. Pick-Mangiagalli. *Metropolitan Opera House, Dec. 2, 1920, preceded by Mascagni's one-act opera, "Cavalleria rusticana" and followed by Leoni's one-act opera, "L'oracolo."

Carmen.

French opera in 4 acts, libretto by Henri Meilhac and Ludovic Halévy, founded on the story by Prosper Mérimée; music by G. Bizet. (Paris, Opéra Comique, March 3, 1875.) *Academy of Music, Oct. 23, 1878, in Italian; Haverly's Fifth Avenue Theatre, March 2, 1881, in English; Metropolitan Opera House, Nov. 25, 1885, in German.

This opera was broadcast by radio on April 14, 1925, in French, in tabloid form, with reduced orchestra, through station WEAF, New York.

This opera was performed on May 14, 1900, at the Lexington Opera House, by a Negro troupe, the Theo. Drury Opera Co.

Performed in Philadelphia, Academy of Music, Oct. 25, 1878; New Orleans, French Opera House, Jan. 14, 1881.

Il Carnevale di Venezia; ovvero, Le precauzioni.

Italian opera in 3 acts, libretto by Marco d'Arienzo; music by E. Petrella. (Naples, Teatro Nuovo, May 20, 1851.) *Academy of Music, April 3, 1867, in Italian.

Performed in Chicago, Crosby's Opera House, 1867; Philadelphia, Academy of Music, Jan. 10, 1868.

La Casa da vendere.

Italian opera, music by C. Salvioni. First performed: March 24, 1834, in Italian, at a benefit for the composer, followed by the overture to Rossini's opera, "Semiramide," and a duet from the opera arranged for bassoon and trumpet, and the second act of Rossini's two-act opera, "La cenerentola."

The composer was the conductor of the orchestra of Lorenzo da Ponte's opera troupe at the Italian Opera House, New York.

The Cats in the larder; or, The maid with a parasol. *See* La Gazza ladra.

Cavalleria rusticana.

Italian opera in 1 act, libretto by Giovanni Targioni-Tozzetti and Guido Menasci, founded on the story by Giovanni Verga; music by P. Mascagni. (Rome, Teatro Costanzi, May 17, 1890.) Casino Theatre, at a matinée, preceded by an English version of Carl Zeller's two-act comic opera, "The Tyrolean (Der Vogelhändler)," and Lenox Lyceum, in the evening, Oct. 1, 1891, rival performances, both in English; Metropolitan Opera House, Dec. 30, 1891, in Italian.

The first open air presentation in New York of this opera was given on Sept. 21, 1916, in Italian, followed by Leoncavallo's two-act opera, "Pagliacci." at the Lewisohn Stadium of the College of the City of New York. Another open-air performance of this opera was given on Aug. 5, 1925, in Italian, followed by "Pagliacci," at Ebbets Field, Brooklyn. This performance was broadcast by radio through

Grand Opera in New York, 1825–1925, cont'd.

station WNYC, New York. This opera was also broadcast by radio on June 9, 1925, in Italian, in tabloid form, through station WJZ, New York. This opera was again heard over the radio on Oct. 16, 1925, in Italian, in tabloid form, through station WRNY, New York.

First performed in America: Philadelphia, Grand Opera House, Sept. 9, 1891.
Performed in Chicago, Sept. 30, 1891; New Orleans, Jan. 3, 1892, in English; Jan. 21, 1897, in French.

Cendrillon.

French opera in 3 acts, libretto by Charles Guillaume Étienne; music by Nicolo. (Paris, Théâtre Feydeau, Feb. 22, 1810.) Park Theatre, July 13, 1827, in French, with N. Dalayrac's one-act opera, "Maison à vendre."

Cendrillon.

French opera in 4 acts, libretto by Henri Cain, founded on the fairy tale by Charles Perrault; music by J. Massenet. (Paris, Opéra Comique, May 24, 1899.) Metropolitan Opera House, Feb. 26, 1912, in French.

First performed in America: New Orleans, French Opera House, Dec. 23, 1902.
Performed in Montreal, His Majesty's Theatre, Dec. 24, 1912.

La Cenerentola; ossia, La bonta in trionfo.

Italian opera in 2 acts, libretto by Jacopo Ferretti; music by G. Rossini. (Rome, Teatro Valle, Jan. 25, 1817.) *Park Theatre, June 27, 1826, in Italian; Park Theatre, Jan. 24, 1831, in an English adaptation, entitled "Cinderella; or, The fairy and the little glass slipper," by Michael Rophino Lacy.

Rossini's opera was exceedingly popular in New York during the first half of the 19th century. The opera was constantly revived in various arrangements and adaptations. Rophino Lacy's version proved an unprecedented success and was performed at the Park Theatre as late as 1845. Another English adaptation was performed at the Broadway Theatre in Jan., 1855, and an arrangement, in 3 acts, with Rossini's music and songs by other composers, was performed at Niblo's Garden early in August of the same year. A pot-pourri production, called "Cinderella," with Rossini's music arranged by Max Maretzek, was performed at Booth's Theatre, Oct. 12, 1880.
Rophino Lacy's version was published in London by Goulding & D'Almaine.

Le Châlet (The Swiss cottage).

French opera in 1 act, libretto by Augustin Eugène Scribe and Mélesville [pseud. of Anne Honoré Joseph Duveyrier]; music by A. Adam. (Paris, Opéra Comique, Sept. 25, 1834.) Niblo's Garden, July 7, 1843, in French; Buckley's Serenaders Hall, Oct. 29, 1855, in an English translation by Edward Seguin.

The compiler has not been able to establish the date of the first performance of this little opera in New York. An abridged English version was performed on Sept. 22, 1836 at the Park Theatre, New York. The performance was preceded by a play, "Lucille; or, The story of a heart," and followed by a farce, "The two Gregories." The opera was performed a number of times that year.

Charles VI.

French opera in 5 acts, libretto by Casimir and Germain Delavigne; music by L.

Halévy. (Paris, Académie royale de musique, March 15, 1843.)
Never performed in its entirety in New York.

Selections from this opera were sung in French on July 30, 1849, in costume, preceded by Donizetti's opera, "La Favorita," at the Chinese Assembly Rooms, New York.
Performed in New Orleans, Théâtre d'Orléans, April 22, 1847.

Le Chemineau.

French opera in 4 acts, libretto by Jean Richepin; music by X. Leroux. (Paris, Opéra Comique, Nov. 6, 1907.) Lexington Theatre, Jan. 31, 1919, in French.

First performed in America: New Orleans, French Opera House, Feb. 11, 1911.

Cherevicky (Christmas eve).

Russian opera in 3 acts, libretto by Polonsky, founded on Nicholas Gogol's story, "Christmas eve revels;" music by P. I. Tchaikovsky. New Amsterdam Theatre, May 26, 1922, in Russian.

This opera is a revision by the composer of his "Vakoula, the smith," performed at the Maryinsky Theatre, St. Petersburg, Dec. 6, 1876. It was again revised by the composer and performed at the Imperial Opera House, Moscow, Jan. 27, 1887, under the title, "Les caprices d'Oxane."

Le Cheval de bronze (The bronze horse).

French opera in 3 acts, libretto by Augustin Eugène Scribe; music by D. Auber. (Paris, Salle de la Place de la Bourse, March 23, 1835.) Park Theatre, May 9, 1842, preceded by a farce, "The anatomist."

An operatic piece of the same name with several characters not in Auber's opera was performed in English at the Bowery Theatre, New York, Oct. 23, 1838.

Chiara di Rosemburgh.

Italian opera in 2 acts, libretto by Gaetano Rossi, founded on Mme. de Genlis's novel, "Le Siège de La Rochelle;" music by L. Ricci. (Milan, Teatro alla Scala, Oct. 11, 1831.) *Palmo's Opera House, Nov. 18, 1844, in Italian.

The Child of the Regiment. *See* La **Fille du régiment.**

Christmas eve. *See* Cherevicky.

Le Cid.

French opera in 4 acts, libretto by Adolphe Philippe Dennery, Édouard Blau and Louis Gallet; music by J. Massenet. (Paris, Opéra, Nov. 30, 1885.) Metropolitan Opera House, Feb. 12, 1897, in French.

First performed in America: New Orleans, French Opera House, Feb. 23, 1890.

Cinderella. *See* Cendrillon; *also* La **Cenerentola.**

La Clemenza di Tito (Titus).

Italian opera in 2 acts, libretto by Caterino Mazzola, founded on that by Pietro Antonio

Grand Opera in New York, 1825–1925, cont'd.

Domenico Metastasio; music by W. A. Mozart. (Prague, Nationaltheater, Sept. 6, 1791.)

Never performed in New York.

The overture of this opera was played at the annual concert of the Euterpean Society on Jan. 29, 1835 at the City Hotel, New York.

The soprano aria, "Deh per questo istante solo," was sung on Jan. 11, 1845 by Mrs. George Loder at the second concert of third season of the Philharmonic Society of New York at the Apollo Rooms, New York.

The overture was played in Baltimore on Jan. 15, 1835 under J. Nenninger.

Cleopatra's night.

American opera in 2 acts, libretto by Alice Leal Pollock, founded on Théophile Gautier's story, "Une nuit de Cléopâtre;" music by H. K. Hadley. First performed: Metropolitan Opera House, Jan. 31, 1920, in English, followed by Leoncavallo's two-act opera, "Pagliacci."

Cléopâtre.

French opera in 4 acts, libretto by Louis Payen [pseud. of Albert Liénard]; music by J. Massenet. (Monte Carlo, Théâtre, Feb. 23, 1914.) Lexington Theatre, Feb. 11, 1919, in French.

First performed in America: Chicago, Auditorium, Jan. 10, 1916.

I Compagnacci.

Italian opera in 1 act, libretto by Giovacchino Forzano; music by P. Riccitelli. *Metropolitan Opera House, Jan. 2, 1924, in Italian, preceded by Laparra's three-act opera, "La Habanera."

Le Comte Ory.

French opera in 2 acts, libretto by Augustin Eugène Scribe and Charles Gaspard Delestre-Poirson; music by G. Rossini. (Paris, Académie royale de musique, Aug. 30, 1828.) Park Theatre, Aug. 19, 1833, in French, followed by a vaudeville, "La famille Riguebourg."

Comus.

English masque by John Milton; music by G. F. Handel and T. Arne, arranged by George Loder. Burton's Theatre, Sept. 11, 1848, in English, followed by a farce, "Poor Pillicoddy," and a play, "The capture of Capt. Cuttle and Bunsby's wedding."

According to O. G. Sonneck's "Early opera in America" (Schirmer, cop. 1915), performances of Milton's masque, presumably in the Dalton-Arne version, took place on March 9, 1770 at Southwark Theatre, Philadelphia, and on June 21, 1773 at the John Street Theatre, New York.

Conchita.

Italian opera in 4 acts, libretto by Maurice Vaucaire and Carlo Zangarini, founded on Pierre Louÿs's novel, "La femme et le pantin;" music by R. Zandonai. (Milan, Teatro

dal Verme, Oct. 11, 1911.) Metropolitan Opera House, Feb. 11, 1913, in Italian.

First performed in America: Buenos Aires, Coliseo, June 18, 1912.

First performed in the United States: San Francisco, Sept. 28, 1912.

Performed in Chicago, Auditorium, Jan. 30, 1913; Philadelphia, Metropolitan Opera House, Feb. 6, 1913.

Conrad and Medora; or, The pacha's bride.

English opera. National Theatre, Feb. 28, 1839, in English, followed by a farce, "Nicholas Nickleby."

The Conspirators. *See* Der Häusliche Krieg.

Les Contes d'Hoffmann (The tales of Hoffmann).

French opera in 4 acts and an epilogue, libretto by Jules Barbier, founded on the play by Jules Barbier and Michel Carré; music by J. Offenbach. (Paris, Opéra Comique, Feb. 10, 1881.) *Fifth Avenue Theatre, Oct. 16, 1882, in French; Century Opera House, Sept. 30, 1913, in an English translation by Charles Henry Meltzer.

This opera was broadcast by radio on June 16, 1925, in French, through station WEAF, New York.

Le Coq d'or.

Russian opera in 3 acts, libretto by Vladimir Bielsky, founded on the poem by Alexander Pushkin; music by N. Rimsky-Korsakoff. (Moscow, Zimin's Private Theatre, May, 1910.) *Metropolitan Opera House, March 6, 1918, in the French translation by Michel D. Calvocoressi, as an opera-pantomime arranged by Michael Fokine, and preceded by Mascagni's one-act opera, "Cavalleria rusticana."

Coriolanus before Rome; or, Filial love.

Italian scena, music by C. Salvioni.

This tenor scena was sung in Italian by Signor Luigi Ravaglia and a chorus, "in full costume," at the former's benefit on Feb. 1, 1834, between one of the acts of Pacini's four-act opera "Gli Arabi nelli Gallie." The scena was repeated at Eugène Guillaud's benefit on Feb. 15, 1834 at the City Hotel, New York.

The Corsican bride.

German opera, libretto by Dr. A. Koehler, founded on De Walden's play, "Rosa Gregorio;" music by E. Mollenhauer. First performed: Winter Garden, June 15, 1863, in German.

This opera was originally to have been performed at the German Opera House, New York.

The overture and the music of the second act of the opera were performed in a concert in Jan., 1863 in New York, the composer conducting.

For De Walden's play, "Rosa Gregorio," upon which the libretto of the opera is founded, Edward Mollenhauer had composed the incidental music. The play was performed during the previous year at the Winter Garden, New York, where Mollenhauer was the conductor of the orchestra.

Cosi fan tutte.

Italian opera in 2 acts, libretto by Lorenzo da Ponte; music by W. A. Mozart. (Vienna,

Grand Opera in New York, 1825–1925, cont'd.

Burgtheater, Jan. 26, 1790.) *Metropolitan Opera House, March 24, 1922, in Italian.

Cosimo.

French opera in 2 acts, libretto by Amable Villain de Saint Hilaire and Paul Duport; music by E. Prevost. (Paris, Opéra Comique, Oct. 13, 1835.) Niblo's Garden, July 22, 1843, in French, followed by a miscellaneous musical program and Piccinni's one-act opera, "La maison en loterie."

The composer of this little opera was the musical director of the French troupe then playing at Niblo's Garden.

Crispino e la comare.

Italian opera in 3 acts, libretto by Francesco Maria Piave; music by Luigi and Federico Ricci. (Venice, Teatro San Benedetto, Feb. 28, 1850.) *Academy of Music, Oct. 24, 1865, in Italian.

Performed in Chicago, Crosby's Opera House, May, 1866; Philadelphia, Academy of Music, Oct. 15, 1866; New Orleans, French Opera House, Nov. 7, 1866.

Il Crociato in Egitto.

Italian opera in 2 acts, libretto by Gaetano Rossi; music by G. Meyerbeer. (Venice, Teatro La Fenice, March 7, 1824.)

Never performed in New York.

The overture of this opera was played on May 9, 1833, at Signor G. B. Montresor's benefit, between the acts of Rossini's opera, "Il barbiere di Siviglia," at the Bowery Theatre, New York. According to the advertisement, this was the first performance of music by Meyerbeer in America.

The **Crown diamonds.** *See* Les **Diamants de la couronne.**

Cyrano.

American opera in 4 acts, libretto by William James Henderson, after Edmond Rostand's play, "Cyrano de Bergerac;" music by W. Damrosch. First performed, Metropolitan Opera House, Feb. 27, 1913, in English.

Czar und Zimmermann; oder, Die zwei Peter (Czar and carpenter).

German opera in 3 acts, libretto and music by A. Lortzing. (Leipzig, Stadttheater, Dec. 22, 1837.) *Broadway Theatre, Jan. 13, 1857, in German; Booth's Theatre, Feb. 8, 1882, in English.

The first performance of this opera in America was announced for Jan. 9, 1857, but postponed until the 13th.

According to F. L. Ritter's "Music in America" (New York, 1884), p. 297, followed by H. E. Krehbiel in his "Review of the New York musical season 1888–1889" (New York, 1889), p. 151, and H. C. Lahee in his "Annals of music in America" (Boston, 1922), p. 45, this opera was incorrectly supposed to have been first performed in New York at Niblo's Garden in 1855 by a German company under the musical conductorship of Julius Unger.

Performed in Philadelphia, Academy of Music, June 20, 1857.

The Czar's bride.

Russian opera in 3 acts, libretto by N. F. Tyumenev, founded on the play by Lev Alexandrovitch Mey; music by N. Rimsky-Korsakoff. (Moscow, Imperial Opera House, Nov., 1899.) New Amsterdam Theatre, May 9, 1922, in Russian.

La Dame blanche (The white lady; Die Weisse Dame).

French opera in 3 acts, libretto by Augustin Eugène Scribe; music by A. Boieldieu. (Paris, Opéra Comique, Dec. 10, 1825.) Park Theatre, Aug. 24, 1827, in French; Park Theatre, May 21, 1832, in an English translation by John Howard Payne, with Boieldieu's music and additions from C. M. von Weber, G. Rossini, D. Auber and P. Guglielmi, followed by a farce, "It is the devil;" Academy of Music, Jan. 15, 1864, in German.

An opera, so-called, "The white lady," with characters different than in Boieldieu's opera, but founded on the same subject, was performed in English on April 23, 1828 at the Park Theatre, New York. According to the announcement, the piece was produced "as performed at Drury Lane."

A German performance of this opera was announced to take place at Niblo's Garden, New York, early in Nov., 1856, but the company disbanded before the time of production.

Le Damnation de Faust.

French oratorio in 4 parts, libretto by Hector Berlioz and Almire Gandonnière, adapted from Gérard de Nerval's French version of Johann Wolfgang von Goethe's dramatic poem, "Faust;" music by H. Berlioz, op. 24. (Paris, Opéra Comique, Dec. 6, 1846; Monte Carlo, Théâtre du Casino, Feb., 1893, in operatic form, arranged by Raoul Gunsbourg.) *Metropolitan Opera House, Dec. 7, 1906, in French, in Raoul Gunsbourg's arrangement.

First sung in America as an oratorio on Feb. 14, 1880, at Steinway Hall, New York, by the New York Oratorio and Arion Societies under Dr. Leopold Damrosch. Sung in Boston, May 14, 1880, under Benjamin Lang.

The **Dance in Place Congo.** *See under* **Shanewis.**

Daphne; or, The pipes of Pan.

American opera, libretto by Marguerite Merington; music by A. Bird. First performed: Waldorf Astoria Hotel, Dec. 13, 1897, in English, at Albert Morris Bagby's morning musicale.

The **Daughter of the regiment.** *See* La **Fille du régiment.**

The Daughter of St. Mark.

English opera in 3 acts, libretto by Alfred Bunn, adapted from Halévy's five-act opera, "La reine de Chypre;" music by W. M. Balfe. (London, Drury Lane Theatre, Nov. 27, 1844.) Niblo's Garden, June 18, 1855, in English.

Grand Opera in New York, 1825–1925, cont'd.

The Demon.

Russian opera in 3 acts, comprising a prologue, 6 scenes and an epilogue, founded on the poem by Michael Lermontoff; libretto prepared by A. N. Maikov and written by Wiskovatoff; music by A. Rubinstein. (St. Petersburg, Maryinsky Theatre, Jan. 25, 1875.) New Amsterdam Theatre, May 13, 1922, in Russian.

Deseret; or, A saint's affliction.

American comic opera in 3 acts by William Augustus Croffut; music by D. Buck. First performed, Haverly's Fourteenth Street Theatre, Oct. 11, 1880.

Performed in Cincinnati, Pike's Opera House, Nov., 1880; Baltimore, Academy of Music, Nov., 1880.

The Desert flower.

English opera, libretto by George Frederick Harris, founded on Jacques François Fromental Élie Halévy's opera, "Jaquarita l'indienne;" music by W. V. Wallace. (London, Covent Garden, Oct. 12, 1863.) *Academy of Music, Jan. 15, 1868, in English.

Halévy's opera, "Jaquarita l'indienne" was performed in New Orleans at the Théâtre d'Orléans on Jan. 18, 1859, but never in New York.

Les Deux journées.

French opera in 3 acts, libretto by Jean Nicolas Bouilly; music by L. Cherubini. (Paris, Théâtre Feydeau, Jan. 16, 1800.) Park Theatre, July 23, 1827, in French, followed by a French work, "La sonnambule" (opera by Louis Piccinni?).

First performed in America: New Orleans, Théâtre St. Philippe, March 12, 1811.

The Devil to pay. *See* The Basket maker's wife.

The Devil's in it. *See* The Basket maker's wife.

The Dew drop. *See* La Sylphide.

Le Diable à quatre; ou, La femme Acariate.

French opera in 3 acts, libretto by Michel Jean Sedaine, revised by Augustin François Creuzé de Lesser; music by J. P. Solié. (Paris, Opéra Comique, Nov. 30, 1809.) Park Theatre, Aug. 17, 1827, in French, with a vaudeville, "Le soldat laboureur."

Les Diamants de la couronne (The crown diamonds).

French opera in 3 acts, libretto by Augustin Eugène Scribe and Jules Henri Vernoy de Saint Georges; music by D. Auber. (Paris, Opéra Comique, March 6, 1841.) Niblo's Garden, July 14, 1843, in French, followed by a miscellaneous musical program; Niblo's Garden, Sept. 18, 1851, in English.

Diana von Solange.

German opera in 5 acts, libretto by Otto Prechtler; music by Ernest ii, Duke of Saxe-Coburg Gotha. (Gotha, Hoftheater, Dec. 5 [not 6], 1858.) *Metropolitan Opera House, Jan. 9, 1891, in German.

Dido.

A pasticcio, in English, with music selected and arranged by C. E. Horn, principally from G. Rossini. First performed: Park Theatre, April 9, 1828, in English, with a play, "The haunted inn."

Dido and Aeneas.

English opera in 3 acts, libretto by Nahum Tate; music by H. Purcell. (Chelsey, Josias Priest's Boarding School for Girls, ca. 1680.) *Town Hall, Jan. 13, 1924, in English, in concert form, the music edited, arranged and orchestrated by Artur Bodanzky.

Le Dieu et la Bayadere (The maid of Cashmere.)

French ballet opera in 2 acts, libretto by Augustin Eugène Scribe; music by D. Auber. (Paris, Salle de la rue Le Peletier, Oct. 13, 1830.) National Theatre, late Italian Opera House, Oct. 3, 1836, in an English adaptation by Sir Henry Rowley Bishop.

Auber's ballet opera was mounted in New York in brilliant style and proved to be a popular success. Another English production took place on Dec. 3, 1836 at the Park Theatre, New York, and enjoyed a long run.

Augusta Maywood Williams, the celebrated dancer, better known as "La Petite Augusta," made her debut as a dancer in this ballet opera on Sept. 12, 1838 at the Park Theatre, New York. She was one of the first Americans to be admitted to the Academy of Dancing in Paris.

A burlesque of Auber's ballet opera, "Buy it dear, 'Tis made of Cashmere," by J. Horncastle, was performed on Nov. 2, 1840, in English, at the Olympic Theatre, New York.

Dinorah. *See* Le Pardon de Poërmel.

I Dispettosi amanti (A lover's quarrel).

Italian opera in 1 act, libretto by Enrico Comitti; music by A. Parelli. (Philadelphia, Metropolitan Opera House, March 6 [not 28], 1912.) Hotel Astor, March 9, 1913, in the English translation by Alma Strettel, for the first time, at the musicale and banquet of the musicians' club, The Bohemians.

Performed in Chicago, Auditorium, Feb. 1, 1913, preceded by Massenet's three-act opera, "Le jongleur de Notre Dame."

First performed in Italy: Milan, Teatro Carcano, May 22, 1919.

Le Domino noir (The Black domino).

French opera in 3 acts, libretto by Augustin Eugène Scribe; music by D. Auber. (Paris, Opéra Comique, Dec. 2, 1837.) Niblo's Garden, June 7 (not 17), 1843, in French.

Don Bucephalo.

Italian opera in 3 acts, music by A. Cagnoni. (Milan, Regio Conservatorio di

Grand Opera in New York, 1825–1925, cont'd.

musica, June 28, 1847.) *Academy of Music, Oct. 18, 1867, in Italian.

A scene from this opera was sung in Italian on June 15, 1855, at a concert, at the Academy of Music, New York, which included Auber's five-act opera, "La muette di Portici (Masaniello)," the beggar's song from Meyerbeer's opera, "Le prophète," and an act from Donizetti's three-act opera, "Linda di Chamounix."

Don Carlos.

French opera in 5 acts, libretto by Joseph Méry and Camille DuLocle; music by G. Verdi. (Paris, Opéra, March 11, 1867.) *Academy of Music, April 12, 1877, in Italian.

Don Chisciotti.

Italian opera in 2 acts, music by M. Garcia.

According to Clément and Larousse's "Dictionnaire des opéras" and Hugo Riemann's "Opern-Handbuch," this opera was performed in New York in 1827. The date cannot be substantiated by a search in the New York newspapers and periodicals of the time. Garcia's first and only opera season in New York closed on Sept. 30, 1826. As far as records go, this opera was never performed in New York.

Don Giovanni; ossia, Il dissoluto punito.

Italian opera in 2 acts, libretto by Lorenzo da Ponte; music by W. A. Mozart. (Prague, National Theater, Oct. 29, 1787.) *Park Theatre, May 23, 1826, in Italian; Chatham Theatre, May 29, 1862, in an English adaptation by Sir Henry Rowley Bishop, preceded by a comedy, "Laugh when you can;" Academy of Music, April 23, 1863, in German.

Don Pasquale.

Italian opera in 3 acts, founded on an Italian opera in 2 acts, "Ser Marc' Antonio," with music by Stefano Pavesi, performed in Milan in 1811; libretto and music by G. Donizetti. (Paris, Théâtre Italien, Jan. 4, 1843.) Park Theatre, March 9, 1846, in English, with a play, "Sam Patch in France;" Astor Place Opera House, Nov. 29, 1849, in Italian.

Don Quichotte.

French opera in 5 acts, libretto by Henri Cain, after Jacques Le Lorrain, founded on the novel by Miguel de Cervantes; music by J. Massenet. (Monte Carlo, Opéra, Feb. 19, 1910; Paris, Théâtre de la Gaité Lyrique, Dec. 29, 1910.) Metropolitan Opera House, Feb. 3, 1914, in French.

First performed in America: New Orleans, French Opera House, Jan. 27, 1912. Performed in Philadelphia, Metropolitan Opera House, Nov. 15, 1913; Chicago, Auditorium, Nov. 26, 1913.

Don Quixote, der Ritter von der traurigen Gestalt.

German opera in a prologue and 3 acts, libretto by H. Italiener; music by A. Neuendorff. First performed: Germania Theatre, Jan. 9, 1882, in German.

Don Sébastien, roi de Portugal (Don Sebastiano, re di Portogallo).

French opera in 5 acts, libretto by Augustin Eugène Scribe; music by G. Donizetti. (Paris, Académie royale de musique, Nov. 13, 1843.) *Academy of Music, Nov. 25, 1864, in Italian.

Performed in Chicago, Crosby's Opera House, May 7, 1865; New Orleans, French Opera House, March 11, 1875.

La Donna caritea.

Italian opera in 2 acts, libretto by Pola; music by S. Mercadante. (Venice, Teatro La Fenice, Feb. 21, 1826.)

Never performed in New York.

The overture to this opera was played for the first time in America on Dec. 14, 1832, between the first and second acts of Bellini's opera, "Il pirata," at the Richmond Hill Theatre, New York, at the benefit of Michele Rappetti, the violinist and leader of the orchestra of the theatre.

La Donna del lago.

Italian opera in 2 acts, libretto by Andrea Leone Tottola, founded on Sir Walter Scott's poem, "The lady of the lake;" music by G. Rossini. (Naples, Teatro San Carlo, Oct. 4, 1819.) *Italian Opera House, Dec. 16, 1833, in Italian.

Performed in Philadelphia, Chestnut Street Theatre, April 21, 1834.

Le Donne curiose.

Italian opera in 3 acts, libretto by Luigi Illica, founded on the play by Carlo Goldoni; music by E. Wolf-Ferrari. (Munich, Residenztheater, Nov. 27, 1903, in German, as "Die neugierigen Frauen.") *Metropolitan Opera House, Jan. 3 (not 4), 1912, in Italian.

Les Dragons de Villars (Das Glöckchen des Eremiten).

French opera in 3 acts, libretto by Joseph Philippe Simon Lockroy and Eugène Cormon [pseud. of Pierre Étienne Piestre]; music by A. Maillart. (Paris, Opéra Comique, Sept. 19, 1856.) *Fifth Avenue Theatre, May 10, 1869, in French; Thalia Theatre, Nov. 24, 1885, in German.

Dubrovsky.

Russian opera, libretto by Modeste Tchaikovsky, founded on the story by Alexander Pushkin; music by E. Napravnik. (St. Petersburg, Maryinsky Theatre, Jan., 1895.) Second Avenue Theatre, June 13, 1922, in Russian.

I Due Foscari.

Italian opera in 3 acts, libretto by Francesco Maria Piave; music by G. Verdi. (Rome, Teatro Argentina, Nov. 3, 1844.) *Park Theatre, June 9, 1847 (not 1846), in Italian.

Performed in Philadelphia, Walnut Street Theatre, July 19, 1847; New Orleans, Théâtre d'Orléans, March 6, 1851.

Grand Opera in New York, 1825–1925, cont'd.

L'Ebrea. *See* **La Juive.**

L'Eclair.

Opéra comique in 3 acts, libretto by Jules Henri Vernoy de Saint Georges and François Antoine Eugène de Planard; music by J. Halévy. (Paris, Opéra Comique, Dec. 30, 1835.) Niblo's Garden, June 23, 1843, in French.

First performed in America: New Orleans, Théâtre d'Orléans, Feb. 16, 1837.

Edipo Re.

Italian opera in 1 act, founded on Sophocles's play, "Oedipus Rex (or, Oedipus Tyrannus);" libretto and music by R. Leoncavallo. (Chicago, Auditorium, Dec. 13, 1920.) Manhattan Opera House, Feb. 21, 1921, in Italian, followed by Camille Saint-Saëns's symphonic poem, "Danse macabre," arranged as a ballet by Andreas Pavley and Serge Oukrainsky.

Eduardo e Cristina.

Italian opera, libretto by Gaetano Rossi; music by G. Rossini. (Venice, Teatro San Benedetto, April 24, 1819.) *Italian Opera House, Nov. 25, 1834, in Italian.

Egmont.

German tragedy in 5 acts, by Johann Wolfgang von Goethe; incidental music by L. van Beethoven, op. 84. (Music played, May 24, 1810.)

Beethoven's incidental music to Goethe's play was first played in its entirety in America on May 17, 1856, at the Academy of Music, New York, in concert form, Theodore Eisfeld conducting.

· Beethoven's complete incidental music was played at the German performance of Goethe's play on Jan. 23, 1871 at the New York Stadt Theatre.

Performed in Boston, March 26, 1859, at the Philharmonic Concerts.

Elaine.

French opera in 4 acts, libretto by Paul Ferrier, founded on Alfred, Lord Tennyson's "Idylls of the king;" music by H. Bemberg. (London, Covent Garden, July 6, 1892, in French.) *Metropolitan Opera House, Dec. 17, 1894, in French.

Elektra.

German opera in 1 act, libretto by Hugo von Hofmannsthal; music by R. Strauss, op. 58. (Dresden, Hofoper, Jan. 25, 1909.) *Manhattan Opera House, Feb. 1, 1910, in the French translation by Henry Gauthier-Villars.

Elisa e Claudio.

Italian opera in 2 acts, libretto by Luigi Romanelli; music by G. Mercadante. (Milan, Teatro alla Scala, Oct. 30, 1821.) *Richmond Hill Theatre, Oct. 18 (not 19), 1832, in Italian.

L'Elisir d'amore (The elixir of love).

Italian opera in 2 acts, libretto by Felice Romani; music by G. Donizetti. (Milan, Teatro della Canobbiana, May 12, 1832.) Park Theatre, June 18, 1838, in English, preceded by a comedy, "Promotion," and followed by a farce, "The two queens;" Palmo's Opera House, May 22, 1844, in Italian.

An English version of this opera under the title, "The love spell; or, The mountebank of Ravenna," with "all the original music" by Donizetti, was performed on Feb. 18, 1840, preceded by a comedy, "More blunders than one," and a farce, "The review," at the Park Theatre, New York.

Performed in Philadelphia, Chestnut Street Theatre, May 8, 1841, in English; New Orleans, Théâtre d'Orléans, March 30, 1842.

An English version adapted by Oscar Weil, entitled "Adina," was performed in Boston in 1887.

The Enchanted horse; or, The eastern lovers.

English opera in 3 acts; music by Jones. First performed: Park Theatre, Sept. 30, 1844, in English, followed by a farce, "Raising the wind."

The Enchantress.

English opera in 4 acts, libretto by Alfred Bunn; music by W. M. Balfe. (London, Drury Lane Theatre, Sept. 27, 1845.) Broadway Theatre, March 26 (not 30), 1849, in English.

Performed in Philadelphia, Walnut Street Theatre, Feb. 21, 1846.

L'Enfant prodigue (Azael, the prodigal).

French opera in 5 acts, libretto by Augustin Eugène Scribe; music by D. Auber. (Paris, Salle de la rue Le Peletier, Dec. 6, 1850.) Broadway Theatre, June 2, 1851, in English.

Die Entfuehrung aus dem Serail.

German opera in 3 acts, libretto by Gottlob Stephanie, founded on the play by Christoph Friedrich Bretzner; music by W. A. Mozart. (Vienna, Nationaltheater, July 12, 1782.) Brooklyn, end of Feb., 1860, in Italian, under the title, "Belmonte and Constanze," by the Operatic Circle, Carl Anschütz conducting; German Opera House, Oct. 10, 1862, in German.

A soprano aria from this opera was sung on Dec. 7, 1842 by Mme. Otto at the first concert of The Philharmonic Society of New York at the Apollo Rooms, New York.

A performance of Mozart's opera was given on Jan. 8, 1910, under the title, "Il seraglio," at the Hotel Astor, New York, by the New York Mozart Society.

Performed in Philadelphia, Academy of Music, March 4, 1863.

Ernani.

Italian opera in 4 acts, libretto by Francesco Maria Piave, founded on Victor Hugo's play, "Hernani;" music by G. Verdi.

Grand Opera in New York, 1825–1925, cont'd.

(Venice, Teatro La Fenice, March 9, 1844.) *Park Theatre, April 15, 1847, in Italian.

Performed in Boston, Howard Athenaeum, April 23, 1847; Philadelphia, Walnut Street Theatre, July 14, 1847; New Orleans, Théâtre d'Orléans, April 13, 1858.

A burlesque of Verdi's opera, "Herr Nanny," by Jonas B. Phillips, was performed in English on May 7, 1849 at Burton's Theatre, New York.

This opera was broadcast by radio on Sept. 1, 1925, in Italian, in tabloid form, with a reduced orchestra, through station WEAF, New York.

Ero e Leandro.

Italian opera in 3 acts, libretto by Tobio Gorrio [pseud. of Arrigo Boito]; music by L. Mancinelli. (Norwich Musical Festival, England, Oct. 8, 1896, in English, as an oratorio; Madrid, Teatro Reale, Nov. 30, 1897, in dramatic form, in Italian.) *Metropolitan Opera House, March 10, 1899, in Italian.

Esmeralda.

English opera in 4 acts, libretto by Alberto Randagger and Theodore Marzials, founded on Victor Hugo's novel, "Notre Dame de Paris;" music by A. G. Thomas. (London, Drury Lane Theatre, March 26, 1883.) *Metropolitan Opera House, Nov. 19, 1900, in English.

L'Esule di Roma.

Italian opera, libretto by Domenico Gilardoni; music by G. Donizetti. (Naples, Teatro San Carlo, Jan. 1, 1828.)

Never performed in New York.

A tenor scena and cavatina from this opera was sung in Italian, "with appropriate costume," by Signor G. B. Montresor at his benefit on May 9, 1833 at the Bowery Theatre, New York, between the acts of Rossini's opera, "Il barbiere di Siviglia."

L'Étoile du nord (The star of the north).

French opera in 3 acts, libretto by Augustin Eugène Scribe; music by G. Meyerbeer. (Paris, Opéra Comique, Feb. 16, 1854.) Academy of Music, Sept. 24, 1856, in Italian; Academy of Music, March 3, 1876, in English.

First performed in America: New Orleans, Théâtre d'Orléans, April 1, 1850.

Performed in Philadelphia, Academy of Music, Oct. 22, 1866.

Eugen Onegin.

Russian opera in 3 acts, libretto by the composer and K. S. Shilovsky, founded on the poem by Alexander Pushkin; music by P. I. Tchaikovsky. (Moscow, Small Theatre, March 17 ·29], 1879.) *Carnegie Hall, Feb. 1, 1908, in English, by the Symphony Society of New York; Metropolitan Opera House, March 24, 1920, in Italian, in operatic form.

Euryanthe.

German opera in 3 acts, libretto by Helmina von Chezy; music by C. M. von Weber. (Vienna, Kärthnerthor-Hof-Operntheater, Oct. 25, 1823.) Metropolitan Opera House, Dec. 23, 1887, in German.

According to J. D. Champlin's "Cyclopedia of music and musicians" (New York, 1888–90), v. 2, p. 32, and H. E. Krehbiel's "Review of the New York musical season 1887–1888" (New York, 1888), p. 63, and "More chapters of opera" (New York, 1919), p. 342, this opera was first produced in America under Carl Anschütz in New York at Wallack's Theatre about 1863. The present compiler has not been successful in finding the date or an announcement of this performance. The reviewer of the performance at the Metropolitan Opera House, writing in "Freund's Music and drama," New York, Dec. 24, 1887, p. 4, refers to the presentation as "the first performance in this country," and says: "Though 'Euryanthe' may have had a few sporadic representations in this city at a remote period and in obscure theatres, no record of such representations is in existence."

Evandro.

Italian opera in 1 act, founded on "Il primo di Maggio," by Stefano Guerrieri. Garden Theatre, Nov. 23, 1917.

Performed in Tampa, Fla., at the Italian Club, March 8, 1919.

Der Evangelimann.

German opera in 2 acts, libretto and music by Wilhelm Kienzel. (Vienna, Hofoperntheater, Jan. 11, 1896.) Manhattan Opera House, Jan. 1, 1924, in German.

First performed in America: Chicago, Great Northern Theatre, Nov. 3, 1923.

The Fairies' lake. *See* Le Lac des fées.

Falstaff.

Italian opera in 3 acts, libretto by Arrigo Boito, founded on Shakespeare's play, "The Merry wives of Windsor;" music by G. Verdi. (Milan, Teatro alla Scala, Feb. 9, 1893.) Metropolitan Opera House, Feb. 4, 1895, in Italian.

First performed in America: Buenos Aires, July 9, 1893.

The performance at the Metropolitan Opera House, New York, was the first in the United States.

Il Fanatico per la musica (Il trionfo della musica).

Italian opera in 1 act, music by S. Mayr, V. Pucitta and G. Pacini. (Paris, Théâtre Italien, 1815; Palermo, Teatro Carolino, 1825.) *Bowery Theatre, April 20, 1829, in Italian, preceded by a comedy, "Two friends," and followed by a moving diorama of the scenery of the Hudson River.

La Fanciulla del West.

Italian opera in 3 acts, libretto by Guelfo Civinini and Carlo Zangarini, founded on David Belasco's play, "The girl of the golden west;" music by G. Puccini. First performed: Metropolitan Opera House, Dec. 10, 1910, in Italian.

Performed in Chicago, Auditorium, Dec. 27, 1910; Milwaukee, Auditorium, Dec. 30, 1910; St. Louis, Coliseum, Jan. 3, 1911; Boston, Boston Opera House, Jan. 17, 1911.

Grand Opera in New York, 1825–1925, cont'd.

Faust.

French opera in 5 acts, libretto by Jules Barbier and Michel Carré, founded on the dramatic poem by Johann Wolfgang von Goethe; music by C. Gounod. (Paris, Théâtre Lyrique, March 19, 1859.) Academy of Music, Nov. 25 (not 26), 1863, in Italian; Academy of Music, Dec. 18, 1863, in German; French Theatre [Théâtre Français], May 18, 1868, in English; Academy of Music, April 27, 1881, in French (first time?).

After its first presentation in New York, Gounod's "Faust" immediately became one of the major operas in the managerial rivalries of the 60's, 70's and 80's. During these stormy periods, it was apparently always sung in Italian. Whether or not the opera was produced in French earlier than the above date, the present compiler has been unable to determine. Gustav Kobbé, in his "Complete opera book" (New York, 1919), p. 563, says: "Popular in this country from the night of its American production, Gounod's 'Faust' nevertheless did not fully come into its own here until during the Maurice Grau régime at the Metropolitan Opera House." The Grau régime belongs to the 90's. The above French performance was given by a French troupe from New Orleans under the management of De Beauplan: the company only played a few nights and then went on strike.

The first open air presentation in New York of this opera was given on Aug. 8, 1925, in English, at Ebbets Field, Brooklyn. The performance was broadcast by radio through station WNYC, New York. This opera was also broadcast by radio on April 7, 1925, in French, in tabloid form, with reduced orchestra, through station WEAF, New York.

According to W. G. Armstrong's "A Record of the opera in Philadelphia" (Philadelphia, 1884), p. 121, this opera was performed for the first time in America in Philadelphia, Nov. 18, 1863, by a German company.

La Favorite (La favorita).

French opera in 4 acts, libretto by Alphonse Royer and Gustave Waez, founded on Baculard-Darnand's play, "Le Comte de Comminges;" music by G. Donizetti. (Paris, Académie royale de musique, Dec. 2, 1840.) Park Theatre, June 25, 1845, in French; Park Theatre, Oct. 4, 1847 (not 1848), in English, followed by a farce, "Shocking events;" Academy of Music, Dec., 1855, in Italian.

First performed in America: New Orleans, Théâtre d'Orléans, Feb. 9, 1843.

Fedora.

Italian opera in 3 acts, libretto by Arturo Colautti, founded on the play by Victorien Sardou; music by U. Giordano. (Milan, Teatro Lirico Internazionale, Nov. 17, 1898.) *Metropolitan Opera House, Dec. 5, 1906, in Italian.

Performed in New Orleans, French Opera House, Jan. 29, 1908, in Italian.

Die Feen.

German opera in 3 acts, libretto and music by R. Wagner. (Munich, Hoftheater, June 29, 1888.)

Never performed in New York.

A chorus and quintet from this opera were sung in German at the Liederkranz Hall, Nov. 18, 1888.

Fernand Cortez; ou, La conquête du Mexique.

French opera in 3 acts, libretto by Étienne Jouy and Joseph Étienne Esménard, founded on the drama by Alexis Piron; music by G. Spontini. (Paris, Théâtre de l'Académie royale de musique, Nov. 28, 1809.) Metropolitan Opera House, Jan. 6, 1888, in German.

The overture of this opera was played on Dec. 28, 1833, between the acts of Rossini's opera, "La donna del lago," at Signorina Clementina Fanti's benefit, at the Italian Opera House, corner Church and Leonard streets, New York.

La Fiancée.

French opera in 3 acts, libretto by Augustin Eugène Scribe, founded on the story, "Les Contes de l'atelier," by Michel Masson and Raymond Brucker; music by D. Auber. (Paris, Salle de la rue Feydeau, Jan. 10, 1829.) Park Theatre, Aug. 14, 1833, in French, followed by a vaudeville, "Les Viets pebhes."

Fidelio; oder, Die eheliche Liebe.

German opera in 2 acts, libretto by Joseph Sonnleithner, founded on Jean Nicholas Bouilly's French libretto, "Léonore; ou, L'amour conjugal;" music by L. van Beethoven. (Vienna, Theater an der Wien, Nov. 20, 1805.) *Park Theatre, Sept. 9, 1839, in English, followed by a farce, "The deep, deep sea;" Broadway Theatre, Dec. 29, 1856, in German.

Performed in New Orleans, French Opera House, Dec. 11, 1877, in Italian.

Figaros Hochzeit. *See* Le Nozze di Figaro.

La Figlia dell' aria (Semiramide).

Italian opera in 2 (?) acts, libretto by Paolo Rosich; music by M. Garcia. First performed: Park Theatre, April 25, 1826, in Italian.

This opera has been confused by many writers with Rossini's opera, "Semiramide." The latter was never produced in the United States by Garcia.

La Fille du régiment (La figlia del reggimento; Marie, die Tochter des Regiments; Die Regimentstochter).

French opera in 2 acts, libretto by Jean François Alfred Bayard and Jules Henri Vernoy de Saint-Georges; music by G. Donizetti. (Paris, Opéra Comique, Feb. 11, 1840.) Niblo's Garden, July 19, 1843, in French, followed by a miscellaneous musical program; Niblo's Garden, June 5, 1844, in English, under the title, "Vivandiere; or, The daughter of the regiment;" Broadway Theatre, Oct. 16, 1848, in English, under the title, "The child of the regiment," with Donizetti's "original" music; Niblo's Garden, Jan. 10, 1853, in Italian; New York Stadt Theatre, May 15, 1855, in German.

First performed in America: New Orleans, Théâtre d'Orléans, March 6, 1843.

Grand Opera in New York, 1825–1925, cont'd.

Il **Flauto magico.** *See* Die **Zauberflöte.**

Der **Fliegende Holländer** (The Flying Dutchman; Il vascello fantasma).

German opera in 3 acts, libretto and music by R. Wagner. (Dresden, Hoftheater, Jan. 2, 1843.) Academy of Music, Jan. 26, 1877, in English; Metropolitan Opera House, Nov. 27, 1889, in German; Metropolitan Opera House, March 31, 1892, in Italian.

First performed in America: Philadelphia, Academy of Music, Nov. 8, 1876, in Italian. That Wagner's opera should have been introduced to the American opera public in the Italian language is a curious fact, about which there has been some doubt. According to W. G. Armstrong's "A record of the opera in Philadelphia" (Philadelphia, 1884), p. 199, the title of Wagner's opera at this performance was given in Italian, the German soprano, Mme. Eugenie Pappenheim singing the part of Senta. On p. 225, Armstrong specifies an Italian production of the opera on April 16, 1883, at the Academy of Music, as the "first time here in Italian," Mme. Albani singing the part of Senta. The report of the first performance in the "Signale" (Leipzig, Jan., 1877), p. 19, clearly states that the language sung at the first rendition of Wagner's opera in America was Italian. The opera was performed three times, according to Armstrong. The company, of which Mme. Pappenheim was a member, was headed for New York, but disrupted before reaching its destination. Gotthold Carlberg was the musical director of the troupe. An English performance of Wagner's opera took place in Philadelphia at the Academy of Music on March 7, 1877.

Performed in New Orleans, French Opera House, Nov. 29, 1877.

The **Flying Dutchman.** *See* Der **Fliegende Holländer.**

Les **Folies amoureuses.**

French opera in 3 acts, libretto by Jean François Regnard, arranged by Castil Blaze [pseud. of François Henri Joseph Blaze]; music selected from W. A. Mozart, D. Cimarosa, F. Paër, G. Rossini, P. Generali, and D. Steibelt. (Paris, Gymnase, April 3, 1823.) Park Theatre, Aug. 21, 1833, in French, followed by a vaudeville, "Phillibert mariage".

The **Forest.** *See* Der **Wald.**

Forest rose; or, American farmers.

American pastoral operatic farce in 2 acts, libretto by Samuel Woodworth; music by J. Davies. First performed: Chatham Theatre, Oct. 7 (not 6), 1825, in English, preceded by a melo-drama, "The lady of the lake."

The writer of the libretto of this pastoral farce was the author of the words of the song, "The old oaken bucket."

La **Forza del destino.**

Italian opera in 4 acts, libretto by Francesco Maria Piave; music by G. Verdi. (St. Petersburg, Imperial Opera House, Nov. 10, 1862; Milan, Teatro alla Scala, Feb. 27, 1869.) *Academy of Music, Feb. 24, 1865, in Italian.

This opera was broadcast by radio on Aug. 25, 1925, in Italian, in tabloid form, with a reduced orchestra, through station WEAF, New York.

Performed in Philadelphia, Academy of Music, March 24, 1865; Chicago, Crosby's Opera House, June 13, 1865.

Verdi's opera was performed in America before it was produced in Italy.

Fra Diavolo; ou, L'hôtellerie de Terracine.

French opera in 3 acts, libretto by Augustin Eugène Scribe; music by D. Auber. (Paris, Salle Ventadour, Jan. 28, 1830.) *Park Theatre, June 20, 1833, in an English adaptation by J. T. Reynoldson, a singer from Covent Garden, London, followed by a comedy, "The chimney piece;" Park Theatre, Aug. 23, 1833, in French, followed by a vaudeville, "L'Heretière;" German Opera House, Feb. 26, 1863, in German; Academy of Music, Dec. 21, 1864, in Italian.

Performed in New Orleans, Théâtre d'Orléans, Dec. 15, 1836; Philadelphia, Chestnut Street Theatre, March 10, 1838; Chicago, Crosby's Opera House, May 17, 1865.

Francesca di Rimini.

Italian opera in 4 acts, libretto by Tito Ricordi, founded on the play by Gabriele d'Annunzio; music by R. Zandonai. (Turin, Teatro Reggio, Feb. 19, 1914.) *Metropolitan Opera House, Dec. 22, 1916, in Italian.

Performed in Chicago, Auditorium, Jan. 5, 1917.

The **Freebooters.** *See* Il **Fuorusciti di Firenze.**

Der **Freischütz.**

German opera in 3 acts, libretto by Johann Friedrich Kind, founded on a story in v. 1 of the "Gespensterbuch," edited by Johann August Apel and Friedrich Laun; music by C. M. von Weber. (Berlin, Schauspielhaus, June 18, 1821.) *Park Theatre, March 2, 1825, in English, followed by a farce, "A Roland for an Oliver;" Park Theatre, Nov. 8, 1827, in a new English version with all of Weber's "original" music, followed by a play, "The Cataract of the Ganges;" Park Theatre, Aug. 13, 1827, in French, followed by a vaudeville, "Jean qui pleure et Jean qui rit;" Palmo's Opera House, Dec. 8, 1845, in German; Astor Place Opera House, Oct. 21, 1850, in Italian.

The opera bore at its first English production in America the subtitle, "The Wild huntsman of Bohemia."

The soprano aria, "Und ob die Wolke sie verhülle," from the third act of this opera, was sung on Oct. 19, 1827, in German, by Mme. Malibran, at the Bowery Theatre, New York, at her American farewell performance, at which she sang Boieldieu's two-act opera, "Jean de Paris," for the first time in English in America.

An alto scena and aria "with piano accompaniment, by particular desire" was sung on Jan. 9, 1834, in German, by Signora Schneider-Moroncelli, at the

Grand Opera in New York, 1825–1925, cont'd.

concert of the Italian Opera Co. at the Euterpean Hall (410 Broadway), New York.

The date of the first performance of this opera in America has been incorrectly reported as March 2, 1824, March 3, 1825, and March 12, 1825. The above date has been verified in the newspapers of the day.

A rehearsal of this opera in Boston was announced by the local newspapers of Dec. 17, 1827, by a company which included Charles Edward Horn and Mrs. Edward Knight. Probably the first English performance of this opera in Boston occurred on Feb. 19, 1828 at the Boston Theatre. The overture of this opera had been played in Boston on Feb. 9, 1826.

Performed in Philadelphia, Chestnut Street Theatre, end of 1827.

Froehlich [or, The life of a Berlin chorister].

German operetta in 2 acts, music by L. Schneider. Palmo's Opera House, Jan. 5, 1846, in German, preceded by a farce, "List und Phlegma."

Il Fuorusciti di Firenze (The freebooters).

Italian opera, music by F. Paer. (Vienna, Kärnthnerthor Theater, July 31, 1804.) *Bowery Theatre, Dec. 24, 1827, in English, followed by a farce, "Peter Wilkins."

Le Furie de Arlecchino.

Italian opera in 1 act, libretto by Luigi Orsini; music by A. Lualdi. (Milan, Teatro Carcano, 1915.) *Hotel Pennsylvania, Dec. 20, 1924, in Italian, preceded by Pedrollo's one-act opera, "La veglia," and followed by a miscellaneous musical and dance program.

This little Italian opera or intermezzo was performed for the first time in America under the auspices of the Manufacturers Trust Co., New York, in honor of its stockholders.

Gabriella.

Italian opera in 1 act, libretto by Charles Alfred Byrne and Fulvio Fulgonio; music by E. Pizzi. (London, St. George's Hall, Nov. 25, 1893.) *Music Hall, March 16, 1894, in Italian.

Gagliarda of a merry plague.

Chamber opera in 1 act, founded on Edgar Allan Poe's story, "The masque of the red death," libretto and music by L. Saminsky. First performed: Times Square Theatre, Feb. 22, 1925, followed by "The Daniel jazz" for voice and small orchestra by Louis Gruenberg and "Pierrot Lunaire," a melodrama by Arnold Schönberg.

Galatée (Galatea).

French opera in 2 acts, libretto by Jules Barbier and Michel Carré; music by V. Massé. (Paris, Opéra Comique, April 14, 1852.) Academy of Music (Brooklyn), Dec. 30, 1886, in an English translation by Frederick A. Schwab, followed by a ballet presentation of Anton Rubinstein's piece, op. 103, "Bal costumé;" Academy of Music (New York), March 17, 1887, in Frederick

A. Schwab's English translation, followed by Léo Delibes' two-act ballet, "Coppelia."

Performed in Boston, Boston Theatre, Jan. 5, 1887, in one act, in Frederick A. Schwab's English translation.

A composite production entitled, "The beautiful Galatea," made up of this opera and Franz von Suppé's one-act operetta, "Die schöne Galatea," arranged by J. W. Norcross, was played in English on Sept. 14, 1882 at Tony Pastor's New Fourteenth Street Theatre, followed by Sir Arthur Sullivan's one-act dramatic cantata, "Trial by jury." The performance was announced for Sept. 11, 1882, but postponed until the 14th.

The Garden of mystery.

American opera in 1 act, libretto by Nelle Richmond Eberhart, founded on Nathaniel Hawthorne's story, "Rappaccini's daughter," from his "Mosses from an old manse;" music by C. W. Cadman. First performed: Carnegie Hall, March 20, 1925, in English.

La Gazza ladra (The thieving magpie).

Italian opera in 2 acts, libretto by Tommaso Gherardi del Testa, founded on a French play, "La pie voleuse; ou, La servante de Palaiseau," by Louis Charles Caigniez and Jean Marie Théodore Baudouin; music by G. Rossini. (Milan, Teatro alla Scala, May 31, 1817.) Park Theatre, Aug. 7, 1833, in French, followed by a vaudeville, "La second année;" Italian Opera House, Nov. 18, 1833, in Italian; Park Theatre, Jan. 14 (not 11), 1839, in English, followed by a farce, "Tom Noddy's secret."

The overture of this opera was played on the piano "by a young lady, with an accompaniment" on Oct. 12, 1825 at Mr. Huerta's concert at the Concert Room, corner Reed street and Broadway, opposite Washington Hall, New York.

Another English version of this opera, "La gazza ladra; or, The maid of Paillaiseau," was performed on Oct. 4. 1839 at the Park Theatre.

A burlesque of Rossini's opera, "The cats in the larder; or, The maid with a parasol," was performed on Dec. 24, 1840 at the Olympic Theatre, New York.

Der Geigenmacher von Cremona (Le luthier de Crémona).

German opera in 2 scenes, libretto by Max Kalbeck, founded on the French play by François Coppée and Henry Beauclair; music by J. Hubay. (Budapest, Nov. 10, 1894.) *Waldorf Astoria Hotel, Dec. 20, 1897, in French, at Albert Morris Bagby's 89th morning musicale.

At the first performance in Budapest, the composer played behind a screen the violin solo which the instrument maker is supposed to render.

Gemma di Vergy.

Italian opera in 2 acts, libretto by Giovanni Emmanuele Bidera; music by G. Donizetti. (Milan, Teatro alla Scala, Dec. 26, 1834.) *Niblo's Theatre (not Garden), Oct. 2 (not 3), 1843, in Italian.

Performed in Philadelphia, Chestnut Street Theatre, Nov., 1843.

Germania.

Italian opera in a prologue, 2 scenes and an epilogue, libretto by Luigi Illica; music

Grand Opera in New York, 1825–1925, cont'd.

by A. Franchetti. (Milan, Teatro alla Scala, March 10, 1902.) *Metropolitan Opera House, Jan. 22, 1910, in Italian.

First performed in America: Buenos Aires, Coliseo, July 13, 1902.
Performed in Boston, Boston Opera House, March 9, 1912.

Die Geschoepfe des Prometheus.

Allegorical ballet in 2 acts, libretto by Salvatore Vigano; music by L. van Beethoven, op. 43. (Vienna, Hoftheater, March 28, 1801.)

The overture of this ballet was played on March 20, 1823, William Taylor conducting, under the title, "Men of Prometheus," as the first number on the program, at P. H. Taylor's concert at the City Hotel, New York. According to the announcements, the overture was played for the "first time in New-York." It was repeated under the same auspices on March 4, 1824 at the City Hotel, New York.

Gianni di Calais.

Italian opera, libretto by Domenico Gilardoni; music by G. Donizetti. (Naples, Teatro del Fondo, Aug. 2, 1828.)

Never performed in New York.

The barcarolle, "Una barchetta in mar' solcando va," for alto, from this opera was sung, in Italian, on Dec. 18, 1834, by Signora Schneider-Maroncelli, at the City Hotel, New York, at the second and last concert by the Musical Fund Society of New York.

Gianni Schicchi.

Italian opera in 1 act, libretto by Gioacchino Forzano; music by G. Puccini. First performed: Metropolitan Opera House, Dec. 14, 1918, in Italian, preceded by "Il tabarro" and "Suor Angelica," Italian operas in 1 act by G. Puccini.

Performed in Chicago, Auditorium, Dec. 6, 1919.

La Gioconda.

Italian opera in 4 acts, libretto by Tobia Gorrio [pseud. of Arrigo Boito], founded on Victor Hugo's play, "Angelo," music by A. Ponchielli. (Milan, Teatro alla Scala, April 8, 1876.) *Metropolitan Opera House, Dec. 20 (not 21), 1883, in Italian; Century Opera House, Sept. 23, 1913, in English.

This opera was broadcast by radio on July 28, 1925, in Italian, in tabloid form, with reduced orchestra, through station WEAF, New York.

Performed in Chicago, 1884; San Francisco, California Theatre, Nov. 2, 1897; New Orleans, French Opera House, Jan. 28, 1902.

I Giojelli della Madonna (The jewels of the Madonna).

Italian opera in 3 acts, libretto by Carlo Zangarini and Enrico Golisciani; plot and music by E. Wolf-Ferrari. (Berlin, Kurfürsten Oper, Dec. 23, 1911, as "Der Schmuck der Madonna," in a German translation by Hans Liebstoeckl.) Metropolitan Opera House, March 5, 1912; Century Opera House, Oct. 14, 1913, in English.

First performed in America: Chicago, Auditorium, Jan. 16, 1912.

Performed in Philadelphia, Feb. 14, 1912; Boston, Boston Opera House, Jan. 17, 1913; Montreal, His Majesty's Theatre, Oct. 6, 1917.

Giovanna 1ma di Napoli.

Italian opera in 3 acts, music by M. Strakosch. First performed: Astor Place Opera House, Jan. 6, 1851, in Italian.

Giovanni Gallurese.

Italian opera in 3 acts, libretto by Francesco d'Angelantonio; music by I. Montemezzi. (Turin, Teatro Vittorio Emanuele, Jan. 28, 1905.) *Metropolitan Opera House, Feb. 19, 1925, in Italian.

La Gioventù d'Enrico V.

Italian opera in 2 acts, music by M. Garcia.

According to Clément and Larousse's "Dictionnaire des opéras" and Hugo Riemann's "Opern-Handbuch," this opera was performed in New York in 1827. The date cannot be substantiated by a search in the New York newspapers and periodicals of the time. Garcia's first and only opera season in New York closed on Sept. 30, 1826. As far as records go, this opera was never performed in New York.

The Gipsy's warning.

English opera in 3 acts, libretto by George Linley and Richard Brinsley Peake; music by J. Benedict. (London, Drury Lane Theatre, April 19, 1838.) Park Theatre, April 20, 1841, in English.

The Girl of the golden West. *See* La Fanciulla del West.

Giselle; ou, Les Wilis. *See* The Night dancers.

Gismonda.

French opera in 3 acts, libretto by Henri Cain and Louis Payen [pseud. of Albert Liénard], founded on the play by Victorien Sardou; music by H. Février. (Chicago, Auditorium, Jan. 14, 1919, in French.) Lexington Theatre, Jan. 27, 1919, in French.

Giuditta (Judith).

Italian opera, libretto by Marco Marcelliano Marcello; music by A. Peri. (Milan, Teatro alla Scala, March 26, 1860.) *Academy of Music, Nov. 11, 1863, in Italian.

Giulietta e Romeo.

Italian opera, libretto by Felice Romani; music by N. Vaccai. (Milan, Teatro della Canobbiana, Oct. 31, 1825.)

Never performed in New York.

The last act of this opera was sung on June 15, 1855, in Italian, at the benefit of Mlle. Vestvali at the Academy of Music, New York, preceded by the fourth act of Verdi's opera, "Rigoletto," and followed by the second and fourth acts of his opera "Il Trovatore." The act was repeated at Signora Vietti's benefit on June 22, 1855.

Giulietta e Romeo. *See* Romeo e Giulietta.

Il Giuramento.

Italian opera in 3 acts, libretto by Gaetano Rossi; music by G. Mercadante. (Milan,

Grand Opera in New York, 1825–1925, cont'd.

Teatro alla Scala, March 11, 1837.) *Astor Place Opera House, Feb. 14, 1848, in Italian.

Performed in Philadelphia, Chestnut Street Theatre, March 20, 1848.

Das **Gloeckchen des Eremiten**. *See* Les Dragons de Villars.

Die **Goetterdaemmerung**. *See* Der **Ring des Nibelungen**.

Das **Goldene Kreuz**.

German opera in 2 acts, libretto by Solomon Hermann Mosenthal; music by Ignaz Brüll. (Berlin, Königliches Opernhaus, Dec. 22, 1875.) *Metropolitan Opera House, Nov. 19, 1886, in German, followed by a ballet divertissement, "Vienna waltzes," in three tableaux by Louis Frappert, arranged for the American stage by Ambroggio, re-arranged and adapted by Walter Damrosch; music by Joseph Bayer.

Performed by the Arion Singing Society in Brooklyn, at Arion Hall, Oct. 23, 1899 and by the students of the vocal department of the New England Conservatory of Music in Boston, at Jordan Hall, May 18, 1906, in English.

Goyescas.

Spanish opera in 3 scenes, libretto by Fernando Periquet y Zuaznabar; music by E. Granados y Campina. First performed: Metropolitan Opera House, Jan. 28, 1916, in Spanish, followed by Leoncavallo's two-act opera, "Pagliacci."

This was the first opera sung in Spanish at the Metropolitan Opera House.

Griselides.

French opera in a prologue and 3 acts, libretto by Paul Armand Silvestre and Eugène Édouard Morand; music by J. Massenet. (Paris, Opéra Comique, Nov. 20, 1901.) *Manhattan Opera House, Jan. 19 (not 9), 1910, in French.

Performed in Chicago, Auditorium, Jan. 12, 1917.

Il **Guarany**.

Italian opera in 4 acts, libretto by Antonio Scalvini; music by A. C. Gomes. (Milan, Teatro alla Scala, March 19, 1870.) Star Theatre, Nov. 3, 1884, in Italian.

The performance of this opera at the Star Theatre, New York, as noted above, was the first in the United States.

The opera was performed on May 6, 1901, at Carnegie Lyceum, New York, by a Negro troupe, the Theo. Drury Opera Co., a white musician, Maurice Arnold, conducting.

Guglielmo Tell. *See* **Guillaume Tell**.

Guillaume Tell (Guglielmo Tell; Wilhelm Tell; William Tell).

French opera in 4 acts, libretto by Hippolyte Louis Florent Bis and Victor Joseph Étienne de Jouy, founded on Friedrich von Schiller's play, "Wilhelm Tell;" music by G. Rossini. (Paris, Opéra, Aug. 3, 1829.) Park

Theatre, Sept. 19, 1831, in English, at Miss Hughes' benefit, preceded by the opera, "Cinderella," and followed by a farce, "'Twas I;" Park Theatre, June 16, 1845, in French; Academy of Music, April 9, 1855, in Italian; Academy of Music, April 18, 1866, in German.

Performed in New Orleans, Théâtre d'Orléans, Dec. 13, 1842; Philadelphia, Academy of Music, April 19, 1858.

Gulistan; ou, Le hulla de Sammarcande.

French opera in 3 acts, libretto by Charles Guillaume and La Chabeaussière; music by N. Dalayrac. (Paris, Opéra Comique, Sept. 30, 1805.) Park Theatre, Aug. 1, 1827, in French, with a vaudeville, "Frontin mari garçon."

Gustavus III; ou, Le bal masqué (or, The masked ball).

French opera in 5 acts, libretto by Augustin Eugène Scribe; music by D. Auber. (Paris, Salle de la rue Le Peletier, Feb. 27, 1833.) *Park Theatre, July 21, 1834, in an English adaptation by James Robinson Planché, the music arranged by Thomas Simpson Cooke, preceded by a comedy, "Petticoat government," and followed by a farce, "Uncle John;" National Theatre, Oct. 21 (not 15), 1839, in English, with Auber's original music, followed by a farce, "My young wife and an old umbrella."

Performed in Philadelphia, Chestnut Street Theatre, May 28, 1844.

The overture and eight songs of this opera were published by E. C. Riley, New York, in 1834. The publication was reviewed in "The American musical journal," Dec., 1834, v. 1, no. 2, p. 42.

La **Habanera**.

French opera in 3 acts, libretto and music by R. Laparra. (Paris, Opéra Comique, Feb. 26, 1908.) Metropolitan Opera House, Jan. 2, 1924, in French, followed by Riccitelli's one-act opera, "I Compagnacci."

First performed in America: Boston, Boston Opera House, Dec. 14, 1910.

Haensel und Gretel.

German opera in 3 acts, libretto by Adelheid Wette, founded on the fairy tale by Jakob Ludwig Karl Grimm; music by E. Humperdinck. (Weimar, Hoftheater, Dec. 23, 1893.) *Daly's Theatre, Oct. 8, 1895, in English; Metropolitan Opera House, Nov. 25, 1905, in German.

A pantomimic adaptation of this opera was performed on June 5, 1911 at New York University, New York.

Performed in Chicago, Auditorium, April 4, 1906; Boston, Hollis Street Theatre, Jan. 21, 1896, in English; Boston Theatre, April 6, 1907, in German; New Orleans, French Opera House, Dec. 25, 1909.

Der **Haeusliche Krieg (Die Verschworenen)**.

German operetta in 1 act, libretto by Ignaz Franz Castelli, adapted from the French; music by F. Schubert. (Vienna,

Grand Opera in New York, 1825-1925, cont'd.

Konzertsaal, March 1, 1861, in concert form; Frankfurt, Oct. 19, 1861, in dramatic form.)

Schubert's operetta, which was never performed in Europe during his lifetime, was produced in America, probably for the first time, in March (?), 1863, under the title, "The conspirators; or, The domestic strife," in 2 acts, in Hoboken, N. J., by the Concordia Singing Society, Friedrich Adolf Sorge conducting.

Halka.

Polish opera in 4 (originally 2) acts, libretto by Vladimir Wolski; music by S. Moniuszko. (Vilna, 1851, in 2 acts; Warsaw, 1858, in 4 acts.) People's Theatre, June, 1903, in Russian.

A performance of the opera was given in Milwaukee, Pabst Theatre, May 13, 1923, by the Polish Opera Club of Milwaukee.

Hamlet.

French opera in 5 acts, libretto by Michel Carré and Jules Barbier, founded on the play by Shakespeare; music by A. Thomas. (Paris, Opéra, March 9, 1868.) *Academy of Music, March 22, 1872, in Italian; Metropolitan Opera House, Feb. 10, 1892, in French.

Performed in Philadelphia, Academy of Music, April, 1872; Boston, Boston Theatre, March 3, 1884.

Hans, le joueur de flûte (Hans, the flute player).

French opera in 3 acts, libretto by Maurice Vaucaire and Georges Mitchell; music by L. Ganne. (Monte Carlo, Théâtre de Monte Carlo, April 14, 1906.) *Manhattan Opera House, Sept. 20, 1910, in the English translation by Algernon Brennan.

Performed for the first time in America: Buenos Aires, Politeama, May 10, 1910.

Hérodiade.

French opera in 4 acts, libretto by Paul Milliet, Henri Grémont and Zamadini; music by J. Massenet. (Brussels, Théâtre de la Monnaie, Dec. 19, 1881; Paris, Théâtre Italien, Feb. 1, 1884, in Italian; Paris, Théâtre de la Gaîté, Oct. 2, 1903, in French.) Manhattan Opera House, Nov. 8, 1909, in French.

A soprano aria from this opera was sung on Dec. 8, 1888, in French, by Mme. Emmy Fursch-Madi at a concert by The Philharmonic Society of New York at the Metropolitan Opera House, New York.
First performed in America: New Orleans, French Opera House, Feb. 13, 1892.
Performed in Chicago, Auditorium. Dec. 16, 1912.

Herr Nanny. *See* **Ernani.**

L'Heure espagnole.

French opera in 1 act, libretto by Franc Nohain; music by M. Ravel. (Paris, Opéra Comique, May 19, 1911.) Lexington Theatre, Jan. 28, 1920, in French, followed by Leoncavallo's two-act opera, "I Pagliacci."

First performed in America: Chicago, Auditorium, Jan. 5, 1920.

Die Hochzeit des Figaro. *See* Le **Nozze di Figaro.**

Home, sweet home! or, The ranz des vaches.

English operatic entertainment in 2 acts, libretto by Isaac Pocock; music by H. R. Bishop. (London, Covent Garden, March 19, 1829.) Park Theatre, May 25 (not 22), 1829, in English, preceded by an operetta, "No," and followed by a farce, "The invincibles."

Les Huguenots (Gli Ugonotti; Die Hugenotten; The Huguenots).

French opera in 5 acts, libretto by Augustin Eugène Scribe and Émile Deschamps; music by G. Meyerbeer. (Paris, Académie royale de musique, Feb. 29, 1836.) Park Theatre, Aug. 11, 1845, in French; Astor Place Opera House, June 24, 1850, in Italian; Academy of Music, April 23, 1866, in German; Grand Opera House, Dec. 6, 1869, in English.

First performed in America: New Orleans, Théâtre d'Orléans, April 29, 1839.

Ida della torre.

Italian opera, music by A. Nini. (Venice, Teatro San Benedetto, Nov. 11, 1837.)

Never performed in New York.
A cavatina, "Quando quell' uom quell' unico," from this opera was sung in Italian on Nov. 18, 1843, by Signora Castellan, at the first concert of the second season of The Philharmonic Society of New York, at the Apollo Rooms, New York.

The Impresario.

German operetta in 1 act, libretto adapted and arranged by Louis Schneider, founded on the one-act comic opera, "Der Schauspieldirektor," libretto by Stephanie, jr.; music by W. A. Mozart. (Schönbrunn, in the Orangery, Feb. 7, 1786, in Mozart's original version; Vienna, 1847, in L. Schneider's adaptation.) Empire Theatre, Oct. 26, 1916, in an English adaptation and version by Henry Edward Krehbiel, preceded by Mozart's one-act operetta, "Bastien und Bastienne."

The Impresario. *See also* **Mozart und Schikaneder.**

In a well. *See* **V studni.**

L'Inganno felice; o, Le miniere di Polonia (The lucky mistake; or, The miners of Poland).

Italian opera in 1 act, libretto by Giuseppe Foppa; music by G. Rossini. (Venice, Teatro Santo Moisè, Jan. 9, 1812.) *Bowery Theatre, May 11, 1833, in French.

The overture of this opera was played on Dec. 22, 1830, Mr. Segura conducting, at a concert for the benefit of St. Mary's Institution for Orphans, at the Masonic Hall, New York.

Grand Opera in New York, 1825–1925, cont'd.

Ione.

Italian opera in 4 acts, libretto by Giovanni Peruzzini, founded on Bulwer-Lytton's novel, "The last days of Pompeii;" music by E. Petrella. (Milan, Teatro alla Scala, Jan. 26, 1858.) *Academy of Music, April 6 (not March 7), 1863, in Italian.

Performed in Philadelphia, Academy of Music, Dec. 2, 1863; New Orleans, French Opera House, Feb. 8, 1867.

Iphigenia in Aulis.

Greek drama by Euripides; incidental music by W. Damrosch. Manhattan Opera House, April 7 and 8, 1921, in an English translation by H. D. (Mrs. Richard Aldington).

Iphigénie en Tauride (Iphigenia auf Tauris).

French opera in 4 acts, libretto by Nicolas François Guillard; music by C. W. von Gluck. (Paris, Académie royale de musique, May 18, 1779.) *Metropolitan Opera House, Nov. 25, 1916, in German.

Iris.

Italian opera in 3 acts, libretto by Luigi Illica; music by P. Mascagni. (Rome, Teatro Costanzi, Nov. 22, 1898; Milan, Teatro alla Scala, Jan., 1899, in revised form.) Metropolitan Opera House, Oct. 16, 1902, in Italian.

First performed in America: Buenos Aires, June 22, 1899; Montevideo, Aug. 10, 1901.

First performed in the United States: Philadelphia, Oct. 14, 1902.

Performed in Baltimore, Music Hall, Oct. 26, 1902; Chicago, Auditorium, April 25, 1908.

Isabeau.

Italian opera in 3 acts, libretto by Luigi Illica; music by P. Mascagni. (Buenos Aires, Coliseo, June 2, 1911.) Lexington Theatre, Feb. 13, 1918.

Performed in Italy: Milan, Teatro alla Scala, and Venice, Teatro La Fenice, contemporaneously, Jan. 20, 1912.

First performed in the United States: Chicago, Auditorium, Nov. 12, 1917; performed in Boston, Boston Opera House, Feb. 21, 1918.

Isidore di Merida.

English opera, music by C. E. Horn. First performed: Park Theatre, June 9, 1828, in English.

The Israelites in Egypt; or, The passage of the Red Sea.

Sacred music drama, libretto and music by M. R. Lacy; music adapted and arranged from G. F. Handel and G. Rossini. First performed: Park Theatre, Oct. 31, 1842, in English.

Performed in Philadelphia, Chestnut Street Theatre, Dec. 15, 1842.

L'Italiana in Algeri.

Italian opera in 2 acts, libretto by Angelo Anelli; music by G. Rossini. (Venice, Teatro San Benedetto, May 22, 1813.) *Richmond Hill Theatre, Nov. 5 (not 17), 1832, in Italian.

The overture of this opera was played in New York on Sept. 21, 1829, by the New York Sacred Music Society.

Performed in Philadelphia, "Italian Opera-House, late Chestnut Street Theatre," Feb. 4, 1833.

Jacquerie.

Italian opera in 3 acts, libretto by A. Donaudy; music by G. Marinuzzi. (Chicago, Auditorium, Nov. 17, 1920.) Manhattan Opera House, Feb. 4, 1921, in Italian.

Jaquarita l'indienne. *See under* The Desert flower.

Jean de Paris (John of Paris; Johann von Paris).

French opera in 2 acts, libretto by Claude Godard d'Aucour de Saint-Just; music by A. Boieldieu. (Paris, Théâtre Feydeau, April 4, 1812.) Park Theatre, Aug. 6, 1827, in French, followed by the overture of Rossini's opera, "Tancredi," and a vaudeville, "Monsieur Blaise; ou, Les deux châteaux;" Bowery Theatre, Oct. 29, 1827, in English, with a program of miscellaneous songs in Italian and German; German Opera House, Oct. 22, 1862, in German.

Mme. Malibran, the daughter of Manual Garcia who introduced Italian opera in the United States, made her last appearance in America in the first English performance of this opera at the Bowery Theatre, New York, Oct. 29, 1827 (not Sept. 28, 1827).

The overture of this opera was played on March 20, 1823, William Taylor conducting, at P. H. Taylor's concert at the City Hotel, New York, and on May 15, 1823, Mr. Gentil conducting, at Keene's twice postponed concert at the City Hotel.

Jeannot et Colin.

French opera in 3 acts, libretto by Charles Guillaume Étienne; music by Nicolo. (Paris, Opéra Comique, Oct. 17, 1814.) Park Theatre, Aug. 10, 1827, in French, followed by a vaudeville, "Les deux Edmon."

Jenufa (Jeji pastorkyňa).

Bohemian opera in 3 acts, libretto and music by Leoš Janáček, founded on the play by Gabriela Preissova. (Brno, 1904; Prague, 1916; Vienna, 1918.) *Metropolitan Opera House, Dec. 6, 1924, in German.

Jessonda.

German opera in 3 acts, libretto by Eduard Gehe, founded on "Le veuve du Malabar;" music by L. Spohr, op. 63. (Cassel, Hoftheater, July 28, 1823.)

Never performed in New York.

The overture of this opera was played for the "first time" in New York on Jan. 11, 1845 by the Philharmonic Society of New York, Uriah C. Hill

Grand Opera in New York, 1825–1925, cont'd.

conducting, at the second concert of the third season, in the Apollo Rooms, New York.

This opera was performed, probably for the first time in America, in Philadelphia, Academy of Music, Feb. 15, 1864, in German.

The Jewels of the Madonna. *See* **I Giojelli della Madonna.**

Joconde; ou, Les coureurs d'aventures.

French opera in 3 acts, libretto by Charles Guillaume Étienne; music by Nicolo. (Paris, Opéra Comique, Feb. 28, 1814.) Park Theatre, July 27, 1827, in French, with a play, "Les deux Edmon."

Johann von Paris. *See* **Jean de Paris.**

John of Paris. *See* **Jean de Paris.**

Le Jongleur de Notre Dame.

French opera in 3 acts, libretto by Maurice Lena, founded on Anatole France's story, "Etui de nacre;" music by J. Massenet. (Monte Carlo, Théâtre, Feb. 18, 1902.) *Manhattan Opera House, Nov. 27, 1908, in French.

Performed in New Orleans, French Opera House, Dec. 14, 1909.

Joseph.

French opera in 3 acts, libretto by Alexandre Duval; music by E. Mehul. (Paris, Théâtre Feydeau, Feb. 17, 1807.) German Opera House, Feb. 16, 1863, in German.

Performed in Philadelphia, Academy of Music, March 7, 1863.

Judith.

English operatic spectacle in 5 tableaux, music composed and arranged by J. N. C. Bochsa, selected from G. Verdi. First performed: Astor Place Opera House, Aug. 20, 1850, in English, followed by a ballet divertissement.

Judith. Italian opera by A. Peri. *See* **Giuditta.**

La Juive (L'Ebrea; Die Jüdin).

French opera in 5 acts, libretto by Augustin Eugène Scribe; music by F. Halévy. (Paris, Opéra, Feb. 23, 1835.) Park Theatre, July 16, 1845, in French; Winter Garden, April 30, 1860, in Italian; Academy of Music, Sept. 23, 1864, in German; Lexington Opera House, May 20, 1921, in Yiddish; Second Avenue Theatre, June 16, 1922, in Russian.

First performed in America: New Orleans, Théâtre d'Orléans, Feb. 13, 1844.

Julien; ou, La vie du poète.

French opera in a prologue and 4 acts, libretto and music by G. Charpentier, sequel to his "Louise." (Paris, Opéra Comique, June 4, 1913.) *Metropolitan Opera House, Jan. 27, 1914, in French.

Khovanstchina.

Russian opera in 5 acts, libretto and music by M. Moussorgsky.

This opera has not yet been performed in America. The third act of this opera was sung in concert form on Dec. 23, 1925, in Russian, by the Schola Cantorum of New York, Kurt Schindler conducting, at Carnegie Hall, New York. The program included the fourth and sixth acts of Rimsky-Korsakoff's seven-act opera, "Sadko."

Kiralyfogas.

Hungarian opera, libretto by Gregory Cziky; music by Joseph Kouti. Terrace Garden, April 2, 1898, in Hungarian.

Die Koenigin von Saba (The Queen of Sheba).

German opera in 4 acts, libretto by Solomon Hermann Mosenthal; music by C. Goldmark, op. 27. (Vienna, Hofoper, March 10, 1875.) *Metropolitan Opera House, Dec. 2, 1885; Academy of Music, April 3, 1888, in English.

Die Koenigskinder.

German opera in 3 acts, libretto by Ernst Rosmer [pseud. of Elsa Bernstein]; music by E. Humperdinck. First performed: Metropolitan Opera House, Dec. 28, 1910, in German.

This opera is a revision of the composer's melodrame of the same name, performed on Jan. 23, 1897 at the Hoftheater, Munich. This version was performed for the first time in America on April 29, 1898, in German, at the Irving Place Theatre, New York, and on Nov. 3, 1902, in English, at the Herald Square Theatre, New York.

Performed in Boston, Boston Opera House, April 16, 1912.

Der Kuhreigen (Le ranz des vaches).

German opera in 3 acts, libretto by Richard Batka, founded on Rudolf Hans Bartsch's story, "Die kleine Blanchefleure," from his collection, "Vom sterbenden Rokoko;" music by W. Kienzl. (Vienna, Volksoper, Nov. 23, 1911.) Metropolitan Opera House, Feb. 25, 1913, in French.

First performed in America: Philadelphia, Metropolitan Opera House, Feb. 21, 1913, in French.

Le Lac des fées (The fairies' lake).

French opera in 5 acts, libretto by Augustin Eugène Scribe and Mélesville [pseud. of Anne Honoré Joseph Duveyrier]; music by D. Auber. (Paris, Académie royale de musique, April 1, 1839.) Olympic Theatre, end of Nov., 1845, in an English adaptation by George Loder.

Lakmé.

French opera in 3 acts, libretto by Edmond Goudinet and Philippe Émile François Gille; music by L. Delibes. (Paris, Opéra Comique, April 14, 1883.) Academy of Music, March 1, 1886, in English; Metropolitan Opera House, April 2, 1890, in Ital-

Grand Opera in New York, 1825–1925, cont'd.

ian; Metropolitan Opera House, Feb. 22, 1892, in French.

Performed in Chicago, Auditorium, March 13, 1890; New Orleans, French Opera House, Feb. 1, 1893.

The Legend.

American opera in 1 act, libretto by Jacques Byrne; music by J. Breil. First performed: Metropolitan Opera House, March 12, 1919, in English, followed by Hugo's one-act opera, "The temple dancer," and Cadman's two-act opera, "Shanewis."

Die Legende der heiligen Elizabeth. *See* Saint Elizabeth.

Leonora.

American opera in 4 acts, libretto and music by W. H. Fry, founded on Bulwer-Lytton's play, "The lady of Lyons." (Philadelphia, Chestnut Street Theatre, June 4, 1845, in English.) Academy of Music, March 29, 1858, in Italian.

La Lettre de change.

French opera in 1 act, libretto by François Antoine Eugène de Planard; music by N. C. Bochsa. (Paris, Théâtre Feydeau, Dec. 11, 1815.) Park Theatre, July 20, 1827, in French, followed by Fetis's one-act opera, "La Vieille."

Lili-Tsee.

German opera in 1 act, libretto by Wolfgang Kirchbach; music by F. Curti. (Mannheim, Hoftheater, Jan. 12, 1896.) *Daly's Theatre, Feb. 17, 1898, in an English translation by Sydney Rosenfeld.

Performed in Boston, Tremont Theatre, April 25, 1898.

The Lily of Killarney.

English opera in 3 acts, libretto by Dion Boucicault and John Oxenford, founded on Dion Boucicault's play, "Colleen Bawn;" music by J. Benedict. (London, Covent Garden, Feb. 8. 1862.) Academy of Music, Jan. 1, 1868, in English.

Linda di Chamounix.

Italian opera in 3 acts, libretto by Gaetano Rossi, founded on the French play, "La grâce de Dieu;" music by G. Donizetti. (Vienna, Kärnthnerthor Theater, May 19, 1842.) *Palmo's Opera House, Jan. 4, 1847, in Italian; Park Theatre, Aug. 2, 1847, in English.

Lobetanz.

German opera in 3 acts, libretto by Otto Julius Bierbaum; music by L. Thuille. (Karlsruhe, Hoftheater, Feb. 6, 1898.) *Metropolitan Opera House, Nov. 18 (not 17), 1911, in German.

Lodoïska.

French opera in 3 acts, libretto by Claude François Fillette-Loraux; music by L. Cherubini. (Paris, Théâtre Feydeau, July 18, 1791.) Lafayette Theatre, Dec. 4, 1826 (not 1827), in English, the music arranged by R. Honey, leader of the orchestra of the theatre, preceded by a comedy, "Midnight hour."

Cherubini's "Lodoïska" became a popular production in New York during the second and third decades of the nineteenth century, especially with equestrian troupes. The opera afforded the managers of the day a grand opportunity for theatrical display and the introduction of much stage business; for instance, an advertisement of a performance of the opera at the Lafayette Theatre on Oct. 19, 1827 in the Evening Post of the date, the announcement declared: "In the 3rd act, Mr. Burroughs & Mr. Wallack, will fight a broad-sword combat, to the music of the Overture of Lodoïska." Apparently even in those days the overture was sometimes placed elsewhere in an operatic production and Gustav Mahler's procedure at the Metropolitan Opera House, New York, was antedated by more than three-quarters of a century!

Lodoletta.

Italian opera in 3 acts, libretto by Giovacchino Forzano, founded on Ouida's story, "Two little wooden shoes;" music by P. Mascagni. (Rome, Teatro Costanzi, April 30, 1917.) *Metropolitan Opera House, Jan. 12, 1918, in Italian.

First performed in America in Buenos Aires, Montevideo, Rio de Janeiro and São Paulo in 1917.

Lohengrin.

German opera in 3 acts, libretto and music by R. Wagner. (Weimar, Hoftheater, Aug. 28, 1850.) *New York Stadt Theatre, April 3, 1871, in German; Academy of Music, March 23, 1874, in Italian; Academy of Music, Jan. 20, 1886, in an English translation by Natalie Macfarren.

The date of the first performance of this opera has been incorrectly reported as March 12, 1871 and April 15, 1871. The above date has been verified in the newspapers of the day.

The wedding march from this opera was played on June 25, 1855, Carl Bergmann conducting, at the Grand German Musical Festival at the Metropolitan Theatre, New York.

Performed in Philadelphia, Academy of Music, April 16, 1874; Boston, March 27, 1877, in German; New Orleans, Dec. 3, 1877, in Italian; March 4, 1889, in French.

I Lombardi alla prima crociata.

Italian opera in 4 acts, libretto by Temistocle Solera, founded on the poem by Tommaso Grossi; music by G. Verdi. (Milan, Teatro alla Scala, Feb. 11, 1843.) *Palmo's Opera House, March 3, 1847, in Italian.

Loreley.

Italian opera in 3 acts, libretto by Carlo d'Ormeville and Angelo Zanardini; music by A. Catalani. (Turin, Teatro Reggio, Feb. 16, 1890.) Lexington Theatre, Feb. 13, 1919, in Italian.

First performed in America: Buenos Aires, Opera House, May 21, 1910.

First performed in the United States: Chicago, Auditorium, Jan. 17, 1919.

Grand Opera in New York, 1825–1925, cont'd.

Louise.

French opera in 4 acts, libretto and music by G. Charpentier. (Paris, Opéra Comique, Feb. 3, 1900.) *Manhattan Opera House, Jan. 3, 1908, in French; Century Opera House, Dec. 30, 1913, in an English translation by Charles Alfred Byrne.

Performed in Boston, Boston Opera House, Dec. 18, 1912.

The **Love spell; or, The mountebank of Ravenna.** See L'Elisir d'amore.

Lover's pilgrimage. See **Mireille.**

A **Lover's quarrel.** See I **Dispettosi amanti.**

Lucia di Lammermoor (The bride of Lammermoor).

Italian opera in 3 acts, libretto by Salvatore Cammarano, founded on Sir Walter Scott's novel, "The bride of Lammermoor;" music by G. Donizetti. (Naples, Teatro San Carlo, Sept. 26, 1835.) Niblo's Garden, Sept. 15, 1843, in Italian; Park Theatre, Nov. 17, 1845, in English; Academy of Music, Oct. 9, 1869, in French.

Performed in New Orleans, Théâtre d'Orléans, Dec. 28, 1841; Chicago, Chicago Theatre, Oct. 27, 1853.

This opera in its entirety was broadcast by radio on May 5, 1925, in Italian, through station WGBS, New York. This opera was broadcast by radio on June 9, 1925, in Italian, in tabloid form, with reduced orchestra, through station WEAF, New York.

A burlesque of Donizetti's opera, "Lucy-did-Sham-amour," libretto by Dr. Northall and the music arranged by George Loder, was performed on July 28, 1848 at Burton's Theatre, New York. Another burlesque, "Lucy of Lammermoor," in 4 acts, was performed Jan. 22, 1855 at Buckley's Serenaders Hall, New York, preceded by a program of Negro minstrelsy.

Lucrezia Borgia.

Italian opera in 3 acts, libretto by Felice Romani, founded on Victor Hugo's play, "Lucrèce Borgia;" music by G. Donizetti. (Milan, Teatro alla Scala, Dec. 2, 1834.) Palmo's Opera House, Nov. 25, 1844, in Italian; New York Stadt Theatre, Oct. 19, 1870, in German; Academy of Music, Oct. 13, 1871, in English.

A burlesque of Donizetti's opera was performed on Feb. 12, 1855, in English, at Buckley's Serenaders Hall, New York, preceded by a program of Negro minstrelsy.

First performed in America: New Orleans, Théâtre d'Orléans, April 27, 1844.

Performed in Philadelphia, Chestnut Street Theatre, March 7, 1848.

Lucy-did-Sham-amour. See **Lucia di Lammermoor.**

Luisa Miller.

Italian opera in 3 acts, libretto by Salvatore Cammarano, founded on Friedrich von Schiller's play, "Kabale und Liebe;" music by G. Verdi. (Naples, Teatro San Carlo,

Dec. 8, 1849.) *Castle Garden, July 20, 1854, in Italian.

Performed in Philadelphia, Walnut Street Theatre, Oct. 27, 1852.

Lully et Quinault; ou, Le déjeuner impossible.

French opera in 1 act, libretto by Gaugiran-Nanteuil; music by Nicolo. (Paris, Opéra Comique, Feb. 27, 1812.) Park Theatre, Sept. 1, 1827, in French, preceded by a play, "La vieille."

Il Lupo d'Ostenda.

Italian opera in 2 acts, music by M. Garcia.

According to Clément and Larousse's "Dictionnaire des opéras" and Hugo Riemann's "Opern-Handbuch," this opera was performed in New York in 1827. The date cannot be substantiated by a search in the New York newspapers and periodicals of the time. Garcia's first and only opera season in New York closed on Sept. 30, 1826. As far as records go, this opera was never performed in New York.

Lurline.

English opera in 3 acts, libretto by Edward Fitzball, founded on the legend of the Loreley; music by W. V. Wallace. (London, Covent Garden, Feb. 23, 1860.) Academy of Music, May 13, 1869, in Italian; Academy of Music, May 15, 1869, in English.

This opera was performed in concert form on June 1, 1863 in Cambridge, Mass., at the City Hall, Miss Addie S. Ryan singing the part of Lurline.

Selections from this opera were given on May 22, 1860 in Jersey City at the Metropolitan Hall and in New York on July 11, 1860 at the music rooms of Wm. Hall & Son, music publishers. The composer who had just come to America was present at this performance.

Die Lustigen Weiber von Windsor.

German opera in 3 acts, libretto by Solomon Hermann Mosenthal, founded on Shakespeare's play, "The merry wives of Windsor;" music by O. Nicolai. (Berlin, Hofoper, March 9, 1849.) Academy of Music, April 27, 1863, in German; Academy of Music, Feb. 5, 1886, in an English translation by Henry Edward Krehbiel.

First performed in America: Philadelphia, Academy of Music, March 16, 1863.

The overture of this opera was played on Jan. 9, 1858 by The Philharmonic Society of New York, at the Academy of Music.

Le **Luthier de Crémona.** See Der **Geigenmacher von Cremona.**

Ma tante Aurore; ou, Le roman impromptu.

French opera in 2 acts, libretto by Longchamp, founded on a French comedy, "Le séducteur amoureux;" music by A. Boieldieu.. (Paris, Théâtre Feydeau, Jan. 13, 1803.) Park Theatre, Aug. 28, 1827, in French, with a vaudeville, "Monsieur Pique Assiette."

The overture to this opera was played at Manuel Garcia's concert on May 4, 1826 at the City Hotel.

Macbeth.

Italian opera in 4 acts, libretto by Francesco Maria Piave and Andrea Maffei,

Grand Opera in New York, 1825–1925, cont'd.

founded on the play by Shakespeare; music by G. Verdi. (Florence, Teatro della Pergola, March 17, 1847.) *Niblo's Garden, April 24, 1850, in Italian.

Le Maçon (Der Maurer und der Schlosser).

French opera in 3 acts, libretto by Augustin Eugène Scribe and Germain Delavigne; music by D. Auber. (Paris, Opéra Comique, May 3, 1825.) Park Theatre, Aug. 3, 1827, in French, followed by Piccinni's one-act opera, "La maison en loterie;" Broadway Theatre, Jan. 8, 1857, in German.

Madame Butterfly.

Italian opera in 3 acts, libretto by Luigi Illica and Giuseppe Giacosa, founded on the story by John Luther Long and the play by David Belasco; music by G. Puccini. (Milan, Teatro alla Scala, Feb. 17, 1904.) Garden Theatre, Nov. 12, 1906, in an English translation by Rosie Helen Elkin; Metropolitan Opera House, Feb. 11, 1907, in Italian.

First performed in America: Buenos Aires, July 2, 1904. Performed at Montevideo, Aug. 27, 1904.

First performed in the United States: Washington, D. C., Columbia Theatre, Oct. 15, 1906, in the English translation by Rosie Helen Elkin. The first Italian performance of Puccini's opera in the United States took place at the Metropolitan Opera House, as noted above.

Puccini's opera was produced in America in English by Henry Savage's opera company. The itinerary was published in "The Musical courier," New York, Dec. 19, 1906, p. 26a.

A performance of this opera on June 19, 1920 at the Staats-Oper, Berlin, was broadcast by radio through the Königswusterhausen station. According to the "Radio digest" (Chicago, Aug. 29, 1925, p. 24), this was "the first complete opera broadcast to the world."

Madame Chrysanthème.

French lyric comedy in a prologue, 4 acts and an epilogue, libretto by Georges Hartmann and André Alexandre, founded on the novel by Pierre Loti [pseud. of Julien Viaud]; music by A. Messager. (Paris, Théâtre Lyrique [Renaissance], Jan. 30, 1893.) Lexington Theatre, Jan. 28, 1920, in French.

First performed in America: Chicago, Auditorium, Jan. 19, 1920.

Madame Sans-Gêne.

Italian opera in 4 acts, libretto by Renato Simoni, founded on the play by Victorien Sardou and Émile Moreau; music by U. Giordano. First performed: Metropolitan Opera House, Jan. 25, 1915, in Italian.

Madeleine.

American opera in 1 act, libretto by Grant Stewart, founded on the play, "Je dine chez ma mère," by Adrien Decourcelles and L. Thibaut; music by V. Herbert. First performed: Metropolitan Opera House, Jan. 24, 1914, in English, followed by Leoncavallo's two-act opera, "Pagliacci."

I Maestri cantori di Norimberga. *See* Die Meistersinger von Nüremberg.

Il Maestro di cappella. *See* Le Maître de chapelle.

The Magic flute. *See* Die Zauberflöte.

The Maid of Artois.

English opera in 3 acts, libretto by Alfred Bunn; music by W. M. Balfe. (London, Drury Lane Theatre, May 27, 1836.) *Park Theatre, Nov. 5, 1847, in English.

Performed in Philadelphia, Walnut Street Theatre, Dec. 29, 1847.

The Maid of Cashmere. *See* Le Dieu et la Bayadere.

The Maid of Judah; or, The Knights Templars.

English opera in 3 acts, founded on Sir Walter Scott's novel, "Ivanhoe;" music adapted by Rophino Lacy, mostly from Rossini's opera, "Mosè in Egitto." *Park Theatre, Feb. 27, 1832, in English.

Performed in Philadelphia, Chestnut Street Theatre, March 6, 1834; Boston, Tremont Theatre, Oct., 1835.

The Maid of Paillaiseau. *See* La Gazza ladra.

The Maid of Saxony.

American opera in 3 acts, libretto by George Pope Morris, founded on Miss Edgeworth's story, "The Prussian vase," and incidents from the life of Frederick II, of Prussia, as narrated by Zimmerman, Latrobe and others; music by C. E. Horn. First performed: Park Theatre, May 23, 1842, in English.

La Maison en loterie.

French opera in 1 act, libretto by Jean Baptiste Radet and Picard; music by A. Piccinni. (Paris, Gymnase, Dec. 23, 1820.) Park Theatre, Aug. 3, 1827, in French, preceded by Auber's three-act opera, "Le maçon."

Maison à vendre.

French opera in 1 act, libretto by Alexandre Duval; music by N. Dalayrac. (Paris, Salle Favart, Oct. 23, 1800.) Park Theatre, July 13, 1827, in French, with Nicolo's three-act opera, "Cendrillon."

Le Maître de chapelle (Il maestro di cappella).

French opera in 2 acts, libretto by Sophie Gay; music by F. Paër. (Paris, Théâtre Feydeau, March 29, 1821.)

The compiler has not been able to establish the date of the first performance of this little opera in New York. According to his records, performances of this opera were given at Niblo's Garden, June 25, 1852, in French, preceded by a play, "Le meunière de Marly," and followed by afterpiece, "Brelan de troupiers;" Castle Garden, Aug. 25, 1852, in French; Théâtre Français, Oct. 11, 1866, in French; Waldorf-Astoria, Jan. 11, 1898, in a double bill with Harvey Worthington Loomis's pantomime, "The traitor mandolin;" New Theatre, Dec. 9, 1909, in Italian, followed by Mascagni's one-act opera "Cavalleria rusticana."

Grand Opera in New York, 1825–1925, cont'd.

Mandragola.

German opera in 3 acts, libretto by Paul Eger, founded on the play by Niccolo di Bernardi dei Macchiavelli; music by I..Waghalter. (Charlottenburg, 1914.) *Princess Theatre, March 4, 1925, in the English translation by Alfred Kreymborg.

Manfred.

Dramatic poem in 3 parts by George Gordon Noël Byron; incidental music for soli, chorus and orchestra by R. Schumann, op. 115. (Leipzig, Gewandhaus, March 24, 1859, in concert form; Leipzig, Stadttheater, Nov. 23, 1863, with scenery.) Thalia Theatre, March 3, 1888, in German.

Schumann's overture to Byron's poem was played on Nov. 21, 1857, by the Philharmonic Society of New York, Theodore Eisfeld conducting, at the Academy of Music, New York.

Schumann's music was played in its entirety in New York, in concert form, on May 8, 1869, Carl Bergmann conducting, at the Academy of Music.

Manon.

French opera in 4 acts, libretto by Henri Meilhac and Philippe Gille, founded on Antoine François Prévost d'Exiles's story, "Histoire de Manon Lescaut;" music by J. Massenet. (Paris, Opéra Comique, Jan. 19, 1884.) *Academy of Music, Dec. 23, 1885, in Italian; Metropolitan Opera House, Jan. 16, 1895, in French.

Performed in New Orleans, French Opera House, Jan. 4, 1894; Chicago, Auditorium, March 27, 1900.

Manon Lescaut.

Italian opera in 4 acts, founded on the novel, "Histoire de Manon Lescaut," by Antoine François Prévost d'Exiles; libretto planned by Giacomo Puccini, written by Domenico Oliva, and revised by Marco Praga, Luigi Illica, Giulio Ricordi and the composer; music by G. Puccini. (Turin, Teatro Regio, Feb. 1, 1893.) Wallack's Theatre, May 27, 1898, in Italian.

First performed in America: Philadelphia, Grand Opera House, Aug. 29, 1894.

Manru.

German opera in 3 acts, libretto by Alfred Nossig; music by I. Paderewski. (Dresden, Königliches Opernhaus, May 29, 1901.) *Metropolitan Opera House, Feb. 14, 1902, in German.

Performed in Boston, Boston Theatre, March 15, 1902; Chicago, Auditorium, April 5, 1902.

Maria di Rohan.

Italian opera in 3 acts, libretto by Salvatore Cammerano; music by G. Donizetti. (Vienna, Kärnthnerthor Theater, June 5, 1843.) *Astor Place Opera House, Dec. 10, 1849, in Italian.

Marie, die Tochter des Regiments. *See* La Fille du régiment.

Marino Faliero.

Italian opera in 3 acts, libretto by Giovanni Emanuele Bidera, founded on the play by Lord Byron; music by G. Donizetti. (Paris, Théâtre Italien, March 12, 1835.) *Park Theatre, Dec. 15, 1843, in Italian.

Les Maris garçons.

French opera in 1 act, libretto by Gaugiran-Nanteuil; music by H. M. Berton. (Paris, Théâtre Feydeau, July 15, 1806.) Park Theatre, Oct. 26, 1827, in French, preceded by Carafa's three-act opera, "Le Solitaire."

Maritana.

English opera in 3 acts, libretto by Edward Fitzball, founded on the play, "Don Caesar de Bazan," by G. A'Becket and Mark Lemon; music by W. V. Wallace. (London, Drury Lane Theatre, Nov. 15, 1845.) Bowery Theatre, May 4, 1848, in English; Academy of Music, Dec. 20, 1885, in Italian, with recitatives by Tito Mattei.

A burlesque of Wallace's opera, in 3 acts, was performed in English on Sept. 22, 1856, at Buckley's Serenaders Hall, New York.

This opera was broadcast by radio on Sept. 15, 1925, in English, in tabloid form, with reduced orchestra, through station WEAF, New York.

Mârouf, savetier du Caire.

French opera in 5 acts, libretto by Lucien Népoty, from the Arabian nights after the French translation by Dr. J. C. Mardrus; music by H. Rabaud. (Paris, Opéra Comique, May 15, 1914.) *Metropolitan Opera House, Dec. 19, 1917, in French.

A public rehearsal of the opera was given in Paris on May 15, 1914.

The Marriage of Figaro. *See* Le Nozze di Figaro.

The Marriage of Georgette. *See* Les Noces de Jeannette.

The Marriage of Jeannette. *See* Les Noces de Jeannette.

Marta of the lowlands. *See* Tiefland.

Martha; oder, Der Markt zu Richmond.

German opera in 4 acts, libretto by W. Friedrich; music by F. von Flotow. (Vienna, Kärnthnerthor Theater, Nov. 25, 1847.) *Niblo's Garden, Nov. 1, 1852, in English; Niblo's Garden, March 13, 1855, in German; Academy of Music, Jan. 7, 1859, in Italian.

Maruxa.

Spanish opera in 2 acts, libretto by Luis Pascual Frutos; music by A. Vives. *Park Theatre, April 19, 1919, in Spanish, followed by "Cielo español," a revue in 1 act and 3 scenes.

Masaniello. *See* La Muette di Portici.

Grand Opera in New York, 1825–1925, cont'd.

I Masnadieri.

Italian opera in 4 acts, libretto by Andrea Maffei, founded on Schiller's play, "Die Räuber;" music by G. Verdi. (London, Her Majesty's Theatre, July 22, 1847.) *Winter Garden, June 2 (not May 30), 1860, in Italian.

Mataswintha.

German opera in 4 acts, libretto by Dr. Ernst Koppel, founded on Felix Dahn's novel, "Ein Kampf um Rom;" music by X. Scharwenka. (Weimar, Hoftheater, Oct. 4, 1896.) *Metropolitan Opera House, April 1, 1907, in German.

First performed in America in concert form: New York, Feb. 13, 1896, by The Manuscript Society of New York.

Matilde di Shabran; ossia, Bellezza e cuor di ferro.

Italian opera in 2 acts, libretto by Jacopo Ferretti; music by G. Rossini. (Rome, Teatro Apollo, Feb. 24, 1821.) *Italian Opera House, Feb. 10, 1834, in Italian.

Performed in Philadelphia, Chestnut Street Theatre, April 28, 1834.

Il Matrimonio segreto.

Italian opera in 2 acts, libretto by Giovanni Bertatti; music by D. Cimarosa. (Vienna, Hoftheater n.d. Burg, Feb. 7, 1792.) *Italian Opera House, Jan. 4, 1834, in Italian.

Performed in Philadelphia, Chestnut Street Theatre, April 17, 1834.

Matteo Falcone.

German opera in 1 act, founded on the poem by Adelbert von Chamisso; music by H. Zöllner. First performed: Irving Place Theatre, Dec. 18, 1893, followed by Leoncavallo's two-act opera, "Pagliacci," in the German translation, "Der Bajazzo," by Ludwig Hartmann.

Der Maurer und der Schlosser. *See* Le Maçon.

Medea.

Italian opera in 3 acts, libretto by B. Castilla; music by G. Pacini. (Palermo, Teatro Carolino, Nov. 28, 1843.) *Niblo's Garden, Sept. 27, 1860, in Italian.

Le Médecin malgré lui (The mock doctor).

French opera in 3 acts, libretto by Jules Barbier and Michel Carré, founded on the play by Molière; music by C. Gounod. (Paris, Théâtre Lyrique, Jan. 15, 1858.) Lyceum Theatre, May 10, 1917, in an English translation by Alice Mattulath.

Mefistofele.

Italian opera in 4 acts, founded on Goethe's dramatic poem, "Faust;" libretto and music by A. Boito. (Milan, Teatro alla Scala, March 5, 1868.) Academy of Music, Nov. 24, 1880, in Italian; Fifth Avenue Theatre, Feb. 28, 1881, in English.

First performed in America: Boston, Globe Theatre, Nov. 16, 1880, in English.

Performed in Philadelphia, Chestnut Street Opera House, Nov. 27, 1880; Chicago, Haverly's Theatre, Dec. 10, 1880; St. Louis, Grand Opera House, Jan., 1881; New Orleans, French Opera House, Jan. 19, 1891, in Italian; Feb. 17, 1894, in French.

Die Meistersinger von Nüremberg (I maestri cantori di Norimberga).

German opera in 3 acts, libretto and music by R. Wagner. (Munich, Hoftheater, June 21, 1868.) *Metropolitan Opera House, Jan. 4, 1886, in German; Metropolitan Opera House, March 2, 1892, in Italian.

Performed in Boston, Boston Theatre, April 8, 1889.

La Mélomanie.

French opera in 1 act, libretto by Grenier; music by S. Champein. (Paris, Opéra Comique, Jan. 23, 1781.)

This opera was announced for production on July 20, 1827, in French, at the Park Theatre by a French company from New Orleans. The performance was called off on account of the indisposition of one of the interpreters.

Les Mémoires du diable; ou, La sonnette mysterieuse.

French musical drama in 3 acts, libretto by Étienne Arago and Paul Vermoned; music by A. Doche. Niblo's Garden, May 22, 1843, in French, preceded by the overture of Herold's opera, "Zampa."

Merlin.

German opera in 3 acts, libretto by Siegfried Lipiner; music by C. Goldmark. (Vienna, Hofoper, Nov. 19, 1886.) *Metropolitan Opera House, Jan. 3, 1887, in German.

The Merry wives of Windsor. *See* Die Lustigen Weiber von Windsor.

Messaline.

French opera in 4 acts, libretto by Paul Silvestre and Eugène Morand; music by Isidore de Lara. (Monte Carlo, Théâtre du Casino, March 21, 1899.) *Metropolitan Opera House, Jan. 22, 1902, in French.

Performed in New Orleans, French Opera House, Jan. 29, 1903.

Midsummer night's dream.

English play in 5 acts by Shakespeare; incidental music by F. Mendelssohn, op. 21 and 61. (Potsdam, Neue Palais, Oct. 14, 1843.) *Burton's Theatre, Feb. 3 (not 11), 1854, in English.

Another performance of Shakespeare's play with Mendelssohn's music was performed on Feb. 6, 1854 at the Broadway Theatre, New York.

Mendelssohn's overture was played on April 22, 1843 by The Philharmonic Society of New York, in the third concert of its first season, at the Apollo Rooms, New York. Selections from Mendelssohn's incidental music were given with soli, chorus and orchestra on March 2, 1850 by The Philharmonic Society, in the third concert of its eighth season, at the Apollo Rooms.

Grand Opera in New York, 1825-1925, cont'd.

Mignon.

French opera in 3 acts, libretto by Michel Carré and Jules Barbier, founded on Goethe's novel, "Die Leiden des jungen Werther;" music by A. Thomas. (Paris, Opéra Comique, Nov. 17, 1866.) *Academy of Music, Nov. 22, 1871, in Italian; Booth's Theatre, Oct. 11, 1875, in English; Haverly's Fifth Avenue Theatre, March 9, 1880, in French.

Performed in Philadelphia, Academy of Music, April 18, 1872.

Der Minstrel.

German opera in 3 acts, libretto by Heinrich Urban; music by A. Neuendorff. First performed: Amberg Theatre, May 18, 1892, in German.

Mireille (Mirella).

French opera in 5 acts, libretto by Michel Carré, founded on Frédéric Mistral's poem, "Mireio;" music by C. Gounod. (Paris, Théâtre Lyrique, March 19, 1864.) Academy of Music (Brooklyn), Dec. 18, 1884, in Italian; Academy of Music (New York), Dec. 20, 1884, in Italian.

This opera was announced for production in Italian at the Academy of Music during the season 1864, by Max Maretzek, the manager. However, "Gounod's interesting opera," as the advertisements described it, was not performed.

Performed in Philadelphia, Academy of Music, Nov. 17, 1864, in German (the first two acts only); New Orleans, Dec. 29, 1884; Boston, Boston Theatre, Jan. 1, 1885.

This opera was performed on Sept. 13, 1880 in an English version under the title, "Lover's pilgrimage," at Hamlin's Opera House, Chicago, by the Emma Abbott Opera Company.

I Miserabili.

Italian opera in 4 acts, founded on Victor Hugo's novel, "Les miserables;" libretto and music by C. Bonsignore. First performed: Academy of Music (Brooklyn), Oct. 24, 1925, in Italian.

The Mock doctor. *See* Le Médecin malgré lui.

Mona.

American opera in 3 acts, libretto by Brian Hooker; music by H. Parker. First performed: Metropolitan Opera House, March 14, 1912, in English.

Mona Lisa.

German opera in a prologue, 2 acts and an epilogue, libretto by Beatrice Dovsky; music by M. Schillings. (Stuttgart, Hoftheater, Sept. 26, 1915.) *Metropolitan Opera House, March 1, 1923, in German.

Monna Vanna.

French opera in 4 acts, libretto by Maurice Maeterlinck; music by H. Février. (Paris,

Opéra, Jan. 13, 1909.) Metropolitan Opera House, Feb. 17, 1914, in French.

First performed in America: Boston, Boston Opera House, Dec. 5, 1913.
Performed in Chicago, Auditorium, Jan. 28, 1914; Philadelphia, Metropolitan Opera House, Feb. 14, 1914.

Moïse en Égypte. *See* Mosè in Egitto.

Mosè in Egitto.

Italian opera in 3 acts, libretto by Andrea Leone Tottola; music by G. Rossini. (Naples, Teatro San Carlo, March 5, 1818.) *Italian Opera House, March 2, 1835, in Italian.

First performed in America in concert form as an oratorio: Masonic Hall, Dec. 22, 1832, in Italian, by the Italian Opera House Company. The opera was sung by them in concert form as an oratorio in Feb., 1833 at the Musical Fund Hall, Philadelphia. The opera was again sung in concert form as an oratorio on June 19, 1847 at the Tabernacle, New York. Rossini afterwards revised this opera in French. It was called "Moïse en Égypte," or "Il nuovo Mosè," in Italian. The libretto was prepared by Giuseppe Luigi Balochi and Victor Joseph Étienne, called Jouy. In this form the opera was first performed on March 26, 1827 at the Académie royale de musique, Paris. This version was first heard in New York on May 7, 1860, in Italian, at the Academy of Music.

Mosè in Egitto. *See also* The Maid of Judah.

The Mountain sylph.

English opera in 2 acts, libretto by J. T. Thackeray; music by J. Barnett. (London, English Opera House [Lyceum], Aug. 25, 1834.) *Park Theatre, May 11, 1835, the music arranged by William Penson, violinist and leader of the orchestra of the theatre; Park Theatre, Sept. 15, 1835, with Barnett's original music, followed by a farce, "The Quaker."

Performed in Philadelphia, Chestnut Street Theatre, Jan. 27, 1836.

Les Mousquetaires de la reine (The Queen's musketeers).

French opera in 3 acts, libretto by Jules Henri Vernoy de Saint-Georges; music by L. Halévy. (Paris, Opéra Comique, Feb. 3, 1846.) Théâtre Français, Oct. 9, 1866, in French; Fifth Avenue Theatre, Feb. 20, 1883, in English.

Mozart und Schikaneder; oder, Der Schauspieldirektor.

German operetta in 1 act, libretto by Louis Schneider, adapted from the one-act Stephanie's "Singspiel," "Der Schauspieldirektor;" music by W. A. Mozart. (Schönbrunn, in the Orangery, Feb. 7, 1786, in Mozart's original version; Vienna, 1847, in L. Schneider's adaptation.) New York Stadt Theatre, Nov. 9, 1870, in German.

La Muette di Portici [Masaniello] (Die Stumme von Portici).

French opera in 5 acts, libretto by Augustin Eugène Scribe and Germain Delavigne;

Grand Opera in New York, 1825–1925, cont'd.

music by D. Auber. (Paris, Académie royale de musique, Feb. 29, 1828.) Park Theatre, Nov. 28, 1831, in an English adaptation in 3 acts by Thomas Simpson Cooke; Park Theatre, Aug. 27, 1833, in French, followed by a one-act vaudeville, "La ligue des femmes; ou, Le bal de faction;" Academy of Music, June 18, 1855, in Italian, followed by the beggar's song from Meyerbeer's opera "Le Prophète" in Italian, a scene from Cagnoni's three-act opera, "Don Bucephalo" and an act from Donizetti's three-act opera, "Linda di Chamounix;" Wallack's Theatre, June 30, 1855, in German.

According to Miss Esther Singleton, "History of the opera in New York" (Musical courier, New York, 1897), this opera was performed for the first time in America on Nov. 7, 1829. On that date, a comedy, "A race for a dinner," a drama, "She would be a soldier," and a farce, "The Anatomist," were played. According to the same writer, the opera was repeated on the 16th with Mlle. Celeste as Fenella. On that date, a comedy, "To marry or not to marry," and a farce, "The Invincibles," were acted.

The present compiler believes that Miss Singleton's first date, Nov. 7, 1829, was meant for Nov. 9, 1829. A production, bearing a title similar to Auber's opera, was performed on that day at the Park Theatre, New York. It was, however, not Auber's opera, a Paris novelty of the preceding year, but a "new historical drama" in 3 acts, entitled "Masaniello; or, The Dumb girl of Portici," which Miss Singleton apparently confuses with the opera. The drama was played in English, preceded by a farce, "Nature and philosophy."

The English performance noted above was advertised as the "first time in America."

Le Muletier de Tolède. *See* The Rose of Castile.

Nabucco [Nabucodonosor].

Italian opera in 4 acts, libretto by Temistocle Solera; music by G. Verdi. (Milan, Teatro alla Scala, March 9, 1842.) *Astor Place Opera House, April 4, 1848, in Italian.

Das Nachtlager in Granada.

German opera in 2 acts, libretto by Johann Karl von Braun, founded on the play by Johann Friedrich Kind; music by C. Kreutzer. (Vienna, Josephstadt Theater, Jan. 12, 1834.) *German Opera House, Dec. 15, 1862, in German.

Performed in Philadelphia, Academy of Music, Jan. 17, 1863.

Nadir and Zuleika.

English opera, music composed and selected by C. E. Horn. First performed: Park Theatre, Dec. 27, 1832.

This opera was performed for the second time in New York on Jan. 7, 1833, at Mrs. Sharpe's benefit, at the Park Theatre, followed by a comedy, "A Day after the wedding," and a farce, "The Rent day."

Native land; or, Return to slavery.

English ballad opera in 3 acts, libretto by William Dimond, founded on Rossini's opera, "Tancredi;" music by H. R. Bishop, with selections from N. Zingarelli, A. Boieldieu and G. Rossini. (London, Covent Garden, Feb. 10, 1824.) *Park Theatre, Jan. 12, 1827, in English.

Natoma.

American opera in 3 acts, libretto by Joseph Deighn Redding; music by V. Herbert. (Philadelphia, Metropolitan Opera House, Feb. 25, 1911.) Metropolitan Opera House, Feb. 28, 1911, in English.

Performed in Baltimore, Lyric Theatre, March 9, 1911; Chicago, Auditorium, Dec. 15, 1911; Los Angeles, March 8, 1913; San Francisco, Tivoli Opera House, March 15, 1913.

La Navarraise.

French opera in 2 acts, libretto by Jules Claretie and Henri Cain; music by J. Massenet. (London, Covent Garden, June 20, 1894; Paris, Opéra Comique, Oct. 8, 1895.) *Metropolitan Opera House, Dec. 11, 1895, in French, preceded by Gluck's three-act opera, "Orfeo ed Euridice."

Performed in New Orleans, French Opera House, Jan. 5, 1897.

Ne touchez pas à la reine.

French opera in 3 acts, libretto by Augustin Eugène Scribe and Gustave Waez; music by X.. Boisselot. (Paris, Opéra Comique, Jan. 16, 1847.) Castle Garden, Aug. 20, 1852, in French.

Nero.

German opera in 4 acts, translated from the French libretto by Jules Barbier; music by A. Rubinstein. (Hamburg, Stadttheater, Nov. 1, 1879.) *Metropolitan Opera House, March 14, 1887, in an English translation by John P. Jackson.

Performed in Boston, Boston Theatre, Jan. 9, 1888.

The New lord of the village. *See* Le Nouveau seigneur du village.

La Niege; ou, Le nouvel Eginhard.

French opera in 4 acts, libretto by Eugène Scribe and Germain Delavigne; music by D. Auber. (Paris, Opéra Comique, Oct. 8, 1823.) Park Theatre, July 30, 1827, in French, with a vaudeville, "Le diner de Madelon."

The Night bell. *See* Il Campanello di notte.

The Night dancers.

English opera in 2 acts, libretto by George Soane, founded on the plot of Adolphe Adam's ballet, "Giselle; ou, Les Wilis;" music by E. J. Loder. (London, Princess's Theatre, Oct. 28, 1846.) Olympic Theatre, Oct. 6, 1847, in English, followed by a farce, "Who do they take me for?"

This opera was first performed in England under the title, "The Wilis; or, The night dancers."

Adolphe Adam's ballet was first performed in Paris, June 28, 1841, at the Opéra, in two acts, the libretto by Théophile Gautier, Jules Henri Vernoy de Saint-Georges and Coralli. The ballet was performed in New York on Feb. 2, 1846, at the Park Theatre.

Grand Opera in New York, 1825-1925, cont'd.

Nina pazza per amore.

Italian opera in 2 acts, libretto by Jacopo Ferretti; music by P. A. Coppola. (Rome, Teatro Valle, Feb. 14, 1835.) *Palmo's Opera House, Feb. 5, 1847, in Italian.

The place of the first performance of this opera in America has been incorrectly reported as the Park Theatre, and the date as Jan. 3, 1847 and Feb. 3, 1847. The performance was announced for Feb. 3, 1847, but postponed until the 5th.

La Niobe.

Italian opera in 2 acts, libretto by Andrea Leone Tottola; music by G. Pacini. (Naples, T. San Carlo, Nov. 19, 1826.)

Never performed in New York.

A soprano scena and cavatina from this opera was sung in Italian by Signorina Adelaide Pedrotti at her benefit on Jan. 2, 1833 at the Bowery Theatre, New York, between the acts of Mercadante's opera, "Elise e Claudio."

Les Noces de Jeannette (The Marriage of Jeannette).

French opera in 1 act, libretto by Michel Carré and Jules Barbier; music by V. Massé. (Paris, Opéra Comique, Feb. 4, 1852.) *Niblo's Garden, April 9, 1855, in an English translation by W. Harrison, as "The marriage of Georgette," preceded by a miscellaneous musical program; Academy of Music, Oct. 28, 1861, in French, followed by Donizetti's two-act opera, "Betly."

Performed in Philadelphia, Academy of Music, Oct. 25, 1861.

Norma.

Italian opera in 2 acts, libretto by Felice Romani, founded on the play by Alexandre Soumet; music by V. Bellini. (Milan, Teatro alla Scala, Dec. 26, 1831.) Park Theatre, Feb. 25, 1841, in English; Niblo's Garden, Sept. 20, 1843, in Italian; New York Stadt Theatre, Nov. 7, 1870, in German.

An aria from this opera was sung in English on Nov. 18, 1840, at the Park Theatre. at the benefit of Mr. Simpson, manager of the theatre, by Mrs. Sutton, who created the title role in the first English performance above.

This opera was broadcast by radio on Aug. 4, 1925, in Italian, in tabloid form, with reduced orchestra through station WEAF, New York.

First performed in America: Philadelphia, Chestnut Street Theatre, Dec., 1840, in an English translation by Joseph Reese Fry. Performed at the same theatre, Nov. 13, 1843, in Italian.

Performed in New Orleans, Théâtre d'Orléans, Dec. 31, 1842.

Le Nouveau seigneur du village (The new lord of the village).

French opera in 1 act, libretto by Augustin François Creuzé de Lesser and Edmé Guillaume François de Favières; music by A. Boieldieu. (Paris, Opéra Comique, June 29, 1813.) Olympic Theatre, Dec. 10, 1849, in English, preceded by Buckstone's play, "Victorine," and followed by Walcot's extravaganza, "Brittania and Hibernia."

Le Nozze di Figaro (Figaros Hochzeit; Die Hochzeit des Figaro; The Marriage of Figaro).

Italian opera in 4 acts, libretto by Lorenzo da Ponte, founded on Pierre Augustin Caron de Beaumarchais's play, "Le Mariage de Figaro;" music by W. A. Mozart. (Vienna, Burgtheater, May 1, 1786.) Park Theatre, May 10, 1824, in English, followed by a melo-drama, "Teresa; or, The Orphan of Geneva;" Academy of Music, Nov. 23, 1858, in Italian; German Opera House, Dec. 18, 1862, in German.

The date of the first performance of this opera in America has been reported by several writers as May 3, 1823, in Sir Henry Rowley Bishop's version, and May 23, 1823, both at the Park Theatre, New York. On the former date, a comedy, "The Soldier's daughter," followed by a melo-drama, "The Forty thieves," was performed. On the latter date, an English version of Rossini's opera "The Barber of Seville." followed by a melo-drama, "The Woodsman's hut," was given.

The English performance noted above was advertised as "for the first time in America." According to Miss Esther Singleton's "History of the opera in New York" (Musical courier, New York, Dec. 7, 1898), Mozart's opera was performed in New York in 1799 under the title, "The Follies of a day." The performance is not mentioned in O. G. Sonneck's "Early opera in America" (Schirmer [1915]).

Mozart's opera in English versions proved to be eminently successful in New York during the first half of the nineteenth century. It was performed in English at the Park Theatre, New York, Jan. 5, 1825, followed by a melo-drama, "Presumption; or, The Fate of Frankenstein;" at the Park Theatre, Nov. 16, 1827, followed by a comedy, "The 100 pound note;" and at the same theatre, Jan. 21 (not 18), 1828, followed by a farce, "Family jars."

A comic opera, "The Two Figaros," with music selected from Mozart and G. Rossini, was performed in English on Nov. 16, 1837, at the National Theatre, New York.

Le Nozze di Figaro. *See also* The Two Figaros.

Il Nuovo Mosè. *See* Mosè in Egitto.

Oberon.

English opera in 3 acts, libretto by James Robinson Planché, founded on Villeneuve's story, "Huon de Bordeaux," and Sotheby's English translation of Wieland's German poem, "Oberon;" music by C. M. von Weber. (London, Covent Garden, April 12, 1826.) *Park Theatre, Oct. 9, 1828 (not 1829), in English, followed by a farce, "The Poachers;" Academy of Music, March 29, 1870, in English; Niblo's Garden, Nov. 2, 1870, in English; Metropolitan Opera House, Dec. 28, 1918, in English, the music arranged by Artur Bodanzky.

The overture of this opera was advertised as played for the "1st time in America" on Aug. 28, 1835 at Niblo's Garden, New York.

A burlesque on Weber's opera, entitled "The Magic horn," was performed on Feb. 13, 1850, in English, at the Olympic Theatre, New York.

Performed in Philadelphia, March 9, 1870, in Italian, with recitatives by Julius Benedict; Boston, Music Hall, May 23, 1870, in English.

Grand Opera in New York, 1825–1925, cont'd.

L'Oiseau bleu.

French opera in 4 acts, libretto by Maurice Maeterlinck; music by A. Wolff. First performed: Metropolitan Opera House, Dec. 27, 1919, in French.

L'Ombre (L'ombra).

French opera in 3 acts, libretto by Jules Henri Vernoy de Saint-Just; music by F. von Flotow. (Paris, Opéra Comique, July 7, 1870.) Academy of Music, April 9, 1875, in Italian.

L'Oracolo.

Italian opera in 1 act, libretto by Camillo Zanoni, founded on Chester Bailey Fernald's story, "The cat and the cherub;" music by F. Leoni. (London, Covent Garden, June 28, 1905.) *Metropolitan Opera House, Feb. 4, 1915, in Italian, followed by Leoncavallo's two-act opera, "Pagliacci."

Performed in Philadelphia, Metropolitan Opera House, April 10, 1917; Chicago, Ravina Park, June 28, 1919.

Orfeo.

Italian opera in 5 acts, libretto by Alessandro Striggio; music by C. Monteverdi. (Mantua, at the ducal court theatre, Feb. 24, 1607.) *Metropolitan Opera House, April 14, 1912, in Italian, in concert form, the music arranged for modern orchestra by Giacomo Orefice.

Orfeo ed Euridice (Orpheus and Eurydice).

Italian opera in 3 acts, libretto by Ranieri de' Calsabigi; music by C. W. von Gluck. (Vienna, Hofburgtheater, Oct. 5, 1762, in Italian; Paris, Académie royale de musique, Aug. 2, 1774, in a French translation by Pierre Louis Moline.) *Winter Garden, May 25, 1863, in an English translation by Fanny Malone Raymond; Metropolitan Opera House, Dec. 30, 1891, in Italian, followed by Mascagni's one-act opera, "Cavalleria rusticana."

This opera bore during the English production at the Winter Garden, New York, the sub-title, "The trial of love."

This opera was sung in concert form on April 12, 1925, in Italian, by the Society of the Friends of Music, New York, Artur Bodanzky conducting, at Town Hall, New York.

Performed in Boston, Boston Theatre, April 11, 1885, in German.

Otello.

Italian opera in 3 acts, libretto by Marquis Berio, founded on Shakespeare's play, "Othello;" music by G. Rossini. (Naples, Teatro del Fondo, Dec. 4, 1816.) *Park Theatre, Feb. 7 (not 11 or 27), 1826, in Italian.

Otello.

Italian opera in 4 acts, libretto by Arrigo Boito, founded on Shakespeare's play, "Othello;" music by G. Verdi. (Milan, Tea-

tro alla Scala, Feb. 5, 1887.) *Academy of Music, April 16, 1888, in Italian; Academy of Music (Brooklyn), Oct. 6, 1903, in English; West End Theatre, Dec. 21, 1903, in English.

Performed in Boston, Grand Opera House, April 30, 1888; Philadelphia, Academy of Music, May 4, 1888; New Orleans, Jan. 22, 1905, in English.

Il Paese dei campanelli.

Italian opera in 3 acts, libretto by Carlo Lombardo; music by V. Ranzato. *Teatro Fourteenth Street and Sixth Avenue [no. 105 West 14th Street], Oct. 17, 1924, in Italian.

Pagliacci (Der Bajazzo).

Italian opera in 2 acts, libretto and music by R. Leoncavallo. (Milan, Teatro dal Verme, May 21, 1892.) *Grand Opera House, June 15, 1893, in Italian; Irving Place Theatre, Dec. 18, 1893, in German, preceded by Heinrich Zöllner's one-act opera, "Matteo Falcone;" Grand Opera House, May 10, 1895, in English (first time?), preceded by Mascagni's one-act opera, "Cavalleria rusticana."

The first open air presentation of this opera in New York was given on Sept. 21, 1916, in Italian, preceded by Mascagni's opera, "Cavalleria rusticana," at the Lewisohn Stadium of the College of the City of New York.

This opera was broadcast by radio on April 25, 1925, in Italian, in tabloid form, with reduced orchestra, through station WEAF, New York. The open air performance of this opera on Aug. 5, 1925, in Italian, preceded by "Cavalleria rusticana," at Ebbets Field, Brooklyn, was broadcast by radio through station WNYC, New York. This opera was also broadcast by radio on June 9, 1925, preceded by "Cavalleria rusticana," through station WJZ, New York; on Sept. 29, 1925 through station WGBS, New York, and on Oct. 16, 1925, followed by "Cavalleria rusticana," through station WRNY, New York.

A performance of this opera in prose without music was given in New York on Jan. 7, 1906, at Public School No. 59, by the women students of the New York School for Teachers. A dramatic version in two acts by H. E. Brookfield was performed on Feb. 20, 1908, in English, at Daly's Theatre, New York.

Paoletta.

American opera in 4 acts, libretto by Paul Jones, founded on his story, "The sacred mirror;" music by P. Floridia-Napolino. (Cincinnati, Music Hall, Aug. 29, 1910.) Capitol Theatre, March 21, 1920, in English, in abridged form.

Paradise Lost. *See* Das **Verlorene Paradies.**

Le Pardon de Poërmel (Dinorah).

French opera in 3 acts, libretto by Jules Barbier and Michel Carré; music by G. Meyerbeer. (Paris, Opéra Comique, April 4, 1859.) Academy of Music, Nov. 24, 1862, in Italian.

Performed in New Orleans, French Opera House, March 4, 1861; Philadelphia, Academy of Music, Dec. 19, 1862.

Parisina.

Italian opera in 3 acts, libretto by Felice Romani, founded on the poem by Lord

Grand Opera in New York, 1825–1925 cont'd.

Byron; music by G. Donizetti. (Florence, Teatro della Pergola, March 17, 1833.) *Astor Place Opera House, Oct. 22, 1850, in Italian.

Performed in Philadelphia, Chestnut Street Theatre, Jan. 4, 1851.

Parsifal.

German opera in 3 acts, libretto and music by R. Wagner. (Bayreuth, Festspielhaus, July 28, 1882.) *Metropolitan Opera House, Dec. 24, 1903, in German; New York Theatre, Oct. 31, 1904, in English.

First performed in America in concert form: New York, Metropolitan Opera House, March 3 and 4, 1886, in German, by the Oratorio Society of New York, Walter Damrosch conducting. The soloists were Frl. Marianne Brandt and Messrs. Krämer, Emil Fischer and Max Heinrich.

The finale of the first act of this opera was performed in concert form on Nov. 3 and 4, 1882 by The Symphony Society of New York, Dr. Leopold Damrosch conducting, at the Academy of Music, New York. The soloists were Messrs. Fr. Remnertz and Max Heinrich. A chorus of 200 men's voices from the Oratorio Society of New York and 75 boys' voices from the choirs of Trinity Church and St. Chrysostom's Chapel, New York, participated.

On the same dates, the music of the Good Friday spell from the third act of this opera was played in concert form by the Brooklyn Philharmonic Society, Theodore Thomas conducting, at the Academy of Music, Brooklyn. Messrs. Werrenrath and Holt-Hansen were the soloists.

The "Vorspiel" or prelude of this opera was played for the first time in America on Nov. 11, 1882 by the Philharmonic Society of New York, Theodore Thomas conducting, at the Academy of Music, New York.

Wagner's opera was again sung in concert form on Feb. 15, 1891, in German, at a Sunday night concert at the Metropolitan Opera House, Anton Seidl conducting. The soloists were Frau Antonia Mielke and Messrs. Reichmann, Emil Fischer and Andreas Dippel. Benjamin Lang brought the New York singers and Seidl's orchestra to Boston for a similar production on April 15, 1891 at the Music Hall. The chorus numbered two hundred singers. The performance was repeated on May 4, 1892 with the same soloists, except Reichmann who was replaced by Georg Henschel.

Dr. L. Kelterborn, conductor of the Fidelio Society, Boston, gave a lecture recital on this opera on April 13, 1891 at Chickering Hall, Boston, with stereopticon views.

Performed in New Orleans, French Opera House, April 24, 1905.

A version of Wagner's opera was announced for performance by a stock company on April 18, 1904 at the Columbia Theatre, Brooklyn, New York, but was withdrawn before the date of production.

An English spoken version of the opera, in 5 acts, founded on Wagner's libretto, by Marie Doran, was performed on May 23, 1904 at the West End Theatre, New York. An earlier dramatization, in English, of Wagner's opera by Edward Locke, the original music arranged by Oscar Radin, was played on March 14, 1904 at the Grand Opera House, Pittsburg.

Il Pasticcio o l'ape musicale. *See* **L'Ape musicale.**

Paul et Virginie.

French opera in 3 acts, libretto by Michel Carré and Jules Barbier, founded on the story by Bernardin de Saint Pierre; music by V. Massé. (Paris, Opéra National Lyrique, Nov. 15, 1876.) Grand Opera

House, Sept. 8, 1879, in English; Casino, March 28, 1883, in French.

Performed in New Orleans, Varieties Theatre, Feb. 7, 1879.

Les Pêcheurs de perles.

French opera in 3 acts, libretto by Michel Carré and Eugène Cormon [pseud. of Pierre Étienne Piestre]; music by G. Bizet. (Paris, Théâtre Lyrique, Sept. 29, 1863.) Metropolitan Opera House, Nov. 13, 1916, in French.

The first two acts of this opera were performed at a matinée at the Metropolitan Opera House on Jan. 11, 1896, with Massenet's two-act opera, "La Navarraise."

First performed in America: Philadelphia, Grand Opera House, Aug. 25, 1893.

Pelléas et Mélisande.

French opera in 5 acts, libretto by Maurice Maeterlinck; music by C. Debussy. (Paris, Opéra Comique, April 30, 1902.) *Manhattan Opera House, Feb. 19, 1908, in French.

Performed in Boston, Boston Theatre, April 1, 1909.

Peri; or, The enchanted fountain.

American opera in 3 acts, libretto by S. J. Burr; music by J. G. Maeder. First performed: Broadway Theatre, Dec. 13, 1852, in English.

Perouze.

Greek opera in 2 acts, libretto by Tsocopoulos; music by Theodore Sakellaridis. (Athens, Municipal Theatre, 191–?) *Terrace Garden, Sept. 27, 1925, in Greek.

La Perruche.

French opera in 1 act, libretto by Dupin and Dumanoir; music by A. L. Clapisson. (Paris, Opéra Comique, April 28, 1840.) Niblo's Garden, May 24, 1843, in French, with a vaudeville, "Moiroud & Co."

Peter the Great. *See* **Il Pietro il grande.**

Le Petit chaperon rouge.

French opera in 3 acts, libretto by Marie Emmanuel Guillaume Marguerite Théaulon de Lambert; music by A. Boieldieu. (Paris, Théâtre Feydeau, June 30, 1818.) Park Theatre, Aug. 31, 1827, in French, followed by a vaudeville, "L'ours et le pacha."

Philemon et Baucis.

French opera in 3 acts, libretto by Jules Barbier and Michel Carré; music by C. Gounod. (Paris, Théâtre Lyrique, Feb. 18, 1860.) Herrmann's Theatre, Nov. 16, 1893, in English; Metropolitan Opera House, Nov. 29, 1893, in French.

Le Philtre.

French opera in 2 acts, libretto by Augustin Eugène Scribe; music by D. Auber. (Paris, Académie royale de musique, June

Grand Opera in New York, 1825–1925, cont'd.

20, 1831.) Park Theatre, Aug. 9, 1833, in French, followed by a vaudeville, "La maraine."

La Pietra del paragone.

Italian opera in 1 act, libretto by Luigi Romanelli; music by G. Rossini. (Milan, Teatro alla Scala, Sept. 26, 1812.)

Never performed in New York.

An "aria buffa" from this opera was "sung by Sig: [Ernesto] Orlandi, in appropriate costume," in Italian, at Signor G. B. Montresor's benefit on May 9, 1833 at the Bowery Theatre, New York, between the acts of Rossini's opera, "Il barbiere di Siviglia."

Pietro il grande (Peter the Great).

Italian opera in 3 acts, libretto translated from the English of Desmond Ryan by Maggioni; music by L. A. Jullien. (London, Covent Garden, Aug. 17, 1852.)

Never performed in New York.

Eight selections from this opera were played on Sept. 22, 1853 at one of Jullien's concerts at Castle Garden, New York.

The Pipe of desire.

American opera in 1 act, libretto by George Edward Barton; music by F. S. Converse, op. 21. (Boston, Jordan Hall, Jan. 31, 1906.) Metropolitan Opera House, March 18, 1910, followed by Leoncavallo's two-act opera, "Pagliacci."

Revived in Boston, Boston Opera House, Jan. 6, 1911.

Pipele.

French opera, founded on Eugène Sue's novel, "Les mystères de Paris;" music by S. de Ferrari. (Venice, Teatro San Benedetto, Nov. 25, 1855.) *Academy of Music, Dec. 10, 1869, in Italian.

Performed in Philadelphia, Academy of Music, Jan. 13, 1870.

Pique Dame.

Russian opera in 3 acts, libretto by Modest Tchaikovsky, founded on the story by Alexander Pushkin; music by P. I. Tchaikovsky. (St. Petersburg, Maryinsky Theatre, Dec. 19, 1890.) *Metropolitan Opera House, March 5, 1910, in German; New Amsterdam Theatre, May 10, 1922, in Russian.

Il Pirata.

Italian opera in 2 acts, libretto by Felice Romani; music by V. Bellini. (Milan, Teatro alla Scala, Oct. 27, 1827.) *Richmond Hill Theatre, Dec. 5, 1832.

The Pirate boy.

English melodramatic opera, music by J. Watson. National Theatre, Jan. 26, 1837, in English, followed by a farce, "My husband's ghost."

Polichinelle.

French opera in 1 act, libretto by Augustin Eugène Scribe and Charles Duveyrier;

music by A. Montfort. (Paris, Opéra Comique, June 14, 1839.) Niblo's Garden, May 19, 1843, in French, preceded by a vaudeville, "Les Nuit aux soufflets."

Poliuto.

Italian opera in 3 acts, libretto by Salvatore Cammarano, founded on Pierre Corneille's play, "Polyeucte;" music by G. Donizetti. (Naples, Teatro San Carlo, Nov. 30, 1848.) *Academy of Music, May (not Jan.) 25, 1859, in Italian.

Der Polnische Jude (The Polish Jew).

German opera in 2 acts, libretto by Richard Batka and Victor Leon, founded on Erckmann-Chatrian's play, "Le juif polonais;" music by K. Weis. (Prague, Deutsches Theater, March 3, 1901.) *Metropolitan Opera House, March 9, 1921, in an English translation by Sigmund Spaeth and Cecil Cowdrey, followed by Wolf-Ferrari's one-act opera, "Il segreto di Susanna."

Le Portrait de Manon.

French opera in 1 act, libretto by Georges Boyer; music by J. Massenet. (Paris, Opéra Comique, May 8, 1894.) *Waldorf Astoria Hotel, Dec. 13, 1897, in French, by The Theatre of Musical Clubs, followed by a pantomime, "Put to the test," libretto by Edwin Star Belknap; music by Harvey Worthington Loomis.

Le Postillon de Lonjumeau.

French opera in 3 acts, libretto by Adolphe de Leuven and Léon Brunswick [pseud. of Léon Lévy]; music by A. Adam. (Paris, Opéra Comique, Oct. 13, 1836.) Park Theatre, March 30, 1840, in English, followed by a comedy, "Catherine and Petrucchio;" Niblo's Garden, June 16, 1843, in English.

The second English performance, noted above, was advertised as the first in New York. It was more adequate than the earlier production.

Le Pré aux clercs.

French opera in 3 acts, libretto by François Antoine Eugène de Planard, founded on Prosper Merimée's "Chroniques de Charles ix;" music by L. Hérold. (Paris, Opéra Comique, Dec. 15, 1832.) Niblo's Garden, July 3, 1843, in French.

Preciosa; oder, Die Zigeuner in Spanien.

German play in 4 acts by Pius Alexander Wolf; incidental music by C. M. von Weber. (Berlin, Königliches Opernhaus, March 14, 1821.) New York Stadt Theatre, Dec. 17, 1870, in German.

Prince Igor.

Russian opera in 4 acts, libretto and music by A. Borodin, the music completed by Nicholas Rimsky-Korsakoff and Alexander Glazounoff. (St. Petersburg, Imperial Opera House, Oct. 23, 1890.) *Metropolitan Opera House, Dec. 30, 1915, in Italian.

Grand Opera in New York, 1825–1925, cont'd.

La **Princesse d'auberge** (**Herbergprinses**).

Flemish opera in 3 acts, libretto by Nestor de Tière; music by Jan Blockx. (Antwerp, Théâtre Lyrique, Oct. 10, 1896.) *Manhattan Opera House, March 10, 1909, in the French translation by Gustave Lagye.

Prinz Eugen; oder, Der Uhrenhändler aus dem Schwarzwalde.

German opera in 3 acts, libretto by the composer and Alexander Rost; music by G. Schmidt. (Frankfurt a M., July 27, 1847.) New York Stadt Theatre, May 26, 1871, in German.

Prinz Waldmeister.

German opera in 3 acts, libretto by Heinrich Italiener, founded on Otto Roquette's story, "Waldmeisters Brautfahrt;" music by A. Neuendorff. First performed: Thalia Theatre, May 2, 1887, in German.

Performed in Berlin, Walhalla Theater, Sept. 3, 1887.

Prodaná nevĕsta. *See* Die **Verkaufte Braut.**

Prometheus. *See* Die **Geschoepfe des Prometheus.**

Le **Prophète** (Il **Profeta;** Der **Prophet**).

French opera in 5 acts, libretto by Augustin Eugène Scribe; music by G. Meyerbeer. (Paris, Théâtre de la Nation [Opéra], April 16, 1849.) Niblo's Garden, Nov. 25, 1853, in Italian; Metropolitan Opera House, Dec. 17 (not 20), 1884, in German; Metropolitan Opera House, Jan. 1, 1892, the principals singing in French and the chorus in Italian.

The date of the first performance of this opera in New York has been incorrectly given as Nov. 25, 1849 and Nov. 25, 1854. The above date has been verified in the newspapers of the day.

Three selections from this opera. "La prêche anabaptiste," the romance (duet) and the "Brindisi," were sung for the first time in America on Dec. 13, 1849 at the Grand Musical Festival, Max Maretzek conducting, at the Tabernacle, New York.

First performed in America: New Orleans, April 2, 1850.

Performed in Philadelphia, Academy of Music, April 2, 1869.

The **Puritan's daughter.**

English opera in 3 acts, libretto by John Vipon Bridgeman; music by W. M. Balfe. (London, Covent Garden, Nov. 30, 1861.) Théâtre Français, Sept. 11, 1869, in English.

I **Puritani.**

Italian opera in 3 acts, libretto by conte Carlo Pepoli; music by V. Bellini. (Paris, Théâtre Italien, Jan. 25, 1835.) Palmo's Opera House, Feb. 3 (not 2), 1844, in Italian.

Performed in Philadelphia, Chestnut Street Theatre, Nov. 20, 1843.

The **Quartette; or, Interrupted harmony.**

English operetta in 1 (?) act, music by C. E. Horn. First performed: Bowery Theatre, April 27, 1829, in English, preceded

by an opera "Il Trionfo della musica" ("Il fanatico per la musica") and followed by a farce, "The Prize; or, 2, 5, 3, 8."

This operetta was again performed at the Park Theatre, New York, April 25, 1832, preceded by the opera "Cinderella."

The **Queen of Sheba.** *See* Die **Koenigin von Saba.**

The **Queen's musketeers.** *See* Les **Mousquetaires de la reine.**

Quo vadis?

French opera in 5 acts, libretto by Henri Cain, founded on the novel by Henry Sienkiewicz; music by Jean Nouguès. (Nice, Feb. 9, 1909.) Metropolitan Opera House, April 4, 1911.

First performed in America: Philadelphia, Metropolitan Opera House, March 23 (not 23 or 24), 1911. Performed in Chicago, Auditorium, Dec. 19, 1911; New Orleans, French Opera House, Jan. 4, 1913.

Le **Ranz des vaches.** *See* Der **Kuhreigen.**

Der **Rattenfaenger von Hameln.**

German opera in 4 acts, libretto by H. Italiener; music by A. Neuendorff. First performed: Germania Theatre, Dec. 14, 1880, in German.

Die **Regimentstochter.** *See* La **Fille du régiment.**

La **Reine de Chypre.**

French opera in 5 acts, libretto by Jules Henri Vernoy de Saint-Georges; music by J. Halévy. (Paris, Opéra, Dec. 22, 1841.) Niblo's Garden, Sept. 10, 1845, in French.

First performed in America: New Orleans, Théâtre d'Orléans, March 25, 1845.

La **Reine de Chypre.** *See also* The **Daughter of St. Mark.**

La **Reine Fiammette.**

French opera in 4 acts, libretto by Catulle Mendès; music by X. Leroux. (Paris, Opéra Comique, Nov. 23, 1903.) *Metropolitan Opera House, Jan. 24, 1919, in French.

Renard.

Marionette opera in 1 act, founded on Russian folk tales; libretto and music by I. Stravinsky. (Paris, salon de Mme. la Princesse Ed. de Polignac, private performance; Paris, Opéra, May, 1922, public performance.) *Vanderbilt Theatre, Dec. 2, 1923, in French, in concert form, by the International Composers' Guild, Leopold Stokowski conducting.

Le **Rendezvous bourgeois.**

French opera in 1 act, libretto by François Benoit Hoffman; music by Nicolo. (Paris, Opéra Comique, May 9, 1807.) Park Theatre, July 25, 1827, in French, with a play, "Therese; or, The Orphan of Geneva."

Grand Opera in New York, 1825–1925, cont'd.

El Retablo de Maese Pedro.

Spanish marionette opera in 1 act, founded on Miguel de Cervantes's story, "Don Quixote," by M. de Falla. (Seville, March 23, 1923, by the Sociedad sevillana de conciertos; Paris, salon de Mme. la Princesse Ed. de Polignac, June 25, 1923; Paris, Nov. 13, 1923, at the Concerts Wiéner.) *Town Hall, Dec. 29, 1925, in Spanish, by the League of Composers, Willem Mengelberg conducting.

Rheingold. *See* Der Ring des Nibelungen.

Rienzi.

German opera in 5 acts, founded on the novel by Bulwer Lytton; libretto and music by R. Wagner. (Dresden, Hoftheater, Oct. 22, 1842.) *Academy of Music, March 4, 1878, in German.

The overture of this opera was played on June 25, 1855, Carl Bergmann conducting, at the Grand German Musical Festival at the Metropolitan Theatre, New York.
Performed in Philadelphia, Academy of Music, March 20, 1878.

Rigoletto.

Italian opera in 3 acts, libretto by Francesco Maria Piave; music by G. Verdi. (Venice, Teatro La Fenice, March 11, 1851.) *Academy of Music, Feb. 19, 1855, in Italian; New York Stadt Theatre, Dec. 14, 1870, in a German translation by Heinrich Proch; Academy of Music, Jan. 27, 1874, in English; Second Avenue Theatre, June 8, 1922, in Russian.

This opera was broadcast by radio on Oct. 2, 1925, in Italian, with piano accompaniment, through station WRNY, New York.
Performed in Philadelphia, Academy of Music, Jan. 25, 1858; New Orleans, March 19, 1860.

Der Ring des Nibelungen.

German tetralogy or trilogy with a prelude, consisting of "Das Rheingold," "Die Walküre," "Siegfried" and "Götterdämmerung," founded on the Eddas and "Das Nibelungenlied;" librettos and music by R. Wagner. (First performance of the cycle: Bayreuth, Festspielhaus, Aug. 13, 14, 16, 17, 1876.) First performance of the cycle in America: Metropolitan Opera House, March 4, 5, 8, 11, 1889, in German.

The operas belonging to this cycle are performed separately.
RHEINGOLD. German opera in 3 acts. Prelude (or "Vorabend," introductory evening) to "Der Ring des Nibelungen." (Munich, Hoftheater, Sept. 22, 1869.) *Metropolitan Opera House, Jan. 4, 1889, in German; Carnegie Hall, Nov. 10, 1924, in English, with scenery.
Performed in Boston, Boston Theatre, April 1, 1889.
DIE WALKÜRE. German opera in 3 acts. Part 2 of "Der Ring des Nibelungen." (Munich, Hoftheater, June 26, 1870.) *Academy of Music, April 2, 1877, in German.
The first open air presentation of this opera in New York was given on Sept. 19, 1916, in German, at the Lewisohn Stadium of the College of the City of New York. This was the first open air production of opera in New York.
Performed in Boston, April 16, 1877.

Der Ring des Nibelungen, continued.

SIEGFRIED. German opera in 3 acts. Part 3 of "Der Ring des Nibelungen." (Bayreuth, Festspielhaus, Aug. 16, 1876.) *Metropolitan Opera House, Nov. 9, 1887, in German.
The music of this opera was adapted by Hugo Riesenfeld for the motion picture, "Siegfried," shown on Aug. 23, 1925 at the Century Theatre, New York.
Performed in Boston, Boston Theatre, April 3, 1889.
DIE GÖTTERDÄMMERUNG. German opera in 3 acts. Part 4 of "Der Ring des Nibelungen." (Bayreuth, Festspielhaus, Aug. 17, 1876.) *Metropolitan Opera House, Jan. 25, 1888.
Performed in Boston, Boston Theatre, April 5, 1889.

Rip van Winkle.

American opera in 3 acts, libretto by Jonathan Howard Wainwright, founded on the story by Washington Irving; music by G. F. Bristow, op. 22. First performed: Niblo's Garden, Sept. 27, 1855, in English.

The opera was performed on Dec. 11, 1898, in concert form, as the second part of a concert by The New York Banks Glee Club, H. R. Humphries conducting.
Performed in Philadelphia, Academy of Music, Nov. 21, 1870.

Rip van Winkle.

American opera in 3 acts, libretto by Percy Mackaye, suggested by Washington Irving's story; music by R. DeKoven. (Chicago, Auditorium, Jan. 2, 1920.) Lexington Theatre, Jan. 30, 1920, in English.

Robert le diable (Robert the devil; Roberto il diavolo; Robert der Teufel).

French opera in 5 acts, libretto by Augustin Eugène Scribe and Germain Delavigne; music by G. Meyerbeer. (Paris, Académie royale de musique, Nov. 21, 1831.) *Park Theatre, April 7, 1834, in an English adaptation by Rophino Lacy; Park Theatre, July 2, 1845, in French; Astor Place Opera House, Dec. 17, 1841, in Italian; Niblo's Garden, Sept. 16, 1856, in German.

The cavatina, "Idol de ma vie," for soprano, was sung on Jan. 9, 1835, in French, by Miss Watson, at the annual concert of the Euterpean Society at the City Hotel, New York.

Roberto Devereux.

Italian opera in 3 acts, libretto by Salvatore Cammarano; music by G. Donizetti. (Naples, Teatro San Carlo, Oct. 2, 1837.) *Astor Place Opera House, Jan. 15, 1849, in Italian.

Le Roi de Lahore.

French opera in 5 acts, libretto by Louis Gallet; music by J. Massenet. (Paris, Opéra, April 27, 1877.) Metropolitan Opera House, Feb. 29, 1924, in French.

First performed in America: New Orleans, French Opera House, 1883–84.

Le Roi d'Ys.

French opera in 3 acts, libretto by Édouard Blau; music by E. Lalo. (Paris, Opéra Comique, May 7, 1888.) Metropolitan Opera House, Jan. 5, 1922, in French.

First performed in America: New Orleans, French Opera House, Jan. 23, 1890.

Grand Opera in New York, 1825–1925, cont'd.

Rokeby; or, A tale of the civil wars.

English operatic piece, libretto by Cox, founded on the poem by Sir Walter Scott; music selected and arranged by F. H. F. Berkeley. *Park Theatre, May 17, 1830, in English.

Romeo e Giulietta [recte Giulietta e Romeo].

Italian opera in 3 acts, libretto by Giuseppe Foppa, founded on Shakespeare's play, "Romeo and Juliet;" music by N. Zingarelli. (Milan, Teatro alla Scala, Jan. 30, 1796.) Park Theatre, July 26, 1826, in Italian.

An opera of the same title, probably Zingarelli's work, was performed on Aug. 6, 1810 in the theatre fronting on St. Peter Street, New Orleans.

Roméo et Juliette (Romeo e Giulietta; Romeo and Juliet).

French opera in 5 acts, libretto by Jules Barbier and Michel Carré, founded on Shakespeare's play, "Romeo and Juliet;" music by C. Gounod. (Paris, Théâtre Lyrique, April 27, 1867.) *Academy of Music, Nov. 15 (not Dec. 14), 1867, in Italian; Park Theatre (Brooklyn), Jan. 14, 1881, in English; Metropolitan Opera House, Dec. 8, 1893, in French.

This opera was announced for performance in English on Jan. 21, 1881, at Haverly's Fifth Avenue Theatre, New York, but was not performed.
This opera was broadcast by radio on Aug. 11, 1925, in French, in tabloid form, with reduced orchestra, through station WEAF, New York.
Performed in Philadelphia, Academy of Music, Jan. 13, 1868.

The Rose of Castile.

English opera in 3 acts, libretto by Augustus Glossop Harris and Edmund Falconer [pseud. of Edmund O'Rourke], founded on A. Adam's opera,. "Le muletier de Tolède;" music by W. M. Balfe. (London, Lyceum Theatre, Oct. 29, 1857.) * Olympic Theatre, July 27, 1864, in English.

Der Rosenkavalier.

German opera in 3 acts, libretto by Hugo von Hofmannsthal; music by R. Strauss, op. 59. (Dresden, Hofoper, Jan. 26, 1911.) *Metropolitan Opera House, Dec. 9, 1913, in German.

Performed in Chicago, Auditorium, Nov. 3, 1925.

Le Rossignol.

French opera in 1 act, libretto by Victor Joseph Étienne de Jouy; music by Louis Sébastien Lebrun. (Paris, Académie royale de musique, April 23, 1816.) Park Theatre, Aug. 26, 1833, in French, preceded by a three-act drama, "Richard d'Arlington."

Russalka; or, The mermaid.

Russian opera in 4 acts, founded on the poem by Alexander Pushkin, libretto and music by Alexander Dargomisky. (St. Petersburg, Imperial Opera House, May 4,

1856.) New Amsterdam Theatre, May 8, 1922, in Russian.

The third act was given in concert form in Dec., 1902, by the Russian Choral Society of East Broadway, New York, at the Educational Alliance, New York.

Ruy Blas.

Italian opera in 4 acts, libretto by Carlo d'Ormeville; music by F. Marchetti. (Milan, Teatro alla Scala, April 3, 1869.) *Academy of Music, March 14, 1879, in Italian.

Sadko.

Russian opera in 7 acts, libretto and music by N. Rimsky-Korsakoff. (Moscow, Private Opera House, Jan. 6, 1898; St. Petersburg, Maryinsky Theatre, Jan., 1901.)

This opera has not yet been performed in America.
The ballet from the sixth act of this opera was danced for the first time in America on Oct. 16, 1916 by Serge Diaghileff's Ballet Russe at the Manhattan Opera House, New York. It was performed by them in Boston on Nov. 9, 1916 at the Boston Opera House.
The fourth act of this opera, "The Novgorod Fair," was sung in concert form on Dec. 23, 1924, in an English translation by Kurt Schindler, by the Schola Cantorum of New York, Kurt Schindler conducting, at Carnegie Hall, New York. This act was repeated in concert form by the Schola Cantorum at Carnegie Hall on Dec. 23, 1925, when the sixth act was sung, in English, for the first time in America. The program included third act of Moussorgsky's five-act opera, "Khovanstchina."

Saffo.

Italian opera in 3 acts, libretto by Salvatore Cammarano; music by G. Pacini. (Naples, Teatro San Carlo, Nov. 29, 1840.) *Park Theatre, June 14 (not 12), 1847, in Italian.

Performed in Philadelphia, Walnut Street Theatre, July 12, 1847.

Saint Elizabeth.

An oratorio or musical legend in a prologue and 4 tableaux, libretto by Otto Roquette; music by F. Liszt. (Weimar, Hoftheater, Oct. 23, 1881, with scenery.) *Metropolitan Opera House, Jan. 3, 1918, with scenery.

This work was originally conceived by the composer as an oratorio and first performed on Aug. 15, 1865 on the twenty-fifth anniversary of the Conservatorium in Buda-Pesth.
The crusaders' chorus from this opera was sung on May 7, 1870, at a concert of The Philharmonic Society of New York, Carl Bergmann conducting, at the Academy of Music, New York.
Performed in America as an oratorio: Academy of Music (Brooklyn), Dec. 18, 1886, in English, in memory of the composer who died on July 31 of that year, at a concert of the Brooklyn Philharmonic Society. The oratorio was again sung on April 25, 1902, Walter Henry Hall conducting, at the Academy of Music, Brooklyn.

Salammbo.

French opera in 5 acts, libretto by Camille du Locle, founded on the novel by Gustave Flaubert; music by E. Reyer. (Brussels, Théâtre de la Monnaie, Feb. 10, 1890.) Metropolitan Opera House, March 20, 1901, in French.

First performed in America: New Orleans, French Opera House, Jan. 25, 1900.

Grand Opera in New York, 1825–1925, cont'd.

Salome.

German opera in 1 act, libretto by Oscar Wilde, translated into German by Hedwig Lachmann; music by R. Strauss, op. 54. (Dresden, Königliches Opernhaus, Dec. 9, 1905.) *Metropolitan Opera House, Jan. 22, 1907, in German; Manhattan Opera House, Jan. 28, 1909, in French.

Performed in Chicago, Auditorium, Nov. 25, 1910; Milwaukee, Auditorium, Dec. 9, 1910; St. Louis, Coliseum, Jan. 2, 1911.

Samson et Delila.

French opera in 3 acts, libretto by Ferdinand Lemaire; music by C. Saint Saëns. (Weimar, Hoftheater, Dec. 2, 1877, in a German translation by Richard Pohl; Rouen, Théâtre des Arts, March 3, 1890; Paris, Opéra, Nov. 23, 1892.) Metropolitan Opera House, Feb. 8, 1895, in French; Century Opera House, Nov. 11, 1913, in English.

First performed in America in concert form as an oratorio: New York, Music Hall (Carnegie Hall), March 25, 1892, in English, the tenor singing in French, by the Oratorio Society of New York, Walter Damrosch conducting.

First performed in America scenically: New Orleans, French Opera House, Jan. 4, 1893.

This opera was broadcast by radio on May 12, 1925, in French, in tabloid form, with reduced orchestra, through station WEAF, New York.

Performed in Boston, Boston Opera House, Nov. 27, 1911.

Sapho.

French opera in 5 acts, libretto by Henri Cain and Arthur Bernède, founded on the novel by Alphonse Daudet; music by J. Massenet. (Paris, Opéra Comique, Nov. 27, 1897.) *Manhattan Opera House, Nov. 17 (not 15 or 18), 1909, in French.

Performed in New Orleans, French Opera House, Dec. 27, 1913; Chicago, Auditorium, Jan. 10, 1918.

Sarrona.

American opera in 1 act and a prologue, libretto and music by L. Howland. (Bruges, Aug. 3, 1903.) *Amsterdam Theatre, Feb. 8, 1910, in English.

Performed in Florence, Teatro Alfieri, Feb. 3, 1906 and during 1906–07 in Piacenza (Municipal Opera House), Trieste, Naples (Teatro Bellini) in June, Padua, Varese, Udine and Pola.

Satanella.

English opera in 4 acts, libretto by Augustus Glossop Harris and Edmund Falconer [pseud. of Edmund O'Rourke], founded on LeSage's story, "Le diable boiteux;" music by W. M. Balfe. (London, Covent Garden, Dec. 20, 1858.) *Niblo's Garden, Feb. 23, 1863, in English.

Performed in Philadelphia, Academy of Music, Oct. 28, 1871.

Le Sauteriot.

French opera in 3 acts, libretto by Henri Pierre Roche and Martial Perier, founded on E. de Keyserling's play, "A sacrifice of springtime," translated into prose by H. P. Roche and into Alexandrian verse by M. Perier; music by S. Lazzari. (Chicago, Auditorium, Jan. 19, 1918.) Lexington Theatre, Feb. 11, 1918.

The Scarlet letter.

American opera in 3 acts, libretto by George Parsons Lathrop, founded on the story by Nathaniel Hawthorne; music by W. Damrosch. (Boston, Boston Theatre, Feb. 10, 1896.) Academy of Music, March 6, 1896, in English.

Der Schauspieldirektor. *See* The Impresario and Mozart und Schikaneder.

Die Schweizer Familie.

German opera in 3 acts, libretto by Ignatz Franz Castelli; music by J. Weigl. (Vienna, Kärnthnerthor Theater, March 14, 1809.) Palmo's Opera House, Dec. 17, 1845, in German.

The Secret of Suzanne. *See* Il Segreto di Susanna.

Il Segreto di Susanna (The Secret of Suzanne; Susannes Geheimnis).

Italian interlude in 1 act, libretto by Enrico Golisciani; music by E. Wolf-Ferrarri. (Munich, Hofoper, Dec. 4, 1909, in the German translation by Max Kalbeck.) *Metropolitan Opera House, March 14, 1911, in Italian, followed by Massenet's three-act opera, "Le jongleur de Notre Dame."

Performed in Philadelphia, Metropolitan Opera House, March 29, 1911; Chicago, Auditorium, Dec. 7, 1911.

Il Seraglio. *See* Die Entfuehrung aus dem Serail.

La Serva padrona (The maid mistress).

Italian opera in 2 acts, libretto by Jacopo Angelo Nelli; music by G. B. Pergolesi. (Naples, Teatro San Bartolomeo, Aug. 28, 1733.) *Academy of Music, Nov. 13, 1858, in Italian, followed by Bellini's two-act opera, "Norma;" Empire Theatre, May 7, 1917, in English, followed by Donizetti's one-act opera, "Il campanello di notte."

This opera was incorrectly ascribed by Bernard Ullmann, manager of the Academy of Music, New York, to Giovanni Paisiello, about whom he published an account in the advertisements of the opera in the newspapers.

Performed in Philadelphia, Academy of Music, Jan. 29, 1859.

Shanewis (The robin women).

American opera in 2 acts, libretto by Nelle Richmond Eberhardt; music by C. W. Cadman. First performed: Metropolitan Opera House, March 23, 1918, in English, followed by "The dance in Place Congo," a ballet pantomime in 1 act, scenario and music by H. F. Gilbert.

Performed in Denver, Civic Auditorium, Dec. 5 and 6, 1924.

Grand Opera in New York, 1825-1925, cont'd.

Si j'étais roi.

French opera in 3 acts, libretto by Adolphe Philippe Dennery and Jules Brésil; music by A. Adam. (Paris, Théâtre Lyrique, Sept. 4, 1852.) Park Theatre, Nov. 29, 1881, in French.

Siberia.

Italian opera in 3 acts, libretto by Luigi Illica; music by U. Giordano. (Milan, Teatro alla Scala, Dec. 19, 1903.) Manhattan Opera House, Feb. 5, 1908, in Italian.

First performed in America: New Orleans, French Opera House, Jan. 13, 1906.

Le Siège de Corinthe. *See* **L'Assedio di Corinto.**

The Siege of Rochelle.

English opera in 3 acts, libretto by Edward Fitzball; music by W. M. Balfe. (London, Drury Lane Theatre, Oct. 29, 1835.) *Park Theatre, April 9, 1838, in English.

Siegfried. *See* **Der Ring des Nibelungen.**

La Sirène (The syren).

French opera in 3 acts, libretto by Augustin Eugène Scribe; music by D. Auber. (Paris, Opéra Comique, March 26, 1844.) Niblo's Garden, Nov. 20, 1854, in English.

Sleepy Hollow.

American opera in 3 acts, libretto by Charles Gaylor, founded on Washington Irving's story, "The legend of Sleepy Hollow;" music by M. Maretzek. First performed: Academy of Music, Sept. 25, 1879, in English.

Performed in Chicago, McVicker's Theatre, Nov. 19, 1879.

Snegourotchka.

Russian opera in a prologue and 4 acts, libretto by Alexander Nicholevich Ostrovsky, founded on an old Russian folk story; music by N. Rimsky-Korsakoff. (Moscow, Jan., 1882.) *Metropolitan Opera House, Jan. 23, 1922, in the French translation by Madame P. Halperine and Pierre Lalo.

Le Solitaire.

French opera in 3 acts, libretto by François Antoine Eugène de Planard, founded on the story by Charles Victor Prévôt, vicomte d'Arlincourt; music by M. E. Carafa. (Paris, Théâtre Feydeau, Aug. 17, 1822.) Park Theatre, Oct. 26, 1827, in French, followed by Berton's one-act opera, "Les Maris garçons."

The Song of David.

Biblical opera in 2 parts by Ira B. Arnstein. First performed: Æolian Hall, May 17, 1925, in concert form, in English, the composer conducting.

Le Songe d'une nuit d'été (A Summer night's dream).

French opera in 3 acts, libretto by N. Rosier and Adolphe de Leuven; music by A. Thomas. (Paris, Opéra Comique, April 20, 1850.) Niblo's Garden, June 21, 1852, in French; Fifth Avenue Theatre, Oct. 15, 1877, in English.

La Sonnambula.

Italian opera in 2 acts, libretto by Felice Romani; music by V. Bellini. (Milan, Teatro Carcano, March 6, 1831.) Park Theatre, Nov. 13, 1835, in English, followed by a farce, "The regent;" Palmo's Opera House, May 13, 1844, in Italian.

This opera was performed as a ballet pantomime on Dec. 18, 1837, at the National Theatre, New York.

A burlesque, "The roof scrambler," founded on Bellini's opera, was performed in English on Dec. 26, 1839 at the Olympic Theatre, New York. An "Ethiopian burlesque," entitled "Lo! som am de beauties," was performed on Feb. 24, 1845 at Palmo's Opera House, New York.

A performance of Bellini's opera was given on Oct. 22, 1847 at the Park Theatre, with an ensemble of Italian, German and English.

Performed in New Orleans, Théâtre d'Orléans, Jan. 14, 1840; Chicago, Rice's Theatre, July 29, 1850.

La Sonnambule. *See under* **Les Deux journées.**

Le Sourd; ou, L'auberge pleine.

French opera in 3 acts, libretto by Pierre Jean Baptiste Choudard Desforges, revised by Adolphe Leuven and Ferdinand Langlé; music by A. Adam. (Paris, Opéra Comique, Feb. 2, 1853.) Théâtre Français, Feb. 18, 1870, in French, preceded by the first act of Jacques Offenbach's three-act comic opera, "Barbe Bleue."

La Spia.

Italian opera in 3 acts, libretto by Filippo Manetta, founded on James Fenimore Cooper's novel, "The spy;" music by L. Arditi. First performed: Academy of Music, March 24, 1854, in Italian.

The Star of the north. *See* **L'Étoile du nord.**

Stradella. *See* **Alessandro Stradella.**

La Straniera.

Italian opera in 2 acts, libretto by Felice Romani; music by V. Bellini. (Milan, Teatro alla Scala, Feb. 14, 1829.) *Italian Opera House, Nov. 10, 1834, in Italian.

Struensee.

German play in 5 acts by Michael Beer; overture and incidental music by G. Meyerbeer. (Berlin, Sept. 19, 1846.)

The overture and incidental music of this drama was performed with recitations for the first time in America on Feb. 28, 1880, Gotthold Carlberg conducting, at Chickering Hall, New York. The tenor solos were sung by Mr. Ch. Fritsch and the harp accompaniments played by Mme. Josephine Chatterton-Bohrer. A chorus of male voices, directed by Ferdi-

Grand Opera in New York, 1825–1925, cont'd.

nand Dulcken, took part. The connecting poetry, translated into English by Hugh Craig, was recited by Miss Genevieve L. Stebbins. The orchestra, according to the advertisements, numbered sixty musicians. Hugo Ulrich's "Symphonie triomphale," op. 9, and Mozart's piano concert no. 8, in D minor, played by Mme. S. A. Rachau, preceded Meyerbeer's music.

The author of the play was a brother of the composer of the music.

Le Sultan de Zanzibar.

French opera in 3 acts, music by A. de Kontski. First performed: Academy of Music, May (not April) 8, 1886, in French.

The composer orchestrated and incorporated in his opera his popular piano piece, "Le reveil du lion," op. 115.

A Summer night's dream. *See* Le Songe d'une nuit d'été.

Suor Angelica.

Italian opera in 1 act, libretto by Gioacchino Forzano; music by G. Puccini. First performed: Metropolitan Opera House, Dec. 14, 1918, in Italian, preceded by "Il tabarro" and followed by "Gianni Schicchi," Italian operas in 1 act by G. Puccini.

Performed in Chicago, Auditorium, Dec. 6, 1919.

Susannes Geheimnis. *See* Il Segreto di Susanna.

The Swiss cottage. *See* Le Châlet.

La Sylphide (The dew drop).

French ballet in 2 acts, libretto by Adolphe Nourrit; music by J. M. Schneitzhoeffer. (Paris, Opéra, March 12, 1832.) Park Theatre, April 23 (not 22), 1832, in operatic form, in English, preceded by a farce, "Our Mary Anne," and followed by a play, "The Sentinel."

The Syren. *See* La Sirène.

Il Tabarro.

Italian opera in 1 act, libretto by Giuseppe Adami, founded on Didier Gold's play, "La houppelande;" music by G. Puccini. First performed: Metropolitan Opera House, Dec. 14, 1918, in Italian, followed by "Suor Angelica" and "Gianni Schicchi," Italian operas in 1 act by G. Puccini.

Performed in Chicago, Auditorium, Dec. 6, 1919.

The Tales of Hoffmann. *See* Les Contes d'Hoffmann.

The Talisman.

English opera in 3 acts, libretto by Arthur Mattheson, founded on the novel by Sir Walter Scott; music by W. M. Balfe. (London, Drury Lane Theatre, June 11, 1874.) *Academy of Music, Feb. 10, 1875, in English.

Performed in Philadelphia, Academy of Music, April, 1875.

The Taming of the shrew. *See* Die Widerspenstigen Zaehmung.

Tancredi.

Italian opera in 2 acts, libretto by Gaetano Rossi, founded on the play by Voltaire; music by G. Rossini. (Venice, La Fenice, Feb. 9, 1813.) *Park Theatre, Dec. 31, 1825, in Italian.

The aria, "Di tanti palpiti," from this opera was sung "by a young lady" at Mr. Huerta's concert in the Concert Room, corner Reed street and Broadway, opposite Washington Hall, New York, on Oct. 12, 1825.

A duet from this opera, arranged for clarinet and bass, was played by Messrs. Martinez and Maurez at Huerta's last concert on Jan. 2, 1826, at the City Hall Assembly Rooms.

Tancredi. *See also* Native land.

Tannhaeuser.

German opera in 3 acts, libretto and music by R. Wagner. (Dresden, Hoftheater, Oct. 20, 1845.) *Stadt Theatre, April 4, 1859, in German; Academy of Music, April 4, 1888, in English; Metropolitan Opera House, Jan. 30, 1889, Paris version; Manhattan Opera House, Dec. 10, 1909, in French.

This was the first of Wagner's operas performed in America.

Performed in Philadelphia, Academy of Music, Feb. 12, 1864; Chicago, McVicker's Theatre, Jan., 1865; Boston, Boston Theatre, Jan. 20, 1871; New Orleans, French Opera House, Dec. 12, 1877, in Italian.

Tebaldo ed Isolina.

Italian opera in 2 acts; music by F. Morlacchi. (Venice, Teatro La Fenice, Feb. 4, 1822.)

Never performed in New York.

The overture of this opera was played on Jan. 25, 1834, at the postponed concert of the Musical Fund Society at the City Hotel, New York.

A romanza for alto was sung on Dec. 19, 1833 by Signora Schneider-Maroncelli at a concert by the Italian Opera Company at the Euterpean Hall, New York. It was repeated on Jan. 30, 1834, at a concert by the Euterpean Society at the City Hotel.

Tell. *See* Guillaume Tell.

The Tempest.

English play in 5 acts by Shakespeare; incidental music adapted from T. Arne, H. Purcell, F. Halévy's opera, "La Tempesta," with additional music, by J. Cooke. Burton's Theatre, April 11, 1854.

According to the advertisements, this was the first performance of Shakespeare's play in New York in its original form. "When the play...was last performed in New York, twenty years ago...Dryden's version furnished the text, and several of Davenport's silly additions were retained."

C. M. von Weber's overture, op. 27, "Der Beherrscher der Geister" ("The ruler of the spirits"), was played before the production. The music from F. Halévy's two-act opera, "La Tempesta" (London, Her Majesty's Theatre, June 14, 1850), was advertised as played "for the first time in America."

The Temple dancer.

American opera in 1 act, libretto by Jutta Bell-Ranske; music by J. A. Hugo. First

Grand Opera in New York, 1825–1925, cont'd.

performed: Metropolitan Opera House, March 12, 1919, in English, preceded by Breil's one-act opera, "The legend," and followed by Cadman's two-act opera, "Shanewis."

Der Templer und die Juedin.

German opera in 3 acts, libretto by Wilhelm August Wohlbrück, founded on Sir Walter Scott's novel, "Ivanhoe;" music by H. Marschner, op. 60. (Leipzig, Stadttheater, Dec. 22, 1829.) New York Stadt Theatre, Jan. 29, 1872, in German.

This opera was announced for production at the Metropolitan Opera House for the season 1890–91, but never performed.

Thaïs.

French opera in 3 acts, libretto by Louis Gallet, founded on the novel by Anatole France; music by J. Massenet. (Paris, Opéra Comique, March 16, 1894.) *Manhattan Opera House, Nov. 25, 1907, in French.

Performed in Chicago, Auditorium, Dec. 6, 1910; New Orleans, French Opera House, Dec. 15, 1910; Milwaukee, Auditorium Theatre, Dec. 23, 1910.

The Thieving magpie. *See* La Gazza ladra.

Der Thurm zu Babel (The tower of Babel).

German sacred opera in 1 act, libretto by Julius Rodenberg; music by A. Rubinstein, op. 80. (Königsberg, Academie, Feb. 9, 1870.) Steinway Hall, Nov. 26, 1881, in English, in concert form by the Oratorio Society of New York, Dr. Leopold Damrosch conducting, preceded by the "Sanctus" from Charles Gounod's "Messe des mortes."

First performed in America in concert form: Chicago, Central Music Hall, Dec. 7, 1880, by the Apollo Club. The date of the New York performance has been generally assumed to be that of the first American production. A performance of the work in concert form had been previously announced for the Cincinnati Music Festival, but did not take place.

Tiefland (Marta of the lowlands).

German opera in a prologue and 2 acts, libretto by Rudolph Lothar, founded on Angel Guimerá's Spanish play, "Terra baixa;" music by Eugen D'Albert. (Prague, Neues Deutsches Theater, Nov. 15, 1903.) *Metropolitan Opera House, Nov. 23, 1908, in German; Century Opera House, March 17, 1914, in English.

Le Toreador; ou, L'accord parfait.

French opera in 2 acts, libretto by Thomas Marie François Sauvage; music by A. Adam. (Paris, Opéra Comique, May 18, 1849.) Théâtre Français, Oct. 18, 1866, in French.

Torquato Tasso.

Italian opera in 4 acts, libretto by Jacopo Ferretti; music by G. Donizetti. (Rome, Teatro Valle, Sept. 9, 1833.)

According to F. L. Ritter ("Music in America," p. 312), this opera was performed for the first time

in America in 1854 at Castle Garden, New York. The present compiler has not been able to substantiate the assertion. According to J. N. Ireland ("Records of the New York stage," v. 2, p. 626), an act from this opera was sung for the first time in America on July 21, 1854, in Italian, at Castle Garden, New York. On that day, however, Verdi's opera, "Luisa Miller," was performed for the second time in America at that theatre.

Torvaldo e Dorliska.

Italian opera in 2 acts, libretto by Pietro Sterbini; music by G. Rossini. (Rome, Teatro Valle, Dec. 26, 1815.)

Never performed in New York.

An aria from this opera was sung on Jan. 25, 1834, at the postponed concert of the Musical Fund Society at the City Hotel, New York.

Tosca.

Italian opera in 3 acts, libretto by Luigi Illica and Giuseppe Giacosa, founded on the play by Victorien Sardou; music by Puccini. (Rome, Teatro Costanzi, Jan. 14, 1900.) Metropolitan Opera House, Feb. 4, 1901, in Italian; Academy of Music (Brooklyn), Sept. 28, 1903, in English; West End Theatre, Jan. 4, 1904, in English.

First performed in America: Buenos Aires, June 16, 1900.

The performance at the Metropolitan Opera House was the first in the United States.

Performed in Boston, Boston Theatre, April 4, 1901, in Italian; Chicago, Auditorium, April 24, 1901, in Italian; New Orleans, Jan. 25, 1905, in English; Dec. 26, 1907, in Italian; Dec. 28, 1911, in French.

Die Tote Stadt.

German opera in 3 acts, libretto by Paul Schott, founded on Georges Rodenbach's play, "Bruges-la-mort;" music by E. W. Korngold, op. 12. (Hamburg, Stadttheater, Dec. 4, 1920.) *Metropolitan Opera House, Nov. 19, 1921, in German.

Die Toten Augen.

German opera in a prologue and 1 act, libretto by Hans Heinz Ewers and Marc Henry; music by E. D'Albert. (Dresden, Hofoper, March 5, 1916.) Manhattan Opera House, Jan. 3, 1924, in German.

First performed in America: Chicago, Great Northern Theatre, Nov. 1, 1923.

The Tower of Babel. *See* Der Thurm zu Babel.

La Traviata.

Italian opera in 3 acts, libretto by Francesco Maria Piave, founded on Dumas fils's play, "Camille;" music by G. Verdi. (Venice, Teatro La Fenice, March 6, 1853.) *Academy of Music, Dec. 3, 1856, in Italian.

Le Tre sultane.

Italian opera in 2 acts, music by M. Garcia.

According to Clément and Larousse's "Dictionnaire des opéras" and Hugo Riemann's "Opern-Handbuch," this opera was performed in New York about 1827. The date cannot be substantiated by a search of the New York newspapers and periodicals of the time. Garcia's first and only opera season in New York closed on Sept. 30, 1826. As far as records go, this opera was never performed in New York.

Grand Opera in New York, 1825–1925, cont'd.

Il **Trionfo della musica.** *See* Il **Fanatico per la musica.**

Tristan und Isolde.
German opera in 3 acts, libretto and music by R. Wagner. (Munich, Hoftheater, June 10, 1865.) *Metropolitan Opera House, Dec. 1, 1886, in German.
Performed in Boston, Boston Theatre, April 1, 1895; Chicago, Auditorium, April 17, 1895.

Der **Trompeter von Säkkingen.**
German opera in 3 acts, founded on the poem by Joseph Victor von Scheffel; music by Emil Kaiser. (Olmütz, Nov., 1882.) *Thalia Theatre, Jan. 2, 1886, in German.

Der **Trompeter von Säkkingen (The Trumpeter of Säkkingen).**
German opera in a prologue and 3 acts, libretto by Rudolf Bunge, ofunded on the poem by Joseph Victor von Scheffel; music by V. Nessler. (Leipzig, Stadttheater, May 4, 1884.) *Metropolitan Opera House, Nov. 23, 1887, in German; Harlem Opera House, Nov. 5, 1889, in English.

The **Troubadour.** *See* Il **Trovatore.**

Le **Trouvère.** *See* Il **Trovatore.**

Il **Trovatore (The Troubadour; Der Troubadour; Le Trouvère).**
Italian opera in 4 acts, libretto by Salvatore Cammarano, founded on A. Garcia's Spanish play, "Guttierez;" music by G. Verdi. (Rome, Teatro Apollo, Jan. 19, 1853.) *Academy of Music, May 2, 1855, in Italian; Burton's Theatre, Oct. 4, 1858, in English; New York Stadt Theatre, Sept. 13, 1870, in a German translation by Heinrich Proch, preceded by a prologue spoken by Otto Brethauer; Lyric Theatre, April 22, 1912, in French.
The first performance of this opera in America was announced at the Academy of Music for April 30, 1855, but postponed until the date noted above.
This opera was broadcast by radio on June 23, 1925 in Italian, in tabloid form, with reduced orchestra, through station WEAF, New York. The performance was repeated on Oct. 20, 1925. The opera was also broadcast by radio on Oct. 9, 1925 in Italian, in tabloid form, through station WRNY, New York.
Performed in Philadelphia, Walnut Street Theatre, Jan. 14, 1856; New Orleans, Théâtre d'Orléans, April 13, 1857.
An English burlesque, "The tearful and tragical tale of the tricky troubadour; or, The truant tracked," in 4 acts, by George Broughall, with Verdi's music, was performed in Sept. and Oct., 1886 in Winnipeg, Canada. The libretto was published by the Manitoba Free Press, Winnipeg, Canada.

Les **Troyens à Carthage (The Trojans at Carthage).**
French opera in a prologue and 5 acts, libretto and music by H. Berlioz. (Paris, Théâtre Lyrique, Nov. 4, 1863.) *Chickering Hall, Feb. 26, 1887, in English, arranged

by Henry Edward Krehbiel, the narrative blank verse by J. S. Tunison, in concert form as an oratorio, Frank van der Stucken conducting.

The **Trumpeter of Säkkingen.** *See* Der **Trompeter von Säkkingen.**

Il **Turco in Italia.**
Italian opera in 2 acts, libretto by Felice Romani; music by G. Rossini. (Milan, Teatro alla Scala, Aug. 14, 1814.) *Park Theatre, March 14, 1826, in Italian.

The **Two Figaros.**
English comic opera in 2 (?) acts, founded on the operas, "Le Nozze di Figaro" and "Il Barbiere di Siviglia;" music selected from W. A. Mozart and G. Rossini. *National Theatre, Nov. 16, 1837, founded by Garrick's play, "Gulliver in Lylliput," and a farce, "The happiest day of my life."
According to the advertisement in "The Evening Post" (New York), "This opera was performed in London at Madame Vestris' theatre, and acted 60 successive nights."
The overture of Rossini's opera, "Il Barbiere di Siviglia," was played before the performance and the overture of Mozart's opera, "Le Nozze di Figaro," introduced between the acts.

Gli **Ugonotti.** *See* Les **Huguenots.**

L'**Ultimo giorno di Pompei.**
Italian opera in 2 acts, libretto by Andrea Leone Tottola, founded on Lord Bulwer Lytton's novel. "The last days of Pompeii;" music by G. Pacini. (Naples, Teatro San Carlo, Nov. 19, 1825.)
Never performed in New York.
The soprano cavatina, "Alfin goder mi è dato," from this opera was sung, in Italian, by Signorina Clementina Fanti at her benefit on Dec. 28, 1833, between the acts of Rossini's two-act opera, "La donna del lago," at the Italian Opera House, New York.

Undine.
German opera in 4 acts, founded on the story by Friedrich Heinrich Karl Fouqué; libretto and music by A. Lortzing. (Leipzig, Stadttheater, April 25, 1846.) *Niblo's Garden, Oct. 9, 1856, in German.

V studni.
Bohemian opera in 1 act, libretto by Karel Sabina; music by W. Blodek. (Prague, Nov. 17, 1867.) *Jan Huss Neighborhood House, March 6, 1920, in Bohemian.

Vakoula, the smith. *See* **Cherevicky.**

Le **Val d'Andorre (The valley of Andorre).**
French opera in 3 acts, libretto by Jules Henri Vernoy de Saint Georges; music by F. Halévy. (Paris, Opéra Comique, Nov. 11, 1848.) Brougham's Lyceum Theatre, March 15, 1851, in English.

Valmondi; or, The tomb of terrors.
English opera by G. Rodwell. First performed: Park Theatre, Oct. 11, 1830, in English.

Grand Opera in New York, 1825–1925, cont'd.

Der **Vampyr.**

German opera in 2 acts, libretto by Wilhelm August Wohlbrück; music by H. Marschner, op. 42. (Leipzig, Stadt Theater, March 29 [not 28], 1828.)

Never performed in New York.

The overture of this opera was played for the "first time" in New York on Jan. 11, 1845 by the Philharmonic Society of New York, Uriah C. Hill conducting, as the last number of the second concert of the third season, in the Apollo Rooms, New York.

Il **Vascello fantasma.** *See* Der **Fliegende Holländer.**

La **Veglia.**

Italian opera in 1 act, libretto by Carlo Linati, founded on J. M. Synge's play, "The wake;" music by A. Pedrollo. (Milan, Teatro Lirico, Jan. 2, 1920.) *Hotel Pennsylvania, Dec. 20, 1924, in Italian, followed by Lualdi's one-act opera "Le furie de Arlecchino," and a miscellaneous musical and dance program.

This little opera was performed for the first time in America under the auspices of the Manufacturers Trust Co., New York, in honor of its stockholders.

Il **Vassalo di Szigeth (Der Vasall von Szigeth).**

Italian opera in 3 acts, libretto by Luigi Illica and F. Pozza; music by A. Smareglia. (Vienna, Hofoperntheater, Oct. 4, 1889, in the German translation by Max Kalbeck.) *Metropolitan Opera House, Dec. 12, 1890, in German.

Die **Verkaufte Braut (Prodaná nevěsta).**

Bohemian opera in 3 acts, libretto by Karel Sabina; music by F. Smetana. (Prague, National Theatre, May 30, 1866.) *Metropolitan Opera House, Feb. 19, 1909, in the German translation by Max Kalbeck.

This opera was announced for production at the Metropolitan Opera House for the season 1903–04 in an English translation by Charles Henry Meltzer, but not performed.

Das **Verlorene Paradies.**

German sacred opera in 3 parts, libretto by Julius Rodenberg, founded on Milton's poem, "Paradise Lost;" music by A. Rubinstein, op. 54. (Düsseldorf, Nov. 8, 1875.) *Academy of Music (Brooklyn), March 12, 1887, in concert form, in English, by the Philharmonic Society of Brooklyn, Theodore Thomas conducting.

A public rehearsal of this work took place on the day preceding its first American performance.

The second part of this work was sung at the twenty-first festival of the North American Sängerbund in Cincinnati in June, 1879.

Versiegelt.

German opera in 1 act, libretto by Richard Batka and Pordes-Milo, founded on the story by Ernst Benjamin Salomon Rauppach; music by Leo Blech, op. 18. (Hamburg, Stadttheater, Nov. 4, 1908.) *Metropolitan Opera House, Jan. 20, 1912, in German, followed by Leoncavallo's two-act opera, "Pagliacci."

I **Vespri Siciliani (Giovanna de Guzman).**

French opera in 5 acts, libretto by Augustin Eugène Scribe and Charles Duveyrier; music by G. Verdi. (Paris, Opéra, June 13, 1855.) *Academy of Music, Nov. 7, 1859, in Italian.

La **Vestale.**

Italian opera, music by V. Puccita. (London, Opera, 1810.)

Never performed in New York.

A scena from this opera was sung by Mrs. Austin at the Park Theatre on Jan. 7, 1828.

La **Vestale.**

French opera in 3 acts, libretto by Victor Joseph Étienne de Jouy; music by G. Spontini. (Paris, Académie royale de musique, Dec. 15, 1807.) Metropolitan Opera House, Nov. 13, 1925, in French.

Performed in Philadelphia, Chestnut Street Theatre, Oct. 30, 1828, by a French company from New Orleans.

Le **Vieil aigle.**

French opera in 1 act, libretto and music by R. Gunsbourg, founded on a story by Maxim Gorki. (Monte Carlo, Opéra, Feb. 13, 1909.) Lexington Theatre, Feb. 28, 1919, in French, preceded by Mascagni's one-act opera, "Cavalleria rusticana."

First performed in America: Chicago, Auditorium, Jan. 19, 1917.

La **Vieille.**

French opera in 1 act, libretto by Augustin Eugène Scribe and Germain Delavigne; music by J. Fetis. (Paris, Opéra Comique, March 14, 1826.) Park Theatre, July 20, 1827, in French, preceded by Bochsa's one-act opera, "La Lettre de change."

Le **Villi.**

Italian opera in 2 acts (originally 1 act), libretto by Ferdinando Fontana; music by G. Puccini. (Milan, Teatro dal Verme, May 31, 1884.) *Metropolitan Opera House, Dec. 17, 1908, in Italian, followed by Mascagni's one-act opera, "Cavalleria rusticana."

Vivandiere; or, The daughter of the regiment. *See* La **Fille du régiment.**

Le **Voyage en Chine.**

French opera in 3 acts, libretto by Eugène Marin Labiche and Alfred Delacour [pseud. of Alfred Charlemagne Lartique]; music by F. Bazin. (Paris, Opéra Comique, Dec. 9, 1865.) Park Theatre, Jan. 11, 1875, in French.

Der **Waffenschmied.**

German opera in 3 acts, libretto and music by A. Lortzing. (Vienna, Theater an der Wien, May 30, 1846.) Deutsches Irving Place Theater, Sept. 26, 1925 (first time in New York?), in German.

Performed in West Hoboken (Union City), N. J., St. Joseph's Auditorium, Oct. 11, 1925.

Grand Opera in New York, 1825–1925, cont'd.

Der Wald (The forest).

Opera in a prologue, 1 act and an epilogue, in English and German; libretto and music by E. Smyth. (Berlin, Königliches Opernhaus, April 9, 1902, in German; London, Covent Garden, July 18, 1902, in German.) *Metropolitan Opera House, March 11, 1903, in German, preceded by Verdi's four-act opera, "Il Trovatore."

Die Walkuere. *See* Der Ring des Nibelungen.

La Wally.

Italian opera in 4 acts, libretto by Luigi Illica; music by A. Catalani. (Milan, Teatro alla Scala, Jan. 20, 1892.) *Metropolitan Opera House, Jan. 6, 1909, in Italian.

Werther.

French opera in 4 acts, libretto by Édouard Blau, Paul Milliet and Georges Hartmann, founded on Goethe's story, "Die Leiden des jungen Werther;" music by J. Massenet. (Vienna, Hof-Operntheater, Feb. 16, 1892; Paris, Opéra Comique, Jan. 16, 1893.) Metropolitan Opera House, April 19 (not 20), 1894, in French.

First performed in America: Chicago, Auditorium, March 29, 1894.

Performed in New Orleans, French Opera House, Nov. 3, 1894.

Die Widerspentigen Zaehmung (The taming of the shrew).

German opera in 4 acts, libretto by Josef Viktor Widmann, founded on the play by Shakespeare; music by H. Goetz. (Mannheim, Hoftheater, Oct. 11, 1874.) *Academy of Music, Jan. 4, 1886, in English; Metropolitan Opera House, March 15, 1916, in German.

Der Wildschuetz; oder, Die Stimme der Natur.

German opera in 3 acts, founded on August Friedrich Ferdinand von Kotzebue's play, "Der Rehbock;" libretto and music by A. Lortzing. (Leipzig, Stadttheater, Dec. 31, 1842.) *German Opera House, Nov. 28, 1862, in German.

Performed in Philadelphia, Academy of Music, Jan. 21, 1863.

Wilhelm Tell. *See* Guillaume Tell.

Zampa; ou, La fiancée de marbre.

French opera in 3 acts, libretto by Mélesville [pseud. of Anne Honoré Duveyrier]; music by L. Hérold. (Paris, Opéra Comique, May 3, 1831.) Park Theatre, Aug. 12, 1833, in French, followed by a vaudeville, "L'Intérieur d'un bureau;" Park Theatre, March 29, 1841, in an English adaptation by W. H. Latham, followed by a farce, "Scan Mag."

The performance of this opera in English, noted above, was advertised as the "1st performance in America" of the work.

A German performance of this opera was announced

in rehearsal at the New York Stadt Theatre early in 1871, but was never given.

Performed in Philadelphia, Chestnut Street Theatre, May 12, 1841, in English.

Zanetto.

Italian opera in 1 act, libretto by Giovanni Targioni-Tozzetti and Guido Menasci; music by P. Mascagni. (Pesaro, Liceo Musicale Rossini, March 2, 1896.) *Waldorf-Astoria, Jan. 4, 1898, in Italian (?), by the Society of Musical Arts.

Performed at the Metropolitan Opera House, New York, Oct. 8 (not 9), 1902, in Italian, by Mascagni's opera company; Baltimore, Music Hall, Oct. 27, 1902.

Die Zauberflöte (Il flauto magico; The magic flute).

German opera in 2 acts, libretto by Emanuel Schikaneder; music by J. W. Mozart. (Vienna, Theater auf der Wieden, Sept. 30, 1791.) *Park Theater, April 17, 1833, in an English adaptation by Charles Edward Horn, followed by a farce, "Everybody's husband;" Academy of Music, Nov. 21, 1859, in Italian; German Opera House, Nov. 10, 1862, in German, without "cuts;" Academy of Music, Jan. 27, 1886, in English, with Mozart's original music.

According to F. L. Ritter ("Music in America," p. 201), this opera was first performed in America on March 17, 1832 at the Park Theatre, New York. According to the newspapers, the twenty-first performance of Auber's opera, "La muette di Portici (Masaniello)," took place on that day. A new grand military spectacle, "Napoleon Buonaparte," followed the opera.

The overture of this opera was played on March 4, 1824 at P. H. Taylor's concert, William Taylor conducting, at the City Hotel, New York.

Zaza.

Italian opera in 4 acts, libretto and music by R. Leoncavallo, founded on the play by Pierre Berton and Charles Simon. (Milan, Teatro Lirico Internazionale, Nov. 10, 1900.) Metropolitan Opera House, Jan. 16, 1920, in Italian.

Excerpts from the opera were given in New York in 1906 at the composer's concerts.

First performed in the United States: San Francisco, Tivoli Opera House, Nov. 27, 1903.

Performed in Montreal, His Majesty's Theatre, Jan. 10, 1913.

Zelmira.

Italian opera in 2 acts, libretto by Andrea Leone Tottola; music by G. Rossini. (Naples, Teatro San Carlo, Feb. 10, 1822.) Never performed in New York.

The scena and cavatina, "Sorte secondami," from this opera was sung in costume by Signor Ferrero at G. B. Montresor's benefit on Jan. 10, 1833 at the Bowery Theatre, New York, between the acts of Bellini's opera, "Il pirata."

Zenobia, queen of Palmyra.

American opera in 4 acts (last act in 2 parts, sometimes described as 5 acts), libretto and music by S. G. Pratt. (Chicago, Central Music Hall, June 15 and 16, 1882, in concert form; Chicago, McVicker's Theatre, March 26, 1883, in operatic form.) Twenty-Third Street Theatre, Aug. 21, 1883, in English.

A CHRONOLOGY OF THE GRAND OPERAS PERFORMED
FROM 1825 TO 1925

1825

Mar. 2. Park Theatre: Der Freischütz.
Oct. 7. Chatham Theatre: Forest rose.
Nov. 29. Park Theatre: Il Barbiere di Siviglia (in Italian; Park Theatre, May 17, 1819, in English).
Dec. 17. Park Theatre: L'Amante astuto.
Dec. 31. Park Theatre: Tancredi.

1826

Feb. 7. Park Theatre: Otello (Rossini).
Mar. 14. Park Theatre: Il Turco in Italia.
Apr. 25. Park Theatre: La Figlia dell' aria.
May 23. Park Theatre: Don Giovanni.
June 27. Park Theatre: La Cenerentola.
July 26. Park Theatre: Romeo e Giulietta (Zingarelli).
Dec. 4. Lafayette Theatre: Lodoïska.

1827

Jan. 12. Park Theatre: Native land.
July 13. Park Theatre: Cendrillon (Nicolo); Maison à vendre.
July 20. Park Theatre: La Lettre de change; La Vieille.
July 23. Park Theatre: Les Deux journées.
July 25. Park Theatre: Le Rendezvous bourgeois.
July 27. Park Theatre: Joconde.
July 30. Park Theatre: Le Niege.
Aug. 1. Park Theatre: Gulistan.
Aug. 3. Park Theatre: Le Maçon; La Maison en loterie.
Aug. 6. Park Theatre: Jean de Paris.
Aug. 10. Park Theatre: Jeannot et Colin.
Aug. 17. Park Theatre: Le Diable à quatre.
Aug. 20. Park Theatre: Le Bouffe et le tailleur.
Aug. 23. Park Theatre: Adolphe et Clara.
Aug. 24. Park Theatre: La Dame blanche.
Aug. 27. Park Theatre: Le Calife de Bagdad.
Aug. 28. Park Theatre: Ma tante Aurore.

1827, continued

Aug. 29. Park Theatre: Aline, reine de Golconde.
Aug. 31. Park Theatre: Le Petit chaperon rouge.
Sept. 1. Park Theatre: Lully et Quinault.
Sept. 8. Park Theatre: Camille.
Oct. 26. Park Theatre: Le Solitaire; Les Maris garçons.
Nov. 5. Park Theatre: Abou Hassan.
Dec. 24. Bowery Theatre: Il Fuorusciti di Firenze (The freebooters).

1828

Jan. 31. Park Theatre: Artaxerxes.
Apr. 9. Park Theatre: Dido (Horn).
June 9. Park Theatre: Isidore di Merida.
Oct. 9. Park Theatre: Oberon.

1829

Apr. 20. Bowery Theatre: Il Fanatico per la musica (Il trionfo della musica).
Apr. 27. Bowery Theatre: The Quartette.
May 25. Park Theatre: Home, sweet home!

1830

Apr. 20. Park Theatre: L'Ape musicale.
May 17. Park Theatre: Rokeby.
Oct. 11. Park Theatre: Valmondi.

1831

Sept. 19. Park Theatre: Guillaume Tell (William Tell).
Nov. 28. Park Theatre: Masaniello (La muette di Portici).

1832

Feb. 27. Park Theatre: The Maid of Judah.
Oct. 18. Richmond Hill Theatre: Elise e Claudio.
Nov. 5. Richmond Hill Theatre: L'Italiana in Algeri.

Chronology, Grand Operas, 1825–1925, cont'd.

1832, continued

Dec. 5. Richmond Hill Theatre: Il Pirata.

Dec. 22. Masonic Hall: Mosè in Egitto (in concert form).

Dec. 27. Park Theatre: Nadir and Zuleika.

1833

Apr. 17. Park Theatre: Die Zauberflöte (The magic flute).

May 11. Bowery Theatre: L'Inganno felice.

June 20. Park Theatre: Fra Diavolo.

Aug. 7. Park Theatre: La Gazza ladra.

Aug. 9. Park Theatre: Le Philtre.

Aug. 12. Park Theatre: Zampa.

Aug. 14. Park Theatre: La Fiancée.

Aug. 19. Park Theatre: Le Comte Ory.

Aug. 21. Park Theatre: Les Folies amoureuses.

Aug. 26. Park Theatre: Le Rossignol.

Dec. 16. Italian Opera House: La Donna del lago.

1834

Jan. 4. Italian Opera House: Il Matrimonio segreto.

Jan. 20. Italian Opera House: Gli Arabi nelli Gallie.

Feb. 1. Italian Opera House: Coriolanus before Rome.

Feb. 10. Italian Opera House: Matilde di Shabran.

Mar. 22. Italian Opera House: La Casa da vendere.

Apr. 7. Park Theatre: Robert le Diable (Robert the Devil).

July 21. Park Theatre: Gustavus III.

Nov. 10. Italian Opera House: La Straniera.

Nov. 25. Italian Opera House: Eduardo e Cristina.

1835

Feb. 6. Italian Opera House: L'Assedio di Corinto.

Mar. 2. Italian Opera House: Mosè in Egitto (with scenery).

May 11. Park Theatre: The Mountain sylph.

Nov. 13. Park Theatre: La Sonnambula.

1836

Oct. 3. National Theatre (Italian Opera House): Le Dieu et la Bayadère (The maid of Cashmere).

1837

Jan. 26. National Theatre: The Pirate boy.

Nov. 16. National Theatre: The Two Figaros.

1838

Apr. 9. Park Theatre: The Siege of Rochelle.

Apr. 23. Park Theatre: La Sylphide (The dewdrop).

June 18. Park Theatre: L'Elisir d'amore (The elixir of love).

Oct. 15. Park Theatre: Amilie.

1839

Feb. 28. National Theatre: Conrad and Medora.

Sept. 9. Park Theatre: Fidelio.

1840

Mar. 30. Park Theatre: Le Postillon de Lonjumeau.

Oct. 12. New National Theatre: Ahmed al Kamel.

1841

Feb. 25. Park Theatre: Norma.

Apr. 20. Park Theatre: The Gipsy's warning.

1842

May 9. Park Theatre: Le Cheval de bronze (The bronze horse).

May 23. Park Theatre: The Maid of Saxony.

Oct. 31. Park Theatre: The Israelites in Egypt.

Nov. 21. Park Theatre: Acis and Galatea.

1843

May 19. Niblo's Garden: Polichinelle.

May 22. Niblo's Garden: Les Mémoires du diable.

May 24. Niblo's Garden: La Perruche.

Chronology, Grand Operas, 1825–1925, cont'd.

1843, continued.

May 26. Niblo's Theatre (Garden): L'Ambassadrice.
June 7. Niblo's Garden: Le Domino noir.
June 23. Niblo's Garden: L'Eclair.
July 3. Niblo's Garden: Le Pré aux clercs.
July 7. Niblo's Garden: Le Châlet.
July 14. Niblo's Garden: Les Diamants de la couronne.
July 19. Niblo's Garden: La Fille du régiment.
July 22. Niblo's Garden: Cosimo.
Aug. 2. Niblo's Garden: Anna Boleyn.
Sept. 15. Niblo's Garden: Lucia di Lammermoor.
Oct. 2. Niblo's Garden: Gemma di Vergy.
Dec. 15. Park Theatre: Marino Faliero.

1844

Feb. 3. Palmo's Opera House: I Puritani.
Feb. 14. Palmo's Opera House: Belisario.
Mar. 18. Palmo's Opera House: Beatrice di Tenda.
Sept. 30. Park Theatre: The Enchanted horse.
Nov. 18. Palmo's Opera House: Chiara di Rosenburgh.
Nov. 25. Palmo's Opera House: Lucrezia Borgia; Park Theatre: The Bohemian girl.

1845

Jan. 3. Palmo's Opera House: Semiramide.
Apr. 7. Palmo's Opera House: Antigone.
June 25. Park Theatre: La Favorite.
July 16. Park Theatre: La Juive.
Aug. 8. Park Theatre: Les Huguenots.
Sept. 10. Niblo's Garden: La Reine de Chypre.
Nov. —. Olympic Theatre: Le Lac des fées (The fairies' lake).
Dec. 17. Palmo's Opera House: Die Schweizer Familie.

1846

Jan. 5. Palmo's Opera House: Fröhlich.
Mar. 9. Park Theatre: Don Pasquale.
Mar. 23. Park Theatre: Le Brasseur de Preston (The brewer of Preston).

1847

Jan. 4. Palmo's Opera House: Linda di Chamounix.
Feb. 5. Palmo's Opera House: Nina pazza per amore.
Mar. 3. Palmo's Opera House: I Lombardi alla prima crociata.
Apr. 15. Park Theatre: Ernani.
June 9. Park Theatre: I Due Foscari.
June 14. Park Theatre: Saffo.
Oct. 6. Park Theatre: The Night dancers.
Nov. 5. Park Theatre: The Maid of Artois.

1848

Jan. 28. Astor Place Opera House: I Capuletti e Montecchi.
Feb. 14. Astor Place Opera House: Il Giuramento.
Apr. 4. Astor Place Opera House: Nabucco.
May 4. Bowery Theatre: Maritana.
Sept. 11. Burton's Theatre: Comus (Handel and Arne).

1849

Jan. 15. Astor Place Opera House: Roberto Devereux.
Mar. 26. Broadway Theatre: The Enchantress.
Dec. 10. Astor Place Opera House: Maria di Rohan; Olympic Theatre: Le Nouveau seigneur de village (The new lord of the village).

1850

Apr. 15. Niblo's Garden: Attila.
Apr. 24. Niblo's Garden: Macbeth (Verdi).
Aug. 20. Astor Place Opera House: Judith (Bochsa).
Oct. 22. Astor Place Opera House: Parisina.

1851

Jan. 6. Astor Place Opera House: Giovanna 1ma di Napoli.
Jan. 15. Brougham's Lyceum Theatre: The Andalusian.
Mar. 15. Brougham's Lyceum Theatre: Le Val d'Andorre (The valley of Andorre).
June 2. Broadway Theatre: L'Enfant prodigue (Azael, the prodigal).

Chronology, Grand Operas, 1825–1925, cont'd.

1852

June 21. Niblo's Garden: Le Songe d'une nuit d'été.

June 28. Niblo's Garden: Le Caïd.

Aug. 20. Castle Garden: Ne touchez pas à la reine.

Nov. 1. Niblo's Garden: Martha.

Dec. 13. Broadway Theatre: Peri; or, The Enchanted fountain.

Dec. 17. Niblo's Garden: The Basketmaker's wife.

1853

Nov. 25. Niblo's Garden: Le Prophète (Il profeta).

1854

Feb. 3. Burton's Theatre: Midsummer night's dream (Mendelssohn).

Mar. 24. Academy of Music: La Spia.

July 20. Castle Garden: Luisa Miller.

Nov. 20. Niblo's Garden: La Sirène (The syren).

1855

Feb. 19. Academy of Music: Rigoletto.

Apr. 9. Niblo's Garden: Les Noces de Jeannette (The marriage of Georgette).

Apr. 12. Niblo's Garden: Alessandro Stradella.

May 2. Academy of Music: Il Trovatore.

June 18. Niblo's Garden: The Daughter of St. Mark.

Sept. 27. Niblo's Garden: Rip van Winkle (Bristow).

1856

May 17. Academy of Music: Egmont.

Sept. 24. Academy of Music: L'Étoile du nord.

Oct. 9. Niblo's Garden: Undine.

Dec. 3. Academy of Music: La Traviata.

1857

Jan. 13. Broadway Theatre: Czar und Zimmermann.

1858

Mar. 29. Academy of Music: Leonora (Fry).

Nov. 13. Academy of Music: La Serva padrona.

Nov. 23. Academy of Music: Le Nozze di Figaro (in Italian; Park Theatre: May 10, 1824, in English).

1859

Apr. 4. New York Stadt Theatre: Tannhäuser.

May 25. Academy of Music: Poliuto.

Nov. 7. Academy of Music: I Vespri siciliani.

1860

Feb. —. Brooklyn: Die Entführung aus dem Serail (Belmonte and Costanze).

June 2. Winter Garden: I Masnadieri.

Sept. 27. Niblo's Garden: Medea.

1861

Feb. 11. Academy of Music: Un Ballo in maschera.

Mar. —. Hoboken, N. J.: Der Häusliche Krieg.

Oct. 28. Academy of Music: Les Noces de Jeannette, and Betly.

1862

Nov. 24. Academy of Music: Dinorah.

Nov. 28. German Opera House: Der Wildschütz.

Dec. 15. German Opera House: Das Nachtlager in Grenada.

1863

Feb. 16. German Opera House: Joseph.

Feb. 23. Niblo's Garden: Satanella.

Apr. 6. Academy of Music: Ione.

Apr. 27. Academy of Music: Die Lustigen Weiber von Windsor.

May 4. Academy of Music: Aroldo.

May 25. Winter Garden: Orfeo ed Euridice.

June 15. Winter Garden: The Corsican bride.

Nov. 11. Academy of Music: Giuditta.

Nov. 25. Academy of Music: Faust.

Chronology, Grand Operas, 1825–1925, cont'd.

1864

July 27. Olympic Theatre: The Rose of Castile.

Nov. 25. Academy of Music: Don Sébastien.

1865

Feb. 24. Academy of Music: La Forza del destino.

Oct. 24. Academy of Music: Crispino e la Comare.

Dec. 1. Academy of Music: L'Africaine.

1866

Oct. 9. Théâtre Français: Les Mousquetaires de la reine.

Oct. 18. Théâtre Français: Le Toreador.

1867

Apr. 3. Academy of Music: Il Carnevale di Venezia.

Oct. 18. Academy of Music: Don Bucephalo.

Nov. 15. Academy of Music: Roméo et Juliette (Romeo e Giulietta).

1868

Jan. 1. Academy of Music: The Lily of Killarney.

Jan. 15. Academy of Music: The Desert flower.

1869

May 10. Fifth Avenue Theatre: Les Dragons de Villars.

May 13. Academy of Music: Lurline.

Sept. 11. Théâtre Français: The Puritan's daughter.

Dec. 10. Academy of Music: Pipele.

Dec. 15. Théâtre Français: Ascold's tomb.

1870

Feb. 18. Théâtre Français: Le Sourd.

Nov. 9. New York Stadt Theatre: Mozart und Schikaneder.

Dec. 17. New York Stadt Theatre: Preciosa.

1871

Mar. 12. New York Stadt Theatre: Lohengrin.

May 26. New York Stadt Theatre: Prinz Eugen.

Nov. 22. Academy of Music: Mignon.

1872

Jan. 29. New York Stadt Theatre: Der Templar und die Jüdin.

Mar. 22. Academy of Music: Hamlet.

1873

Nov. 26. Academy of Music: Aida.

1875

Jan. 11. Park Theatre: Le Voyage en Chine.

Feb. 10. Academy of Music: The Talisman.

Apr. 9. Academy of Music: L'Ombre.

1877

Jan. 26. Academy of Music: Der Fliegende Holländer (The flying Dutchman).

Apr. 2. Academy of Music: Die Walküre.

Apr. 12. Academy of Music: Don Carlos.

1878

Mar. 4. Academy of Music: Rienzi.

Oct. 23. Academy of Music: Carmen.

1879

Mar. 14. Academy of Music: Ruy Blas.

Sept. 8. Grand Opera House: Paul et Virginie.

Sept. 25. Academy of Music: Sleepy Hollow.

1880

Oct. 11. Haverly's Fourteenth Street Theatre: Deseret.

Nov. 24. Academy of Music: Mefistofele.

Dec. 14. Germania Theatre: Der Rattenfänger von Hameln.

1881

Nov. 26. Steinway Hall: Der Thurm zu Babel (in concert form).

Nov. 29. Park Theatre: Si j'étais roi.

Chronology, Grand Operas, 1825–1925, cont'd.

1882

Jan. 9. Germania Theatre: Don Quixote, der Ritter von der traurigen Gestalt.

Oct. 16. Fifth Avenue Theatre: Les Contes d'Hoffmann.

1883

Aug. 21. Twenty-third Street Theatre: Zenobia.

Dec. 20. Metropolitan Opera House: La Gioconda.

1884

Nov. 3. Star Theatre: Il Guarany.

Dec. 18. Academy of Music (Brooklyn): Mireille (Mirella).

1885

Dec. 2. Metropolitan Opera House: Die Königin von Saba.

Dec. 23. Academy of Music: Manon.

1886

Jan. 2. Thalia Theatre: Der Trompeter von Säkkingen (Kaiser).

Jan. 4. Academy of Music: Die Widerspenstigen Zähmung (The taming of the shrew); Metropolitan Opera House: Die Meistersinger.

Mar. 1. Academy of Music: Lakmé.

Mar. 3. Metropolitan Opera House: Parsifal (in concert form).

May 8. Academy of Music: Le Sultan de Zanzibar.

Nov. 19. Metropolitan Opera House: Das Goldene Kreuz.

Dec. 1. Metropolitan Opera House: Tristan und Isolde.

Dec. 30. Academy of Music (Brooklyn): Galatea.

1887

Jan. 3. Metropolitan Opera House: Merlin.

Feb. 26. Chickering Hall: Les Troyens à Carthage (in concert form).

Mar. 12. Academy of Music (Brooklyn): Das Verlorene Paradies (Paradise Lost; in concert form).

Mar. 14. Metropolitan Opera House: Nero.

1887, continued.

Nov. 9. Metropolitan Opera House: Siegfried.

Nov. 23. Metropolitan Opera House: Der Trompeter von Säkkingen (Nessler).

Dec. 23. Metropolitan Opera House: Euryanthe.

1888

Jan. 6. Metropolitan Opera House: Fernand Cortez.

Jan. 25. Metropolitan Opera House: Die Götterdämmerung.

Mar. 3. Thalia Theatre: Manfred (Schumann).

Apr. 16. Academy of Music: Otello (Verdi).

1889

Jan. 4. Metropolitan Opera House: Rheingold.

1890

Jan. 3. Metropolitan Opera House: Der Barbier von Bagdad.

Nov. 26. Metropolitan Opera House: Asreal.

Dec. 12. Metropolitan Opera House: Il Vassalo di Szigeth (Der Vasall von Szigeth).

1891

Jan. 9. Metropolitan Opera House: Diana von Solange.

Oct. 1. Casino Theatre; Lenox Lyceum: Cavalleria Rusticana.

1892

May 18. Amberg Theatre: Der Minstrel.

1893

Jan. 24. Manhattan Opera House: Boabdil.

Jan. 31. Music Hall: L'Amico Fritz.

June 15. Grand Opera House: Pagliacci.

Nov. 16. Hermann's Theatre: Philemon et Baucis.

Dec. 18. Irving Place Theatre: Matteo Falcone.

Chronology, Grand Operas, 1825–1925, cont'd.

1894

Mar. 16. Music Hall: Gabriella.

Apr. 19. Metropolitan Opera House: Werther.

Dec. 17. Metropolitan Opera House: Elaine.

1895

Feb. 4. Metropolitan Opera House: Falstaff.

Feb. 8. Metropolitan Opera House: Samson et Delila.

Oct. 8. Daly's Theatre: Haensel und Gretel.

Dec. 11. Metropolitan Opera House: La Navarraise.

1896

Jan. 11. Metropolitan Opera House: Les Pêcheurs de perles (first two acts).

Feb. 13. Manuscript Society: Mataswintha (in concert form).

Mar. 6. Academy of Music: The Scarlet letter.

Nov. 13. Academy of Music: Andrea Chenier.

1897

Feb. 12. Metropolitan Opera House: Le Cid.

Dec. 13. Waldorf-Astoria Hotel: Daphne (morning); Le Portrait de Manon (evening).

Dec. 20. Waldorf-Astoria Hotel: Der Geigenmacher von Cremona.

1898

Jan. 4. Waldorf-Astoria Hotel: Zanetto.

Feb. 17. Daly's Theatre: Lili-Tsee.

Apr. 2. Terrace Garden: Kiralyfogas.

May 16. Wallack's Theatre: La Bohème.

May 27. Wallack's Theatre: Manon Lescaut.

1899

Mar. 10. Metropolitan Opera House: Ero e Leandro.

1900

Jan. 22. American Theatre: A basso porto.

Nov. 19. Metropolitan Opera House: Esmeralda (A. Goring Thomas).

1901

Feb. 4. Metropolitan Opera House: Tosca.

Mar. 20. Metropolitan Opera House: Salâmmbo.

1902

Jan. 22. Metropolitan Opera House: Messaline.

Feb. 14. Metropolitan Opera House: Manru.

Oct. 16. Metropolitan Opera House: Iris.

1903

Mar. 11. Metropolitan Opera House: Der Wald.

June —. People's Theatre: Halka.

Dec. 24. Metropolitan Opera House: Parsifal (with scenery).

1906

Nov. 12. Garden Theatre: Madame Butterfly.

Dec. 5. Metropolitan Opera House: Fedora.

Dec. 7. Metropolitan Opera House: Le Damnation de Faust.

1907

Jan. 22. Metropolitan Opera House: Salomé.

Apr. 1. Metropolitan Opera House: Mataswintha (with scenery).

Nov. 18. Metropolitan Opera House: Adriana Lecouvreur.

Nov. 25. Manhattan Opera House: Thaïs.

1908

Jan. 3. Manhattan Opera House: Louise.

Feb. 5. Manhattan Opera House: Siberia.

Feb. 19. Manhattan Opera House: Pelléas et Mélisande.

Nov. 23. Metropolitan Opera House: Tiefland.

Nov. 27. Manhattan Opera House: Le Jongleur de Notre Dame.

Dec. 17. Metropolitan Opera House: Le Villi.

Chronology, Grand Operas, 1825–1925, cont'd.

1909

Jan. 6. Metropolitan Opera House: La Wally.

Feb. 19. Metropolitan Opera House: Die Verkaufte Braut.

Mar. 10. Manhattan Opera House: La Princesse d'auberge.

Nov. 8. Manhattan Opera House: Hérodiade.

Nov. 17. Manhattan Opera House: Sapho.

1910

Jan. 19. Manhattan Opera House: Grisélidis.

Jan. 22. Metropolitan Opera House: Germania.

Feb. 1. Manhattan Opera House: Elektra.

Feb. 8. New Theatre: L'Attaque du moulin; Amsterdam Theatre: Sarrona.

Mar. 5. Metropolitan Opera House: Pique Dame.

Mar. 18. Metropolitan Opera House: The Pipe of desire.

Sept. 20. Manhattan Opera House: Hans, le joueur de flûte (Hans, the flute player).

Nov. 14. Metropolitan Opera House: Armide.

Dec. 10. Metropolitan Opera House: La Fanciulla del West.

Dec. 28. Metropolitan Opera House: Die Königskinder.

1911

Jan. 12. Metropolitan Opera House: Lodoletta.

Feb. 28. Metropolitan Opera House: Natoma.

Mar. 3. Carnegie Hall: Briséïs (in concert form).

Mar. 14. Metropolitan Opera House: Il Segreto di Susanna.

Mar. 29. Metropolitan Opera House: Ariane et Barbe Bleue.

Apr. 4. Metropolitan Opera House: Quo vadis?

Nov. 18. Metropolitan Opera House: Lobetanz.

1912

Jan. 3. Metropolitan Opera House: Le Donne curiose.

Jan. 20. Metropolitan Opera House: Versiegelt.

1912, *continued.*

Feb. 26. Metropolitan Opera House: Cendrillon (Massenet).

Mar. 5. Metropolitan Opera House: I Giojelle della Madonna.

Mar. 14. Metropolitan Opera House: Mona.

Apr. 14. Metropolitan Opera House: Orfeo (Monteverdi; in concert form).

1913

Feb. 11. Metropolitan Opera House: Conchita.

Feb. 25. Metropolitan Opera House: Der Kuhreigen (Les ranz des vaches).

Feb. 27. Metropolitan Opera House: Cyrano.

Mar. 9. Hotel Astor: I Dispettosi amanti (A lover's quarrel).

Mar. 19. Metropolitan Opera House: Boris Godounoff.

Dec. 9. Metropolitan Opera House: Der Rosenkavalier.

1914

Jan. 2. Metropolitan Opera House: L'Amore dei tre re.

Jan. 24. Metropolitan Opera House: Madeleine.

Jan. 27. Metropolitan Opera House: Julien.

Feb. 3. Manhattan Opera House: Don Quichotte.

Feb. 17. Metropolitan Opera House: Monna Vanna.

Mar. 25. Metropolitan Opera House: L'Amore medico.

1915

Jan. 25. Metropolitan Opera House: Madame Sans Gêne.

Feb. 4. Metropolitan Opera House: L'Oracolo.

Dec. 30. Metropolitan Opera House: Prince Igor.

Chronology, Grand Operas, 1825–1925, cont'd.

1916

Jan. 28. Metropolitan Opera House: Goyescas.

Oct. 26. Empire Theatre: Bastien und Bastienne, and The Impresario (Der Schauspieldirektor).

Nov. 13. Metropolitan Opera House: Les Pêcheurs de perles (complete).

Nov. 25. Metropolitan Opera House: Iphigénie en Tauride (Iphigenia auf Tauris).

Dec. 22. Metropolitan Opera House: Francesca di Rimini.

1917

Mar. 8. Metropolitan Opera House: The Canterbury pilgrims.

May 7. Empire Theatre: Il Campanello di notte (The night bell).

May 10. Lyceum Theatre: Le Médecin malgré lui (The mock doctor).

Nov. 23. Garden Theatre: Evandro.

Dec. 19. Metropolitan Opera House: Marôuf.

1918

Jan. 3. Metropolitan Opera House: Saint Elizabeth.

Jan. 12. Metropolitan Opera House: Lodoletta.

Jan. 26. Lexington Theatre: Azora.

Feb. 11. Lexington Theatre: Le Sauteriot.

Feb. 13. Lexington Theatre: Isabeau.

Mar. 6. Metropolitan Opera House: Le Coq d'or.

Mar. 23. Metropolitan Opera House: Shanewis, and The Dance in Place Congo.

Oct. 18. Park Theatre: Bianca.

Dec. 14. Metropolitan Opera House: Il Tabarro, Suor Angelica, and Gianni Schicchi.

1919

Jan. 24. Metropolitan Opera House: La Reine Fiammette.

Jan. 27. Lexington Theatre: Gismonda.

Jan. 31. Lexington Theatre: Le Chemineau.

Feb. 11. Lexington Theatre: Cléopâtre.

Feb. 13. Lexington Theatre: Loreley.

Feb. 28. Lexington Theatre: Le Vieil aigle.

1919, *continued.*

Mar. 12. Metropolitan Opera House: The Legend, and The Temple dancer.

Apr. 19. Park Theatre: Maruxa.

Dec. 1. Century Theatre: Aphrodite (Février).

Dec. 27. Metropolitan Opera House: L'Oiseau bleu.

1920

Jan. 16. Metropolitan Opera House: Zaza.

Jan. 28. Lexington Theatre: Madame Chrysanthème (m a t i n e e); L'Heure espagnole (evening).

Jan. 30. Lexington Theatre: Rip van Winkle (DeKoven).

Jan. 31. Metropolitan Opera House: Cleopatra's night.

Feb. 27. Lexington Theatre: Aphrodite (Erlanger).

Mar. 6. Jan Huss Neighborhood House: V studni.

Mar. 21. Capitol Theatre: Paoletta.

Mar. 24. Metropolitan Opera House: Eugen Onegin.

Dec. 2. Metropolitan Opera House: Il "Carillon" magico.

1921

Feb. 4. Manhattan Opera House: Jacquerie.

Feb. 21. Manhattan Opera House: Edipo re.

Mar. 9. Metropolitan Opera House: Der Polnische Jude (The Polish Jew).

Apr. 7. Manhattan Opera House: Iphigenia in Aulis (Damrosch).

Nov. 19. Metropolitan Opera House: Die Tote Stadt.

1922

Jan. 5. Metropolitan Opera House: Le Roi d'Ys.

Jan. 23. Metropolitan Opera House: Snegourotchka.

Feb. 14. Manhattan Opera House: L'Amour des trois oranges.

Mar. 24. Metropolitan Opera House: Cosi fan tutte.

May 8. New Amsterdam Theatre: Russalka.

Chronology, Grand Operas, 1825–1925, cont'd.

1922, *continued.*

May 9. New Amsterdam Theatre: The Czar's bride.

May 13. New Amsterdam Theatre: The Demon.

May 26. New Amsterdam Theatre: Cherevicky (Christmas eve).

June 13. Second Avenue Theatre: Dubrovsky.

1923

Feb. 14. Metropolitan Opera House: Anima allegro.

Mar. 1. Metropolitan Opera House: Mona Lisa.

Dec. 2. Vanderbilt Theatre: Renard (in concert form).

1924

Jan. 1. Manhattan Opera House: Der Evangelimann.

Jan. 2. Metropolitan Opera House: La Habanera, and I Compagnacci.

Jan. 3. Manhattan Opera House: Die Toten Augen.

Jan. 13. Town Hall: Dido and Aeneas (in concert form).

1924, *continued.*

Feb. 29. Metropolitan Opera House: Le Roi de Lahore.

Oct. 17. Teatro Fourteenth Street and Sixth Avenue: Il Paese dei Campanelli.

Dec. 6. Metropolitan Opera House: Jenufa.

Dec. 20. Hotel Pennsylvania: La Veglia, and Le Furie de Arlecchino.

1925

Feb. 19. Metropolitan Opera House: Giovanni Gallurese.

Feb. 22. Times Square Theatre: Gagliarda of a merry plague.

Mar. 4. Princess Theatre: Mandragola.

Mar. 20. Carnegie Hall: The Garden of mystery.

May 17. Aeolian Hall: The Song of David (in concert form).

Sept. 26. Deutsches Irving Place Theater: Der Waffenschmied.

Sept. 27. Terrace Garden: Perouze.

Oct. 24. Academy of Music (Brooklyn): I Miserabili.

Nov. 13. Metropolitan Opera House: La Vestale.

Dec. 29. Town Hall: El Retablo de Maese Pedro.

INDEX

The names of composers are given in full with the years of birth and death, wherever possible. The full names of librettists are given each time they occur in the alphabetical list of the operas, beginning on p. 39. Titles in quotation marks are those of plays performed in connection with operas.

H

Hackett, Mrs., singer, 23.
Hadley, Henry Kimball, 1871–   :
    Azora, 42.
    Bianca, 43.
    Cleopatra's night, 46.
Hagenmacher, Mr., 26.
Haines, T.:
    Amilie, 40.
Halévy, Jacques François Fromental Élie, 1799–1862:
    Charles vi, 45.
    L'Eclair, 50.
    Jaquarita l'indienne. See The Desert flower, 48.
    La Juive, 59.
    Les Mousquetaires de la reine, 65.
    La Reine de Chypre, 71. See also The Daughter of St. Mark, 47.
    La Tempesta. See The Tempest, 76.
    Le Val d'Andorre, 78.
    See also Meilhac, H., and J. F. F. É. Halévy.
Hall, Charles, 32.
Hall, Walter Henry, conductor, 73.
Halleck, Fitz-Greene, poet, 13.
Halperine, Mme. P., and P. Lalo, translators:
    Snegourotchka, 75.
Handel, Georg Friedrich, 1685–1759:
    Acis and Galatea, 39.
    Comus, 46.
    See also The Israelites in Egypt, 58.
"The Happiest day of my life," 78.
The Harmonicon, 16, 17, 18.
Harris, A. G., and E. Falconer, pseud. of E. O'Rourke:
    The Rose of Castile, 73.
Harrison, W.:
    The Marriage of Georgette. See Les Noces de Jeannette, 67.
Hartmann, G., and A. Alexandre:
    Madame Chrysanthème, 62.
Hawthorne, N.:
    Rappaccini's daughter. See The Garden of mystery, 54.
    The Scarlet letter, 74.
Hazelton, G. C., translator:
    Aphrodite, 41.
Heinrich, M., singer, 69.
Henderson, W. J.:
    Cyrano de Bergerac, 47.
Henschel, G., singer, 69.
Herbert, Victor, 1859–1924:
    Madeleine, 62.
    Natoma, 66.
"L'Heretière," 53.
Hérold, Louis Joseph Ferdinand, 1791–1833:
    Le Pré aux clercs, 70.
    Zampa, 64, 80.
Hiemer, F. C.:
    Abou Hassan, 39.
Hill, violinist, 19.
Hill, Uriah C., conductor, 58, 79.
Hoffman, F. B.:
    Le Rendezvous bourgeois, 71.
Hofmannsthal, H. von:
    Elektra, 50.
    Der Rosenkavalier, 73.
Hollaway, sr., viola player, 19.
Hollaway, jr., violinist, 19.
Holt-Hansen, singer, 69.
"L'Homme gris," 44.
Hone, Philip, mayor of New York and patron of opera, 30, 31–32, 34.
Honey, R., adaptation:
    Lodoïska, 60.
Hooker, B.:
    Mona, 65.

Horn, Charles Edward, 1786–1849, 23, 25, 31.
    Ahmed al Kamel, 39.
    Isidore di Merida, 58.
    The Maid of Saxony, 62.
    Nadir and Zuleika, 66.
    The Quartette, 71.
Horn, Charles Edward, adaptations:
    Die Zauberflöte, 80.
Horncastle, J.:
    Buy it, dear, 'tis made of cashmere. See Le Dieu et la bayadere, 48.
Hornung, [John], bassoon player, 19.
Howland, G. C., 31.
Howland, Legrand:
    Sarrona, 74.
Hubay, Jenö, 1858–   :
    Der Geigenmacher von Cremona, 54.
Huerta, musician, 42, 54, 76.
Hugo, John Adam, 1873–   :
    The Temple dancer, 60, 76.
Hugo, Victor:
    Angelo. See La Gioconda, 55.
    Hernani. See Ernani, 50–51.
    Lucrèce Borgia. See Lucrezia Borgia, 61.
    Les Miserables. See I Miserabili, 65.
    Notre Dame de Paris. See Esmeralda, 51.
Humperdinck, Engelbert, 1854–1921:
    Haensel und Gretel, 56.
    Die Koenigskinder, 59.

I

Illica, L.:
    Andrea Chenier, 40.
    Le Donne curiose, 49.
    Germania, 54–55.
    Iris, 58.
    Isabeau, 58.
    Siberia, 75.
    La Wally, 80.
    See also Manon Lescaut, 63.
Illica, L., and G. Giacosa:
    La Bohème, 43.
    Madame Butterfly, 62.
    Tosca, 77.
Illica, L., and F. Pozza:
    Il Vassalo di Szigeth, 79.
Incledon, singer, 23.
"L'Intérieur d'un bureau," 80.
International Composers' Guild, 71.
"The Invincibles," 57.
Ireland, J. N.:
    Records of the New York stage, from 1750 to 1860, 7, 77.
Irving, W.:
    The Legend of Sleepy Hollow. See Sleepy Hollow, 75.
    Rip van Winkle, 72.
    Tales of the Alhambra. See Ahmed al Kamel, 39.
"It is the devil," 47.
Italiener, H.:
    Don Quixote, der Ritter von der traurigen Gestalt, 49.
    Prinz Waldmeister, 71.
    Der Rattenfaenger von Hameln, 71.

J

Jackson, J. P., translator:
    Nero, 66.
Janáček, Leoš, 1854–   :
    Jenufa, 58.
Janacopulos, Véra, translator:
    L'Amour des trois oranges, 40.

Planard, F. A. E. de:
  La Lettre de change, 60.
  Le Pré aux clercs, 70.
  Le Solitaire, 75.
  See also Vernoy de Saint Georges, J. H., and
    F. A. E. de Planard.
Planché, J. R.:
  Oberon, 67.
Planché, J. R., adaptation:
  Gustavus III, 56.
Pocock, I.:
  Home, sweet home!, 57.
Poe, E. A.:
  The Masque of the red death. *See* Gagliarda of a
    merry plague, 54.
Pola:
  La Donna caritea, 49.
Polis Opera Club, Milwaukee, 57.
Pollock, A. L.:
  Cleopatra's night, 46.
Ponchielli, Amilcare, 1834–1886:
  La Gioconda, 55.
Ponta, Giulia da, singer, 25–27, 28.
Ponta, Lorenzo da, 1749–1838, 16, 17, 18–19, 25–26,
    28, 31, 32–34.
  L'Ape musicale, 41.
  Cosi fan tutte, 46–47.
  Don Giovanni, 49.
  Le Nozze di Figaro, 67.
Ponta, Lorenzo L., 28.
"Poor Pillicoddy," 46.
Pordes-Milo. *See* Batka, R., and Pordes-Milo.
Porto, A., singer, 32, 33, 39, 43.
Pozza, F. *See* Illica, L., and F. Pozza.
Praga, M. *See* Manon Lescaut, 63.
Pratt, Silas Gamaliel, 1846–1916:
  Zenobia, 80.
Preissova, G.:
  Jenufa, 58.
"Presumption; or, The Fate of Frankenstein," 67.
Prevost, E.:
  Cosimo, 47.
Prévost d'Exiles, A. F.:
  Histoire de Manon Lescaut. *See* Manon, 63;
    Manon Lescaut, 63.
Prévôt, C. V., vicomte d'Arlincourt:
  Le Renegat. *See* Gli Arabi nelli Gallie, 41.
  Le Solitaire, 75.
Price, Stephen, 13, 16, 17, 18, 34.
Prime, Rufus, 31.
Il Primo di Maggio. *See* Evandro, 51.
"The Prize; or, 2, 5, 4, 8," 71.
Proch, H., translator:
  Rigoletto, 72.
Prod'homme, J. G., 22.
Prokofieff, Sergei, 1891–   :
  L'Amour des trois oranges, 40.
"Promotion," 50.
Puccini, Giacomo, 1858–1924:
  La Bohème, 43.
  La Fanciulla del West, 51.
  Gianni Schicchi, 55, 76.
  Madame Butterfly, 62.
  Manon Lescaut, 63.
  Suor Angelica, 55, 76.
  Il Tabarro, 55, 76.
  Tosca, 77.
  Le Villi, 79.
Pucita, Vincenzo, 1778–1861:
  La Vestale, 79.
  See also Il Fanatico per la musica, 51, 71.
Purcell, Henry, ca. 1658–1695:
  Dido and Aeneas, 48.
  See also The Tempest, 76.

Pushkin, A.:
  Boris Godounoff, 43.
  Le Coq d'or, 46.
  Dubrovsky, 49.
  Eugen Onegin, 51.
  Pique Dame, 70.
  Russalka, 73.

Q

"The Quaker," 65.
Quinault, P.:
  Armide, 41.
Quintero:
  Anima allegra, 40.

R

Rabaud, Henri, 1873–   :
  Mârouf, savetier du Caire, 63.
Rachau, Mme. S. A., pianist, 76.
Radet, J. B., and Picard:
  La Maison en loterie, 62.
Radin, Oscar, arranger:
  Parsifal, 69.
Radio, operas broadcast by:
  Aida, 39.
  Il Barbiere di Siviglia, 42.
  La Bohème, 43.
  The Bohemian girl, 43.
  Carmen, 44.
  Cavalleria rusticana, 44–45.
  Ernani, 50–51.
  Faust, 52.
  La Forza del destino, 53.
  Gioconda, 55.
  Lucia di Lammermoor, 61, Errata and addenda.
  Madame Butterfly, 62.
  Maritana, 63.
  Norma, 67.
  Pagliacci, 68.
  Rigoletto, 72.
  Roméo et Juliette, 73.
  Samson et Delila, 74.
  Il Trovatore, 78.
"Raising the wind," 50.
Randagger, A., and T. Marzials:
  Esmeralda, 51.
Ranzato, V.:
  Il Paese dei campanelli, 68.
Rapetti, Michele, violinist and conductor, 29, 37, 40,
    41, 44, 49.
Rauppach, E. B. S.:
  Versiegelt, 79.
Ravaglio, Luigi, singer, 32, 33, 41, 46.
Ravel, Maurice, 1875–   :
  L'Heure espagnole, 57.
Ray, Robert, 32.
Raymond, Fanny Malone, translator:
  Orfeo ed Euridice, 68.
Redding, J. D.:
  Natoma, 66.
"The Regent," 75.
Regnard, J. F.:
  Les Folies amoureuses, 53.
Reichmann, singer, 69.
Remnertz, F., singer, 69.
"The Rent day," 66.
The Review, 50.
Reyer, Louis Étienne Ernest Rey, called, 1823–1909:
  Salammbo, 73.
Reynoldson, J. T., adaptation:
  Fra Diavolo, 53.
Ricci, Luigi, 1805–1859:
  Chiara di Rosemburgh, 45.